Selected books by Robert Thurman

Infinite Life: Breaking Free from the Terminal Lifestyle

Inner Revolution: Life, Liberty, and the Pursuit of Real Happiness

The Tibetan Book of the Dead

Essential Tibetan Buddhism

Anger

Worlds of Transformation
(With Marilyn M. Rhie)

Wisdom and Compassion: The Sacred Art of Tibet
(With Marilyn M. Rhie)

THE
JEWEL TREE
OF TIBET

❧

The Enlightenment Engine of
Tibetan Buddhism

ROBERT THURMAN

FREE PRESS
NEW YORK   LONDON   TORONTO   SYDNEY

FREE PRESS
A Division of Simon & Schuster, Inc.
1230 Avenue of the Americas
New York, NY 10020

For information about special discounts for bulk purchases,
please contact Simon & Schuster Special Sales:
1-800-456-6798 or business@simonandschuster.com

Designed by Joseph Rutt

Manufactured in the United States of America

10 9 8 7 6 5 4 3 2 1

Library of Congress Control Number: 2004061927

ISBN 0-7432-5762-6

✣

To all my spiritual friends and mentors—
Mentioning their names for a purpose,
Geshe Wangyal,
Kyabjey Ling Rinpochey,
Lhajey Yeshi Dhonden, Gelek Rinpochey,
Tara Tulku Rinpochey, Locho Rinpoche,
My reluctant Vajrayogini,
And those who came down from heaven to share the work—
And the one who may be seen at heart to emanate all,
His Holiness the Dalai Lama, Shakya Bhikshu Tenzin Gyatso.

"You are mentor! You are archetype deity!
You are buddha-angel and protector!
From now 'til my enlightenment, I seek no other savior!
With compassion's goad, please care for me
In this life, the between, and future lives!
Save me from the dangers of either life or liberation!
Grant me all accomplishments!
Be my eternal friend! Protect me from all harm!"

✣

CONTENTS

❧

PREFACE

We held an inspired retreat a few years ago on the Tibetan distillation of the path of enlightenment, which seems, as I am getting older, to be all that I can get excited about continuing to learn myself or teach to others. It is so beautiful, so useful, covering all the important points and practices we need to master in order to make our precious human lives more meaningful, ultimately fruitful, and plain happier. We taped it for the folks at Sounds True, with the kind help of Tami Simon and her wonderful staff. Over the years, I have been pleased at the feedback I have gotten from people of all sorts that they find it inspiring and useful.

I did feel diffident about putting out my version of these teachings, when readers nowadays have access to original discourses on this tradition from His Holiness the Dalai Lama himself and numerous other respected Tibetan mentors. I am keenly aware that I am still learning these principles myself; I do not pretend to myself or to anyone else either to have achieved a real "beginner's mind" or to have achieved the enlightenment of an expert sage.

The version of the stages of the path that I am using as "root text" here is the Fourth Panchen Lama's *Mentor Devotion*, a semiesoteric text, which is taught by mentors to advanced students along with initiations of various kinds. My reasons are fivefold: I just love that text, first of all. It highlights the central role that the lama, the spiritual mentor or teacher, plays in making the Tibetan approach to the path powerfully effective, by making the presence of the Three Jewels of Buddha, Dharma, and Sangha alive and immediate to the practitioner. His Holiness the Dalai Lama allowed the publication of a brief teaching he gave on the text some years ago, so it is now acceptable to divulge this once guarded practice more generally. My way of explaining the text in the light of elements in Western culture that affect the way Westerners might approach it may provide a different kind of introduction to my fellow practitioners. And, because I have already presented it in tape form and people are finding it helpful, I'm encouraged that the text might be helpful as well.

Therefore, when my friend Leslie Meredith suggested we turn the retreat into a book, I agreed with pleasure. I must thank Leslie first of all for her inspiration. My agent, Lynn Nesbit, as always, provided useful advice and practical help. Tami Simon, president of Sounds True, Inc., graciously agreed to participate in the project and coordinate it with the continuing audio publication. My son and colleague at Tibet House US, Ganden Thurman, helped me secure the initial transcription, which was lightly edited by my assistant, Dr. Jensine Andresen. Leslie again did an excellent editing at the next stage, and her assistant, Kit Frick, has been most helpful in the final polishing under the usual pressures. Any errors that remain are mine, of course.

As always, I gratefully thank my wife and inspiring muse, Nena, for her patience and encouragement.

Robert (Tenzin) Thurman
Ganden Dekyi Ling, Woodstock, New York
August 2004

THE
JEWEL TREE
OF TIBET

INTRODUCTION

This book began as an intensive retreat with a small group of students. It is a teaching on the steps on the path of enlightenment that is common to all the forms of Tibetan Buddhism. The Tibetans have taken teachings from all kinds of Buddhism, especially those preserved and developed in India over fifteen hundred years before they traveled to Tibet. But there in Tibet, Buddhism was made into a systematic method for people to practice and perform in order to become perfectly enlightened in this life, or in a short number of lives, starting from wherever they started.

This is what we'll aim to practice on this retreat, on this quest for enlightenment in book form. You'll start wherever you are in your life, today. We'll retreat into one of the greatest sacred wisdom texts of Tibetan knowledge of the soul, called *The Devotion to the Mentor,* in which a glorious wish-fulfilling gem tree is used to focus our minds. We're on a quest to contemplate this great text line by line, so that we come to understand its full, rich meaning, the brilliant reflections of its many facets guiding us, lighting up our awareness. And we'll take this awareness with us, out into the world, into our lives. It is a powerful text, just the reading of which has the capacity to lift you out of your individual self and into a perspective of unity, refreshing your individuality immeasurably. It will help you cultivate the sensitivity and appreciation to love more fully, feel compassion more intensely, and become a fountain of cheerfulness for all you meet and know.

The steps on the path of enlightenment in this text are a distillation of the vast profusion of healing techniques dispensed by the Shakyamuni Buddha—the historical Buddha—to his many thousands of disciples, two thousand five hundred years ago. I first encountered *The Devotion to the Mentor* and the jewel tree, in this life, forty-two years ago, when I met the Very Venerable Geshe Wangyal at his monastery in the Pine Barrens of New Jersey, which was in a little pink tract house on East Third Street in Freewood Acres. He read to me a version of this same enlightenment path, the way to a higher quality of being, that had been written by the great south Indian philosopher sage Nagarjuna in the second century C.E. Nagarjuna had written it as *Letter from a Spiritual Friend* to his friend and disciple the south Indian King Udayibhadra, whose name means "King Happily Good."

My teacher read this text aloud in a Tibetan translation, accompanying it with a commentary written by a great fourteenth-century Tibetan lama, and as he read he would translate and explain in English to me and my friend Chris. The three of us would sit together in the chapel room or out in the yard of the little pink house that served as a monastery in New Jersey, under the spell of the great wish-fulfilling jewel tree of Tibet. Then, in the evening and late into the night, I would memorize the Tibetan, learn the text's meaning, and meditate on the steps and themes—incorporating it all into my mind and psyche and spirit.

The fresh and reasonable vision of life, the deep meaning of existence, the imminence of freedom, the vast horizon of my human potential—all this leapt out at me from these words in the lovely Tibetan script, block-printed on beautiful, long, fibrous pages. I loved Nagarjuna and his friend the king. I loved the Tibetan alphabet, so logical and elegant. I felt totally at home in it.

At that time, I was in the middle of a long pilgrimage that had led me to drop out of college and had taken me across Europe on a motorcycle and across Asia on foot, all the way to India. There, I had met the Tibetans and begun to learn from them and work with them when the death of my father brought me back to New York City for a month of family sadness and mourning, as well as a reimmersion into the hypocrisy and anxiety of the world that I was eager to transcend. Yet there I also met my teacher and went to work with him in the Jersey Pine Barrens, in a Russian Mongolian refugee community. Through him, I met the path of enlightenment. I met a true mentor. I had come home—to myself and my soul—through this great teacher and the jewel tree text he revealed to me.

And it was not just the text and the teachings that affected me so deeply. It was the special context in which Tibetans meditate and use their teachings. I learned to look up with my inner eye, the third eye of imagination, which lies in the middle of our foreheads and opens a channel of vision into a subtle realm of reality. In this inner sky revealed by my third eye, I discovered mystical beings, buddhas, bodhisattvas (persons who strive for enlightenment in order to help others on their quest for their highest development), historical lama mentors, angels, deities mild and fierce, and all the saints and teachers and philosophers from all the world's spiritual traditions. I beheld the shining tree of jewels, decked with living jewel beings.

I recognized the jewel tree as the world tree, Yggdrasil, the great ash tree extending over the entire earth, growing from the well of wisdom, where Odin, the highest god, had to cast one eye as sacrifice in order to receive the eye of wisdom from the goddess of the tree. The jewel tree is the tree of life, the tree of wisdom, and it is also the giant fig tree under which the Buddha attained perfect enlightenment, the bodhi tree. It grows from earth to heaven and is filled with the wish-granting jewels that make up the family of living mentors who have reached immortal life and can share their bliss with you, protect you, bless you, and help you open up your own inner doorway to peace and fulfillment. The jewel tree opens its loving embrace to everyone and promotes happiness—which is our natural state and birthright.

Since that time when I began to enjoy the luminous shelter of the jewel tree of Tibet, I have studied and meditated year after year. I went on to become a monk; I learned more and more advanced teachings, tried to put them into practice, and seemed to succeed with insight after insight. But then I began to realize that last week's insight was superseded by the next one. For a while, all I wanted was to stay in my Buddhist community of seekers of enlightenment, to be embraced as a monk. My inner life was rich, full of insights and delightful visions, with a sense of luck and privilege at having access to such great teachers and teachings and the time to study and try to realize them. Eventually, I realized that there was more I needed to learn from the world, from engagement with others, from developing compassion in my interactions rather than the solitary quest of wisdom. So I resigned as a monk and reentered the university, determined to find a way to continue to study while engaging more actively with others.

As I have grown older and become less sure about everything—and even confused and discouraged when my inherited negative personality traits reemerge in the heat of relationships—I have repeatedly turned back to the beginning of my studies of the jewel tree. I regularly rest under the jewel tree and reflect on the steps it provides us to enlightenment, freedom, and happiness. A golden ladder from earth to heaven, the great jewel tree is an inner space for a retreat, a spiritual vacation, a refreshment and recharging that comes from stepping back from our emotions and habitual perspectives—even for a few moments. You can spend minutes under the jewel tree or you can spend entire days or weeks, depending on the time you can afford to take. Sometimes it helps to meditate with others on the jewel tree, since your thoughts will become amplified and intensified by the resonance of one living mind with another.

INTRODUCTION 5

Whenever I conduct a retreat, I try to remember that the main person who needs the retreat is myself. The person who most needs to learn what I say, even though I may be saying it, is me. So, therefore, I'm very thankful that you're joining me in your reading of this text and on this quest. I don't pretend to be a great teacher, but I do claim that this, the wish-granting jewel tree of Tibet, is a great teaching.

We love and admire Tibet because Tibet is the guardian, custodian, preserver, developer, and utilizer of these great enlightenment teachings. Originally, all the teachings came from what the Tibetans call the Noble Country, Aryavarta, the country of the noble beings. These beings followed the Buddhist tradition and achieved nobility in the spiritual sense, they were selfless beings—beings who did not live enclosed within their own personal, egocentric perspective but lived within a multiperspectival world. The perspectives of the others were to them as important as, or more important than, the perspective of the self. The noble beings realized the meaning and the reality of selflessness. A noble person is defined by the Buddha not in terms of social class or race or nationality or sex or religion but by whether you perceive things only from your own perspective or whether you perceive them simultaneously from all others' perspectives.

So, what we're going to try to do on this quest together is to go from the beginning of the Tibetan path of enlightenment to its end. And we're going to rehearse various short meditations that will help us get deeper along the path. And we're going to learn about what that path is so that we understand it, so that you can do this retreat yourself again and again, and I can do this retreat myself again and again, each time learning something new. We're aiming to develop a tolerance for cognitive dissonance, a greater subtlety of consciousness. You don't want to get all fascinated or obsessed or entranced with one particular thing that you experience as you go along, but keep moving and learning, seeing things freshly again and again.

Even if you are not a Tibetan Buddhist or any kind of Buddhist, I hope you will be able to follow along with this teaching and gain something from it. I follow His Holiness the Dalai Lama. He's my main teacher, my mentor. I follow his view that, in the world today, we don't want millions and millions and millions of new Buddhists. We're not competing with the Christians, the Jews, the Muslims, the Hindus. We're not competing for market share, for a population explosion. But we are looking to the quality of people's lives, hoping that people will become more enlightened, whatever their religious affiliation or secular humanist beliefs. Conversion is not the goal here. Therefore, in teaching a teaching like this, which we hope the public will use widely, we want to make it accessible to as many people as possible.

However, if we teach a spiritual practice in a completely bland, watered down way, then no one will really have much inspiration to use it. I love the Buddha, and I love the Dharma, which is the teaching of the Buddha, and I love the Tibetan versions of it. And I particularly love the version that was perfected by Tsong Khapa, who lived in the fifteenth century. It is the core teaching that the Dalai Lamas have practiced since then, including the current Dalai Lama, the Fourteenth, His Holiness Tenzin Gyatso.* So, I want to share my love for their vision and wisdom with you through the ancient text that inspires this retreat in book form.

---

* The Dalai Lamas are believed to be incarnations of the archangel of universal compassion, Avalokiteshvara, the "God of Sensitive Concern." Their line of incarnations extends at least back to the time of the historical Buddha, and from there back into mythic timelessness. The first of the fourteen Dalai Lamas who have taken responsibility for Tibet was Gendun Drubpa (1391–1474); the Great Fifth Dalai Lama (1617–1682) was the first to be given control of the government; and the present, the Great Fourteenth (1935–) is the first to become known all over the world.

In this book, I will draw from those teachings and focus on the
particularly vivid teaching about the wish-fulfilling jewel tree by the
Fourth Panchen Lama,* called the *Guru Puja,* or the *Devotion to the
Mentor.* A mentor is not considered merely a teacher but is seen rather
as an exemplar of the teaching, a model to follow. So, in each lesson
or subject or verse, I will veer away from my own narrow understanding and Tibetan images, and I will encourage you to meditate,
whether you are Sufi, Christian, or another kind of Buddhist, and to
draw in your own images and ideas to enhance your own understanding. This retreat is divided into six chapters that can serve as retreats in themselves, with different meditations and a regular review
of the principles that form the steps on the path to enlightenment.
I want you to figure out how to enter a kind of jewel space of awareness, to populate and retreat to that jewel space in your own way.
There you will be energized to discover your own feeling of insight
into your own soul—and into the soul of the entire universe. The
wish-fulfilling jewel tree will restore you to yourself and illuminate
your path through life . . . and illuminate your spirit into the next
life.

---

* The Panchen Lamas are believed to be the incarnations of the Buddha Amitabha, Lord
of the Western Heaven, Sukhavati, teacher of Avalokiteshvara. There has been a long line
of these incarnations, but the title of Fourth Panchen Lama was first given by the Great
Fifth Dalai Lama to his teacher, Losang Chogyen (1569–1662), and the current Panchen
Lama is the Eleventh. The Dalai and Panchen Lamas are considered, respectively, the first
and second in holiness among the reincarnated teachers of Tibet.

ONE

BUDDHISM AND THE WAY
Grounding Your Meditation

Let's begin by reading the very first verse of this work that we are going to learn to practice—what the Tibetans would call the root text, the backbone of our time together, the *Mentor Devotion*. This teaching integrates both exoteric and esoteric practices into a method that energizes and accelerates your understanding and experience. The external teacher figure in Tibetan Buddhism is considered more of a friend than a mentor. Your esoteric teacher, by contrast, is one you imagine and visualize to be indivisible from the Buddha himself, someone who is a living exemplar of enlightenment. You use your mental power of imagination to propel you toward the enlightened state, to mobilize you to become like your teacher. This altered focus makes the teaching more accessible and immediate. It gives you a personal guide from the outset, a companion on the path but one who is always ahead of you, motivating you. The mentor figure empowers you, not just to play at self-transformation but actually to realize the teaching, to experience the higher goal state. Thus, "mentor devotion" is a practice of acknowledging or worshiping the Buddha in a model figure of your choice. You envision the mentor as the Buddha and strive to emulate that model until you are able to understand and embody the teaching entirely yourself. Though the teaching integrates this esoteric dimension and power, it can be practiced even by beginners and used by anyone who wants to learn its steps to travel the mainstream path to enlightenment.

As you read the following lines, go into a momentary meditational mode. Read the first verse to yourself:

Through the great bliss state,
I myself become the mentor deity.
From my luminous body,
Light rays shine all around,
Massively blessing beings and things,
Making the universe pure and fabulous,
Perfection in its every quality.

Take a minute to be with this image of light and perfection.

Now I will explain. The great bliss state is the state of reality— where we actually are, right here and now. It is not some elaborate place far away from where we are. The wonderful thing about the Buddha's revelation, the Buddha's insight, is that this reality itself *is* the great bliss state, that which he first called "Nirvana," the extinction of all suffering, which he came to describe as "bliss void indivisible."

The extinction of suffering and the achievement of perfect happiness and the reality of perfect happiness is the reality of our world. This was the Buddha's good news. This is what he realized under the bodhi tree, where he first became enlightened. The bodhi tree was the original wish-granting gem tree. To find happiness or peace or enlightenment, we do not have to create some artificial world, a world apart from this world. We have to understand the nature of *this* world. And the nature of this world, when we do understand it, is revealed to us *through* our understanding, not from some other person just showing us something. Our own understanding reveals the nature of the world to us as the great bliss state of emptiness and openness. The nature of this world is superbliss, intertwined and indivisible.

This great bliss state, therefore, as the first line mentions, is the reality to which the Buddha awoke twenty-five hundred years ago, and to which millions and hundreds of millions of Buddhists over the centuries have awakened. It is also, undoubtedly, the reality that the great founding teachers of other world traditions experienced and tasted in their own ways, and made available to people, sometimes through understanding, sometimes through faith, or sometimes through different experiences. It is the same great bliss state because it is the same reality. All beings dwell in this reality.

Unfortunately, most beings are not aware of it. They think they are dwelling in the reality of insufficiency, a self-centered reality where they are pitted against the world and the world is pitted against them. To them, the world is always suffering and always causes them frustration and always overwhelms them. The Buddha's good news is that you can actually take a break from this struggle. Relax. Ease back. He taught that where you are is actually perfect. But, of course, unfortunately, you can't know it just by my saying it, because you're so caught up in your stream of not knowing. So, the Buddha had to provide a method of education. The great teachers in all traditions provide you with arts of development and education whereby you can come to awaken from the world of delusion, in which you feel you must suffer, to the world of reality, in which you are automatically free from suffering.

The second line says, "I myself become the mentor deity." This is fascinating to put at the very beginning of the teaching, when we are thinking of ourselves as rank beginners. It challenges and empowers us at the outset.

"I myself": although I'm telling this to you, I'm the vessel through which this teaching is coming to you, I myself don't pretend to understand it fully, by any means. I'm also suffering in the world, still struggling with the world, because of my distorted perspective. However, when I say, "I myself become the mentor deity," when you yourself say, "I myself become the mentor deity," at the beginning of our practice, what we are doing is imagining ourselves as being already at the goal of awakening.

You're imagining that you actually are a buddha, you have become a buddha. You have awakened, and you're imagining what it feels like to awaken. You're imagining what it feels like to know that your reality is a great bliss state, indivisible and uninterruptible and indestructible. And you're imagining that in that great bliss state you become for others a mentor and a divine teacher, a mentor who is always present to all others in whatever form they need.

The verse goes on, "From my luminous body"—you imagine your body no longer feels like a body of heavy flesh and blood obstructed and filled with gravity and old age and sickness and limitations and obstacles. "From my luminous body, light rays shine all around"—because once you become aware of the great bliss state that is the nature of reality, then your body itself becomes a teaching. Once you've become, out of your compassionate will, or from automatically wishing to manifest yourself as a mentor deity, a divine educator who can be shiningly present to everyone who needs you—once you have done that, your body becomes a light vehicle. It becomes a lens through which the light emerges from the natural state to all other beings and opens them and blesses them.

The fifth line says, "Massively blessing beings and things." You are blessing them by bringing that light, the light of awakening, to them, causing them to look up from their treadmill, from the tunnels of desire and frustration and aversion and hatred and anger and confusion that they are charging down endlessly, round and round in an endless maze and circle. This light of reality, the light of bliss, shines on them, and they look up from their preoccupation, from their obsession, and they feel blessed by that moment of freedom, by a moment of looking up in wonder, glimpsing "the universe pure and fabulous, perfection in its every quality." You see the universe as helping the beings. You see even the tunnels down which they run as radiating to the beings the light of reality, the light of freedom. Actually, you begin at this very end point. You are invited to taste the experience of already having reached the goal, just as the Buddha invited everyone to become as liberated, blissful, and powerful as himself. He did not hold himself above us.

This is another one of the greatnesses of Tibetan Buddhism— Tibetan Buddhism is not a national thing, something "Made in Tibet," something combined with some local traditions in Tibet— Tibetan Buddhism *is* Buddhism.

What is Buddhism? It is the response of awakened beings to unawakened beings' wish to become awakened. That is what Buddhism is. When you become awakened, you realize your oneness with other beings. When you realize your oneness with them, their suffering becomes your suffering, their delusion becomes your delusion. You feel it, just as they do. You don't imagine how they're feeling it, the way we normally do from within our self-enclosure, you actually feel it. When you feel it, then, you automatically respond to help alleviate it. You recognize, of course, that there's nothing you can do by force. There's nothing you can do by magic. There's nothing you can do *automatically* to relieve beings of that suffering. You can't sort of bliss them out instantaneously, or give them some kind of bliss-bomb explosion.

No matter how intense your own feeling is, within yourself, of joy and freedom and relief and relaxation, you can't automatically force other people into that mode. In fact, if you approach them with the very high energy of your own bliss, they will perceive that as a little bit of pressure, and they will then constrict more, and they will feel more pressure, and they will suffer more. You realize that the only way you yourself awakened and opened was to realize your selflessness, to realize that you are not an isolated, separated, absolute being, cut off from other beings, but that you, yourself, are nothing but a nexus of bliss.

You come to realize that you are empty of any intrinsic reality, separated identity, fixed, static personality, and by being empty of that, you become completely interconnected with all other beings. You don't become nonexistent, as some people fear, but you become a nexus of relationality with all other beings, with nothing resisting the delicate, intimate tendrils of relationality. Once you realize that, you realize that that infinite realm and web of relationality is bliss, and once you realize that as bliss, you have nothing left to do in the universe. Your old life is over, in a way, if in that life you had defined yourself as isolated and separated from the world, or struggling with the world to achieve a good position, to gain some sort of power or control or security or safety, or even if you were trying to flee from that interconnected universe. Instead of that, you now become the universe. Then, nothing is actually wrong in that universe. It is perfect.

But others don't see it that way. So, the one thing that *is* lacking in that perfect universe is their seeing it as perfect, so that everyone would feel perfectly at ease within it. You may automatically wish to free them, which could lead to frustration if, in your initial glimpse of this awakening, you lacked the compassion, the skill in liberative technique, the art to really open to others the world as you see it, to enable them to see their own reality as a reality of bliss.

Originally, the Buddha found this vision under a tree. He went there. He met with the gods. He spent six years there after having been a prince his whole life. He talked to the gods. He asked them the nature of reality. After some questioning, they revealed that they weren't sure what it was, quite. They asked the Buddha to go find out and, if he found out, to let them know. He investigated and explored more and more. Finally, after much investigation and exploring, he discovered the nature of reality, which he called selflessness, which he called profound peace, which he called luminosity, radiance, transparency, which he called uncreated—reality as it is in itself. And when the Buddha discovered that, he said, "Like an elixir is this reality which I have found, an elixir of immortality." And he was ecstatic and joyous. At first, he said, "I don't think I will show anyone this reality. No need to bother, because they will not understand it. So, instead, I'm going to stay in the forest and not speak to anyone." However, in doing that, he was already speaking something, and he was already leaving a teaching for beings.

The first thing the Buddha gave as a teaching, in a way, was silence. The reason that he could afford to be silent was that, in that perception, he did perceive all beings as completely free from suffering. Even beings that perceived themselves as being in hell, he saw them as having an ultimate reality that was freedom from suffering. Even hell is a great bliss state in its reality. That deep vision of reality doesn't ignore, of course, that in its unreality, the way the beings in those hells perceive it, it is hell, with its many forms of agony. But that unreality, luckily, is far less real than the true reality, which is bliss. So, the silence of the Buddha was not a silence of abandoning other beings. It was a silence that affirmed that you, in your deepest being, your deeper, deeper reality of cells, of subatomic energies, your reality of your deepest sensitivity is, in fact, freedom—no matter the theater of pain you have fascinated yourself by, gotten caught up in, or are habitually obsessed with.

Thus, silence is the Buddha's greatest expression. It's the Buddha's great teaching, what the Hindus call "You Are That" in the Upanishads. "You are the ultimate reality. You are God!" the Hindus boldly declare. But the Buddha's way of affirming that fact is by being silent, because if you are *that*, after all, if you are what the theists think is God, you already know it yourself.

Buddhism, as merely a set of responses to the needs of beings, develops as they need them. It isn't some system that emerges as a thing-in-itself out of some reality. It is not a dogma, a structure built up on the basis of reality. Buddhism is, actually, simply, an endless series of methods and arts of opening doors to reality that fit with any particular person's location and place. "Buddhism" can emerge as Christianity. It can emerge as Judaism. It can emerge as humanism. It can emerge as nihilism, even temporarily, in some special cases. It can emerge as absolutisms of various kinds. It isn't that it consists of some rigid view, some orthodox ideology, some dogmatic religion. There is no fixed institution or "religion" that can be pinned down exactly as *the* referent of "Buddhism."

A BRIEF HISTORY OF BUDDHISM

To help you understand this revolutionary concept—revolutionary still today—let me give you a brief history of "Buddhism." During the beginning of Buddhism in India, the Buddha emphasized to people, to individuals, that they needed to break away from conventional society. Conventional society in his time was not the enlightened, beautiful, luminous, exquisite India that we know today, gradually emerging from centuries of colonial oppression. India in Buddha's time was a militaristic country, like ancient Greece or Iran or Egypt, a country of city-states with armies and armor, with a rigid class system, with people enslaving and exploiting other people, with people fighting and killing and conquering other people, with nature being exploited by the beginnings of the Agricultural Revolution. Cities and excessive wealth were being built up by some people, power was sought by vainglorious warrior rulers. Buddha himself was born as such a warrior ruler, and it was predicted, even, that he could conquer that whole world should he turn his mind to worldly power, wealth, and dominion. Fortunately for the world, he didn't do an Alexander the Great number, and instead, he turned inward to conquer himself, to conquer reality. But in the India of his time, in Eurasia of that time, Buddha saw that first of all he had to emphasize individualism for people.

The Buddha asked, "Why should you live your life fighting and struggling and producing, enslaving and being enslaved? Why shouldn't you just leave the conventional world? Why shouldn't you fulfill yourself instead?" Imagine yourself as the Buddha back then. You were a person. You went and sat under a tree. You suffered. You struggled. You analyzed. You meditated. You came to a deep understanding of the essential blissfulness of every element and cell and particle of life, and even the bliss in the rocks and the bliss in the earth and the bliss in the volcanoes and the bliss in the stars. And then you saw these other beings running around madly chasing ephemeral goals, power, and dominion, which they would only lose when soon they died. And then after death, they would suffer from the negative acts they had committed against others in order to get that power and dominion—even if the power were knowledge, as with a yogi, a mage, or a scientist. They would die and forget that they had caused this-and-that disaster in the process of trying to get power, and be reborn, becoming again a deer caught in the headlights in some future world.

If you were the Buddha at that time, you, too, would have asked, "How can I break them out of these routine patterns, the social collective that they are caught in and that tells them to do this and do that by instinct, that tells them God wants them to do this, go from birth to death without ever looking up from the groove down which they are driven or preordained to follow? How can I show them that their own heart is an engine of bliss, their own brain an instrument of deep wisdom?" Well, you would emphasize individualism.

You would say, "Don't just follow these conventional, traditional ideas, even religious ideas. Don't follow them. They are just fitting you into somebody else's scheme. You yourself can be god. You really are that, in fact. You, yourself, are reality. You, yourself, are buddha. So, don't follow these things. Withdraw from them. Seek your own reality. Look inside yourself with mindfulness. Look inside yourself with analysis. Minimize your negative activities and evolutionary actions, and don't harm other beings. Become more helpful. Or, since you can't become helpful right away, because you can't yet see clearly, at least cease to harm."

And then, Buddha did a marvelous thing. He invented the monastic system. He invented being ordained as a monk or a nun so that people would be supported by the collective to escape from the collective. The Buddha chose India for this system because India was the wealthiest place then, and there was enough surplus that people could afford to support people living outside their collective; people had the generosity to support the nonconformist, the individualist. So, Buddha invented the monastic orders for men and women, the Sangha Jewel, the renunciate, transcendent community and their lay supporters. And this system caught on like wildfire in India, because people wanted and valued it and, as all human beings do, intuitively knew that some higher happiness exists that they should be able to get.

No religion can acquire our allegiance without promising that happiness for us, at least in the afterlife, or as a taste in a ritual in this life. Most religions get us to defer that achievement to some afterlife, heaven, the happy hunting ground. Shamanic, indigenous, tribal, nonliterate religions and the great religions alike do that. Secular humanism promises it, too, but only as a sort of stressless oblivion, since they don't have a very colorful heaven but a pretty quiet, dark one, a heavenly rest. But Buddha saw higher happiness as possible for everyone, here and now. So, he created an institution that celebrated that possibility, and it became a doorway to happiness within society.

It was as if the Buddha created holes in the cheese of society—he "Swiss-cheesed" the society. And the holes were the Sangha, the community, the renunciate institution, where people would go for lifelong free lunch. They would be fed free lunch by the lay community to keep their bodies going, and then they would spend their whole life energy liberating themselves, seeking freedom, not having to produce anything for anyone, not doing any agricultural work, not doing any military work, not doing any social work. Initially.

At first, the Buddha very intelligently and practically avoided challenging the cultural and social routines too much; he challenged them only enough to gain some space for the individual. The Buddha didn't dictate to his fellow warrior kings, "You better stop doing this, and you better not do that." But he did respond when they visited him, and he did say, "It would be better if you don't have war, if you don't make violence." He gave a list of ethics, of not killing, not stealing, not committing sexual misconduct, not lying, and so forth, like the Ten Commandments, but ten recommendations rather than commandments. But he didn't expect the kings to follow him too quickly.

Around four hundred years after the Buddha had left his body, the Sangha institution had produced many, many free people. And these free people, in a social feedback loop, had begun to make possible more freedom for the laypeople as well as the monastics. So, the Sangha institution could intervene more actively in society, in the routine lives of Indians. At that point, the less individualistic and more social teachings, which the Buddha had quietly planted earlier with a few disciples, became more useful, and people began to spread them as a kind of social gospel—called the Mahayana, the universal vehicle, or the vehicle of society. Those monastic institutions began to reach out and actually change the routine way of living in society. They unfolded the social dimension of the Buddha's teaching and began to change the social ethic of India. Devotionalism began to arise, cutting across the class system. Universalism began to arise, cutting across the gender system. Vegetarianism began to arise, cutting across the sacrifice system. Pacifism and nonviolence began to arise, cutting across the militaristic system. And India advanced enormously, economically and culturally. It developed the most glorious culture of the ancient world, a culture where even the pursuit of pleasure was developed to a very sophisticated art.

The pursuit of wealth created the legendary riches of India, which brought Alexander the Great to India, later brought all kinds of Central Asian conquerors to India, eventually brought the Muslims, had Columbus drooling fifteen hundred years later, and brought other European conquistadors to India. That tremendous wealth began to develop in this time.

As the wealth and society began to expand more and more, some people decided they couldn't wait for society to achieve freedom over a long period of time, felt they couldn't wait for enlightenment through many, many lifetimes of their own. These people decided they would achieve this perfect freedom and perfect ability to help others achieve freedom in a single lifetime. This was the beginning of the Tantric tradition, which was very esoteric at first. In the Tibetan view, Tantra emerged at the same time as the Mahayana, around one hundred years before the Common Era, but it remained completely esoteric for seven hundred years, without a single book on it being published. In its esoteric tradition, people lived on the fringes, on the margins; they were the magical people, the magicians, the *siddhas*, the adepts.

But after about five hundred years, the kings had become more gentle, relatively speaking, tamed by serious wealth and refined pleasure. Their militaristic habits subdued, the violence level in India became relatively moderate. So the Tantric masters began to emerge into the public because so many people were ready for more immediate realization and there was less need to keep their knowledge a secret. So, the deep exploration of the unconscious, the confrontation with the dark side, the elevation of the spiritual power of woman, and the sublime arts of fierce and gentle transformation that constitute the Vajrayana, the adamantine vehicle, the Tantrayana, the "weaving" vehicle, the "continuum" vehicle—these most astounding spiritual technologies were safely brought out into more general usefulness.

These were the three main stages through which Indian society developed: individualism, universalism, and esotericism. The awakening responses developed in interaction with the culture of India, with the people of India. The more and more open, more and more vulnerable, more and more ready to experience their own bliss, to accept their own reality they became, the less and less afraid of joy they became.

Of course, when a society adopts this kind of view, it becomes vulnerable as a whole. In Western historiography of the nineteenth and twentieth centuries, and even the beginning of the twenty-first, a society that becomes vulnerable and gentle in this way is called "decadent." There's something wrong with it. Its military guard is let down. The individual is no longer pitted violently against himself; he is not violent within the family, against other families. The people are not harshly disciplined in the schools, disciplined in the military academies, and therefore, they are no longer ruthless, capable of inflicting harsh violence on neighbors in conquest or defense. According to the Western view, the whole militaristic structure of life and of the individual heart, mind, soul, body, when weakened, creates decadence. But we must remember, this is the view of a militaristic society. We're the most militaristic society history has ever seen. We have nuclear weapons, germ warfare, incredible instruments of violence. Our culture is permeated with that violence, and our minds are permeated with that violence. Even our physical posture is permeated with that violence.

From the point of view of an enlightenment world history, however, the "decadence" that India had reached was, in fact, civilization. It was gentleness. It was something like a social paradise, heaven on earth, a New Jerusalem, but in India, temporarily. And it could only be temporary in any particular country at that time, because most of the world was still seething with violence and conquest and hordes and great invasion armies.

Inevitably, the gentle culture would eventually be swept over, overwhelmed by hordes of fierce warriors. The hordes themselves, of course, were actually looking for just such gentleness and joy, bliss and peace—for a surcease of suffering. But in thinking that they had to conquer it somehow, by violence, they destroyed what they were seeking. At least they destroyed its surface manifestations. But the great *siddhas*, the adepts, the great enlightened beings, the walking, living buddhas, had foreseen this. They realized that Central Asia was filled with potential yogis who were seeking bliss but thinking wrongly that it could be conquered by violence. The *siddhas* recognized that many of these would sweep into India and topple this gentle civilization, burn the monasteries, libraries, and temples to the goddesses and the male-female union icons, what Freud might have called "primal scene" deities, which frightened them most of all. So, the *siddhas* looked up and said, "Aha! Which among all these Central Asian barbarians may be the ones we can turn to, to save this jewel-like civilization of realization, where it won't be lost for the future?"

They looked, and they saw Tibet, where the people were violent conquerors at this time. The Tibetans were, perhaps, the most fierce of all contenders, powerful emperors and violent warriors, sweeping down from their wild plateau. But they had one saving grace. Their appetite for conquest was not limitless. This was not the result of any religious ideal or any special racial trait but was an accident of their geography. Tibetans like to live at two to three miles in altitude.

Therefore, when they would conquer China, or the Central Asian Silk Route, or northern India, they would feel a little too much oxygen, too much humidity, and they would soon go back up to the high, clear altitudes. So, they didn't ever want to stay anywhere. Once they unified the great giant plateau, large as all of Western Europe, they were happy with that.

And the great adepts saw that the Tibetans were ready to develop a more steady-state society. They thus could go to the Tibetans and turn them around from external conquest to internal conquest, from other-conquest to self-conquest, from territory-conquest to reality-conquest, from sword-conquest to Dharma-conquest—Dharma, in its highest meaning, meaning "reality." In Sanskrit, *dharma* is the jewel of the Buddha's teaching, and the word has a range of meanings, going from "thing," "quality," through "duty," "law," "religion," up to "path," "teaching," "truth," "reality," and even "freedom," or Nirvana itself. Capitalized as an English word, *Dharma* usually means "teaching." The expression "Dharma-conquest" was used by the Indian emperor Ashoka (third century B.C.E.) to describe his new policy of peaceful dialogue with neighbors after giving up military conquest.

So the great adepts began to send emissaries up over the passes into Tibet: Padmasambhava in the eighth century, Maitripa in the tenth, Atisha in the eleventh, and many others. They took with them their great treasury, their wish-granting gem tree, with all of its wish-fulfilling gem fruits, including the monastic vehicle of individual liberation, the universal vehicle of love and compassion, and the adamantine vehicle of depth psychology and inner subtle energy yogas.

They took this wisdom and art up there one by one, and text by text, and tradition by tradition. They dealt with the Tibetans one by one, and they turned these ferocious, individualistic, seminomadic warriors into the great yogis. And once they got the taste for it, many Tibetan seekers began to come down to the Indian plains and cities, braving the difficult journey to find the great adepts and wise teachers.

At first, there was tremendous resistance in the general Tibetan public. The Tibetans did not just say, "Oh, yeah, great, let's all be yogis and meditate." Not at all. The legend is that Padmasambhava had to wrestle and fight with all the mountain deities, the fierce, savage, military deities of Tibet, and one by one, mountain by mountain, he moved into Tibet, not like a shaman but like a supershaman. He overwhelmed them and impressed them by the one thing that the Buddhist deity-wrestlers always do, they never drive the deities out completely. They never eradicate or kill them. They wrestle them down, and then, when they *could* deliver a coup de grâce, and the deities know that, they start having retreats. Of course, at first these deities needed to be pinned down or they would have run away. But once a Buddhist supershaman pinned them down, he didn't hurt them. He gave them endless lectures.

After a month, a year, or a century or two, the deities got sick of the talks and said, "Okay, I guess the Dharma is useful. Buddhism is helpful. I guess I would rather be enlightened than conquer another country or two." And because these fierce deities were used to animal sacrifices, even human sacrifices in the most ancient period, the Buddhists always made them over into vegetarians with new rituals. The deities were a little disgruntled about that at first, but then they got used to it. They lost a little weight. They felt better. It was okay.

So, in this way, from the seventh century to the seventeenth century, the Tibetans were approached by enlightened beings in various manners and ways, men and women, adepts and simple people. Once beings become enlightened, they gain the ability to manifest in whatever way they are needed and can do the most good.

After about a thousand years of self-struggle, of self-investigation, of self-insight, the nation as a whole achieved what the Indians had achieved in about fifteen hundred years. They became demilitarized. They became gentle. They became monasticized. They became tantricized. They became internally and socially compassionate and ethical, you could say. But, it took a thousand years. Of course, some individual Tibetans, even in the first century, even in the first decade, did achieve enlightenment, although the Tibetans themselves like to say that Milarepa was the first Tibetan to achieve perfect buddhahood in a single life. Milarepa lived in the eleventh and twelfth centuries, and thus benefited from more than four hundred years of collective effort by many Tibetan individuals. And still he had to go through an arduous evolutionary process from being a criminal, even a mass murderer, to becoming a perfect buddha. He had to undergo tremendous ordeals to purify his sins, and he made heroic efforts in solitary contemplation for decades to develop all the enlightened qualities.

Just as foreseen by the great adepts at the full flower of Indian civilization from 500–600 c.e. to 900–1000 c.e., India would begin to absorb the great waves of invasion that poured in during the second millennium. With the Iranian, Turkish, and Tajik Muslim invasions followed by the Portuguese, French, and British Christian invasions, the prominence of the enlightenment institutions melted away. Nevertheless, they did remain for the Indian people, apart from the Buddhist institutions, because the enlightenment perspective had become completely absorbed into the village social fabric as "Hinduism" and was able to persist unseen beneath the oppressive weight of the various conquerors. But the monasteries, libraries, temples, and stupa-monuments were all sacked and destroyed, and all evidence of organized Buddhism was wiped out of India—which goes to show you that "Buddhism" does not consist of merely some physical institutions. It is simply the response of enlightened beings to help the unenlightened.

Back in Tibet, the Tibetans had achieved the full measure of social incorporation of Buddhism by the seventeenth century. Only at this time can we say that the culture caught up with the great adepts, the advanced beings who had taught the Tibetans earlier, so only then did the culture as a whole reflect the enlightenment civilization, the enlightenment traditions. In the seventeenth century, after centuries of war and struggles for power, something extraordinary happened, perhaps the only instance in all of Buddhist history. The Tibetan people themselves, including the feuding warlords, with a few exceptions, who fortunately were defeated in the final battles, turned to the monasteries and said, "When we produce governments, we fight each other. We fight with each other for power all the time. To have a lasting peace, why don't you enlightened teachers, with your high reincarnations, focus a bit more on society and take responsibility for the government?"

Speaking to the lamas, speaking to the monks, they said, "We're going to have a buddhocracy now, not a theocracy. We're going to have a lamocracy, a monastocracy, no longer a warlordocracy, no longer will we have feudal militarism running this country. Tibet will be run by lamas, by enlightened beings. Please, be enlightened and run our country for our own individual good, for our own liberation. Let us found a polity based on the individual aspiration of every individual within it, that each being should have maximum opportunity to unfold his or her enlightenment to the maximum degree in this life." The Fifth Dalai Lama accepted this invitation in 1642, and that's when the Tibetans, in celebration of this innovation, built the Potala Palace, a symbol of their choice to live under the aegis of the great bodhisattva of universal compassion. Starting in the 1630s and '40s, and finishing in the 1690s, they spent fifty years building that amazing building, the largest palace in the world.

The Potala is built on top of a fort. Upon the fort, there is a monastery, and the dominant activity within the fort is the monastic activity. Within the monastery is a Mandala Mansion, the ideal abode of the bodhisattva Avalokiteshvara, the bodhisattva of universal compassion. Thus, three levels are fused in one: the monastic, individual vehicle level of individualism, withdrawing from the social routine to achieve individual freedom; the social level, where a bodhisattva king runs the society a certain way and the ethic of compassion becomes the dominant ethic of the society; and the magical level of the Vajrayana, the magical cosmology where time has collapsed, where the individual can achieve perfect enlightenment, can evolve to perfect buddhahood, even within this life, where evolution can be accelerated to achieve buddhahood in a single life rather than the usual process of three incalculable aeons of lifetimes, evolving over millions of years, to develop the compassion, the amazing embodiment of buddhahood, not just the wisdom, the mentality of buddhahood.

Almost all religions try to defer gratification. They say, "Well, yes, you'll be at the throne of God. You'll be with the angels in heaven if you do right, if you work hard, if you give gifts; if you do this and that, you'll be with the buddhas in the pure land." Institutions feel that if people somehow even imagine the goal too much, if they taste it too much, then they'll drop out, and they won't serve the collective. Authoritarian societies, scarcity societies, militaristic societies fear that people won't fight and die for the group, that people will want fulfillment for themselves now, and the society will collapse. But Tibet in the seventeenth century reached the point where the society was organized around more people wanting deep inner fulfillment more than anything else.

Ironically, even if you organize a society where theoretically anyone who wants fulfillment now could try to attain it, and would be supported by everyone else doing so, many people are still afraid of that idea. They work to get a certain quality of fulfillment, then they kind of postpone getting more. They tend to harden their personal paths into institutional forms, settle down as members of an institution, and consider that other personal paths or institutions are not as good as their own. This tendency leads to institutional division and conflict, which even arises between different forms of Buddhism. Centuries ago, the great Tibetan lamas decided that the orders of Tibetan Buddhism were getting too competitive with one another. To counter this trend, they reminded everybody that the orders were all really providing insights and arts for people to open up their own inner awareness, freedom, and joy. In fact, the real Buddhist vision is that people of all religions—even the secular humanists today—are on the Dharma path, the path to reality, the path to their fulfillment, the path to happiness. We must always remember that liberation is attained as much by wisdom, by science, as by faith and religion. Wisdom and science seek experience of reality, aim to find freedom from reality, and do not merely seek a home in a constructed belief system.

There is no such thing as being saved by being a member of some group. That is simply not correct. Being a member of some group usually serves to reinforce egotism, and egotism never can bring salvation, because egotism is, itself, doomed. Egotism is ignorance; it is misknowledge; it is the *cause* of suffering. Therefore, empowering the cause of suffering by egotistically becoming a Buddhist, or egotistically becoming a Christian, will never produce happiness. You'll be a miserable, frustrated Sufi or Buddhist or humanist, Protestant or Catholic, Orthodox or Reformed Jew, Nyingma or Gelukpa Buddhist. Whenever the group membership becomes the thing, you'll be miserable, because the group will intensify your ego, and egotism simply is the key to misery.

Tibetans came to believe that we can all become perfect buddhas. They reversed most religions' and most peoples' sense of history as a process of decay and degeneration. They stopped saying, "Well, there was a Buddha back then, but nowadays we can't really become buddhas. Maybe we can become saints. Maybe we can become bodhisattvas. In a future life, we may be born in a pure land, or in a world ready for buddhas, and we could become buddhas, after more billions of lives of evolution." Tibetans, based on the gift to Tibet of the Tantric insight into the acceleration of evolution, came to feel that people could, *in this life*, become buddhas, and that many had. And so only the Tibetans developed the unique institution of the reincarnated lama—the reincarnation institution.

All Buddhists, Hindus, and most people in the world, actually, believe in some sort of rebirth or reincarnation. In fact, the early Christians did, too, along with the Greeks and the Rabbinic Jews. They called it "transmigration." They believed that there is a continuity of life, that we've been born before, we're born after, and we'll be born again and again, endlessly.

There are different versions of reincarnation in other world teachings. In some, we are always reborn as humans. In others, we weren't born before this life but we'll be reborn after it. But almost everybody subliminally and instinctively recognizes the infinite continuity of life, including individual life as well as collective species life. The form of rebirth or reincarnation particular to Buddhism was part of the "realistic worldview" called "karma," which means "causality" and simply is Darwinian evolution with an individual twist. It is scientific. It is not some mystical idea. It's a scientific description of the continuity of life, and it has an individualistic twist because it involves the soul in that Darwinian evolution, rather than making evolution a material thing that concerns only genes and species, collectives but no individuals.

In fact, that teaching, that evolutionary perspective, that vision changed Tibetan tribalism and egotism and race egotism and clan egotism tremendously. The Tibetans didn't invent Buddhism or reincarnation, but they took them to the next level because of their sense of the immediacy of the possibility of buddhahood. In their culture, many beings became perfect buddhas, and as perfect buddhas, they didn't want to abandon their people, whom they were helping to develop their own buddhahood. They developed the conscious reincarnation tradition so that they would not lose progress or continuity. It's a very ingenious thing. The Dalai Lama, the Karmapa Lama—many, many of them—and, of course, other great beings were reincarnated many times in other ways without being formally recognized but still continued to help and to evolve.

So, that's a general review of Buddhism. This brief introduction explains the mystery of why an elementary teaching, like our jewel tree, begins by reminding us of the goal and that we will be *at* the goal ourselves. It lets us imagine ourselves *being at the goal* to give us the taste or boost that inspires us to achieve it. It was just around 1600 that this work on mentor worship at the foot of the jewel tree was written. It codifies the mainstream path of enlightenment that was used in India and Tibet, in fact, all through the history of Buddhism. This path of enlightenment is like a great conveyor belt, like the moving walkway in an airport, except this is a walkway without walls. So, anyone can get on it anywhere, and then it will take them along. And people can even walk ahead on this great conveyor toward enlightenment, and so go faster, as you do in airports when you're rushing for your flight.

THE THREE JEWELS AND THE JEWEL TREE

Now, we turn back to the text of our quest and retreat, and we begin at the very beginning. And the very beginning is what is called "taking refuge in the Three Jewels." The Three Jewels are the foundation of all forms of Buddhism, and the first jewel is the Buddha. The word *buddha* means "the Awakened One." And it doesn't mean only Shakyamuni Buddha, formerly the prince Siddhartha, who became a perfect buddha in the sixth century before the Common Era in India, whom we sometimes call the "historical buddha." *Buddha* means all those who have awakened from the sleep of ignorance and blossomed into their full potential.

Awakened and blossomed, they are teachers of others. That is their most important name, "teacher," because that role is just as important as the fact that they're awakened themselves. Remember that awakening, freedom from suffering, salvation, if you will, liberation, omniscience, buddhahood, all come from your own understanding, your insight into your own reality. It cannot come just from the blessing of another, from some magical empowerment, from some sort of secret gimmick, or from membership in a group. It can't even come only through your faith, although some good faith may help. It can't come through meditation, either, at least not by meditation alone. So, the most important element of Buddha to us, until we become buddhas ourselves, is that Buddha is a teacher, and he gives us a teaching. Now, teaching is not an indoctrination; it's not imposing a dogma. A teaching gives us a set of methods that we can use to develop ourselves, to learn, to think over, to meditate upon, and finally, to gain deep, profound, transforming insight, wisdom, and understanding.

So, we take refuge in the Buddha: *Namo buddham sharanam gacchami.* We take refuge in the Buddha. We mean, we turn to the teaching of the reality of bliss, the teaching of the possibility of happiness, the teaching of the method of achieving happiness in whatever form it comes to us, whether it comes as Christianity, whether it comes as humanism, whether it comes as Hinduism, Sufism, or Buddhism. The form doesn't matter. The teacher is Buddha to us, one who can point the way to our own reality for us. He could be a scientist; she could be a religious teacher.

Now, the second refuge—we take refuge in the Dharma: *Namo dharmam sharanan gacchami.* The second jewel of refuge is Dharma.

Dharma means "to be held." *Dharma* in its highest meaning means reality itself. Beneath that, it has a wide range of other meanings.

The highest meaning of *Dharma* is the reality that is our own reality—the reality that holds us in freedom from suffering, holds us apart from suffering, holds us in a state of bliss. Dharma is our own reality that we seek to understand fully, to open to fully. Dharma, therefore, also consists of those methods and the teaching of those methods that are the arts and sciences that enable us to open ourselves. They are also Dharma. The practices that we do, which will open us, which follow those teachings, which implement them in our lives, in our practice, and in our performance, which deploy those arts—they are also Dharma.

Virtues and ethics and practices are also Dharma. Even the qualities that we develop, the positive qualities that lead us toward freedom and reality, those are Dharma. That is how *Dharma* came to mean a religion in some contexts, and also "duty" and other kinds of routines in Vedic Brahmanism, before Buddha used it in the liberating way. In later Hinduism, in the *Bhagavad-Gita, Dharma* was used by God to say, "Do your dharma," meaning, "Do your duty." "Follow your role as a warrior, Arjuna!" said God. "Krishna, you warrior, follow your Dharma!" That means, "Follow your duty." But in Buddhist terms, *Dharma* means more like Joseph Campbell's great statement, "Follow your bliss!" Bliss is your freedom. So it means, "Follow your freedom!" And it came more to mean that in India, after Buddha's time, also in another strand in the *Gita*, in Hinduism and Jainism, as well as Buddhism.

So, the second jewel is Dharma, the real jewel of refuge in Buddhism. Ultimately, we take refuge in reality itself, because that is the only secure refuge. If we took refuge in any unrealistic thing, it could be blown down by this-and-that howling wind—but when we take refuge in reality, that is what endures. It is uncreated. It is not made by anyone, reality. It lasts. It is there, and therefore it can give refuge.

The final taking of refuge, the receiving refuge in reality, is embodying reality in our being, realizing that reality is our body and breath and thought and mind. Therefore, the final refuge is only being buddha ourselves. But meanwhile, to whatever extent we can open to reality, we take refuge in reality, the second jewel.

The third jewel is the Sangha, the community of those who enjoy the jewels of refuge, who learn that teaching, seek that understanding, and work to embody that Dharma. They are consciously evolving toward being buddhas, sharing their understanding and bliss with others, as teachers of freedom to other beings, helping them discover these jewels. This includes all Buddhists everywhere and through time, in Sri Lanka, in Thailand, in Burma, in Tibet, in China, Korea, Mongolia, Japan, Vietnam, in ancient time and still now in India.

Namo buddham sharanam gacchami. Namo dharmam sharanam gacchami. Namo sangham sharanam gacchami.

All Buddhists say this, each in his own language. *Namo* means "I bow," meaning by bowing to express trust and faith and respect, to throw yourself on the mercy of another. *Buddham* is "to the Buddha." *Sharanam* means "refuge," a safe place of renewal, a resort. *Gacchami* means "I go." So, "I bow to Buddha and resort to him as refuge." *Resort* has a good double meaning, both "refuge" and "vacation resort," not just some pious act of going someplace and bowing to someone and then entering some sort of prison cell. It's like going to a vacation resort, going for a rest, to relax, restore your energy, enjoy, to get some peace. *Sharanam*, "refuge," is related to the word *shramana*, "ascetic," one who is "world weary," tired of the ordinary round, willing to give up minor pleasures for the great pleasure of release, peace, bliss. A *shramana* is "one who goes to refuge" from suffering. We sometimes translate it as "ascetic." But I like to translate it as "vacationer," one who goes away and takes a break. *Dharmam sharanam gacchami*, "I take refuge in reality." I go there for refuge.

Sangham sharanam gacchami, "I take refuge in the community." I go there to join those friends who are taking a break.

Now because of Tibetans' particular history, in which Tibet became the incubator, preserver, the crucible, the special mountain petal, high lotus where the quintessence of the Indian Buddhist civilization is cradled, Snow-Peak-Petaled White Lotus of Dharma, the Tibetans added a new context for the Three Jewels. Because of their insistence on the immediacy of enlightenment potential, they added the jewel of the lama, the spiritual teacher, the mentor. But the mentor is not a fourth jewel. That would be an incorrect interpretation. The teacher is the one who makes the Three Jewels immediate, accessible to you and me. The teacher is the mentor who embodies the Three Jewels, opens the door for us to get to them. So, that is why in our jewel tree teaching, we say first of all, "I bow to the mentor and go for refuge." This means that you choose to envision that the mentor's body is the living Sangha Jewel, the mentor's speech is the living Dharma Jewel, and the mentor's mind is the living Buddha Jewel. This makes the jewels immediate, alive, present to you. Otherwise, when you say, *"Namo Buddham,"* if you're thinking of the person long ago in history who died and passed away and is gone far away, though you say, "I go for refuge to him," how can you get to such a refuge?

You are saying, "I go to historical memory. I go to my faith that he once was in the world, that maybe another Buddha will come someday." But if you think of the Buddha as long gone, there's no one around in whom you can take refuge. So, instead, for you, the mentor's or teacher's mind becomes the living Buddha. For your personal inspiration, your practical use, you make an icon out of the mentor, just as a Theravada Buddhist temple has an icon or statue of Shakyamuni Buddha. It's not idolatry; they never think that image *is* Shakyamuni Buddha. They think Buddha attained Parinirvana, ultimate Nirvana, thousands of years earlier. But the icon or statue helps their memory—your mind—focus on Shakyamuni Buddha.

The Tibetans have plenty of icons and statues, too, but they also learned from their Indian teachers to take the living teacher as an icon and focus their remembrance on Shakyamuni Buddha by thinking, "The mind of my mentor is Shakyamuni Buddha." This subtle shift in focus works as a way of feeling the living presence of Shakyamuni Buddha, not gone far away but still with you, encouraging your practice.

"I take refuge in the Teaching." The icons of the Dharma are all the texts, the scriptures. The sacred texts are the Word of Buddha. They have been transmitted through history. They were memorized as he spoke, then they were written down. Then they were copied. Then they were edited and they were corrected. But no text, actually, completely, identically, can follow what the Buddha said. They're only a memory, a commemoration, a reminder. Again, if Buddha's not there speaking, I can't find the Buddha's speech, which opens the doorway for me into reality itself. But if the mentor's speech becomes the Dharma for me, if I can see the mentor's speech as the living Dharma, I can go for refuge to that speech, I can find there the living Word of Buddha. It becomes alive for me. Dharma becomes, therefore, realizable by me, here and now. Reality's doorway opens for me, the reality of freedom and liberation comes close to me, here and now.

Namo sangham sharanam gacchami. If you think of the Sangha Jewel, the spiritual community, as great saints long past, then what's the Sangha today, some lost guys wandering around here and there? The mentor is, ideally, a monk. The mentor can certainly be, and often is (perhaps should be more often), a woman, too. He or she's a fully ordained male or female mendicant. The mentor, therefore, is a member of that same, unbroken lineage of the Jewel Community.

His body is the community. Her body is restrained by the vows of individual liberation, her heart is formed by the universal vehicle of love and compassion, the spirit of enlightenment of infinite love and compassion for all beings. So, the mentor's body becomes the living presence of the Jewel Community.

Many people say, "Well, I'm a Christian or a Sufi, a Buddhist or a Jew. But I can't be good. I'm going to be a nasty businessman all day, I'm going to be a nasty egotist. But then I'll go to church or synagogue or temple or mosque, and I'll pray to be cleansed. Jesus, or someone else, will cleanse me, Buddha or Avalokiteshvara will save me later. I'm just a hopeless sinner, and there's no way I'll deal with it." This common way of being religious is actually good, too, because, although you kind of excuse yourself six days a week, at least for a few hours on Saturday or Sunday you'll try to be one with the savior being, however you visualize the mentor being.

Now, today, this moment, I hope we can take some inspiration from Buddhism, from this essence of Buddhism, and aim to live up to our ideals more fully. We must make it twenty-four/seven to be in communion; we must follow the precepts of Muhammad and do the ethical thing and the virtuous thing, twenty-four/seven; we must not kill, not steal, not commit sexual misconduct, not lie, not cause dissension, not speak harshly, not speak meaninglessly, not hold malice, not greedily think of getting something from others, not be prejudiced or fanatical.

INVOKING OUR MENTOR

So, as you invoke your mentor to give you access to the Three Jewels and our jewel tree, you can either say or just think the following: *"I and all space full of mother beings, from now until enlightenment, take refuge in the Mentor and the Three Jewels!"* We repeat this three times, so that our own bodies, our own speech, and our own minds, the three levels of our

being, from exterior to interior, all are seen and all go into the refuge of Buddha, Dharma, and Sangha, made immediate by the presence of the unbroken lineage of the Lama Mentors.

The *Mentor Devotion* says, *"I and all space full of mother beings, from now until enlightenment, take refuge in the Mentor and the Three Jewels! I and all space full of mother beings, from now until enlightenment, take refuge in the Mentor and the Three Jewels! I and all space full of mother beings, from now until enlightenment, take refuge in the Mentor and the Three Jewels!"*

Then, we repeat the refuge resolution three times: *Namo gurubhyoh. Namo buddhaya. Namo dharmaya. Namo sanghaya. Namo gurubhyoh. Namo buddhaya. Namo dharmaya. Namo sanghaya. Namo gurubhyoh. Namo buddhaya. Namo dharmaya. Namo sanghaya.*

Next, we repeat the vow to perform the particular practice of the *Mentor Devotion:*

> *For the sake of all mother beings, I myself will become a mentor deity to install all beings in the supreme exaltation as being mentor deities themselves. For the sake of all mother beings, I will become a mentor deity to install all beings into the supreme exaltation as being mentor deities themselves. For the sake of all mother beings, I will become a mentor deity to install all beings in the supreme exaltation as being mentor deities themselves.*

If you say this as a Christian, you would say, "For the sake of all mother beings, I will become a Christ, in order to lead all beings to becoming a Christ. For the sake of all mother beings, I will become a Christ, in order to lead all beings to becoming a Christ. For the sake of all mother beings, I will become a Christ, in order to lead all beings to becoming a Christ."

This is like the teaching of the *Imitatio Christi* that we have from the medieval Christian monastic period. The "Imitation of Christ" expresses the resolve that "I will live up to the mystical body of Christ. I will embody Christ's virtues." And you don't necessarily

mean that you are vowing you will follow Jesus' physical path, that you're going to have yourself crucified. Some medieval Christians did just that, however. For example, the Jesuits in their Stations of the Cross meditation, which Ignatius taught, visualize themselves carrying the cross and going to Golgotha, going through the whole thing. In that sense, they have a visualization of being crucified.

But when you say, "I will practice a path, I will become a Christ, I will imitate Christ, for the sake of all my mother beings, so that they, too, can come to an understanding where they, too, can become a Christ," you're rising to a spiritual level that is in all the teachings—in which the "kingdom of God is within you."

If you do this as a humanist, you say, "I will become Socrates, the wisest of all, who knows he or she knows nothing but who seeks to harness the soul and the passions and make them work with the Apollonian drive of reason, to harness them to the chariot of reason, so that the intelligent passions guided by the reins of reason lead us to a full and a benevolent and altruistic life, leaving a good legacy to all beings, even though I, myself, think of myself as not having a future life, I think of myself as just part of my lineage as a humanist."

In this way, the Three Jewels can find parallels; "I take refuge in the Buddha" would correspond for a Christian to "I take refuge in the Christ." "I take refuge in the Dharma" to "I take refuge in the Holy Ghost" or "in the Holy Spirit"; that is, "I take refuge in the reality, as God knows it, or the Holy Spirit knows it, not the deluded reality of ignorant beings." And "I take refuge in the Sangha" to "I take refuge in the holy community of all the great saints and all the great monks, and even the laypeople who are trying to do something positive within that tradition."

As a Jew, you would say, "I take refuge in Moses." "I take refuge in the Dharma" would become "I take refuge in the Torah, the law." (Actually, *Dharma*, means "law" in secular India or China, in East

Asian society, and *Dharmashastra* means "law school" in India today.) And, for the Sangha, "I take refuge in the community of the rabbis and saints and Hasidic masters."

In earlier days in all of the Abrahamic traditions, there were plenty of angels and divine beings, many different kinds, not just the one absolutely transcendental God. The Abrahamic One God has all his angels, all his spirits and beings there benevolently to bless you. At Armageddon, Jesus is supposed to come down with an army of them. Today, modern secularism has people pretend there's not much of that. But the Buddhist tradition hopes to inspire other traditions to use their own teachings to live up to their ideals. This is how the *Mentor Devotion* hopes to inspire all Buddhist traditions as well, to make the Buddha's presence more immediate. The Buddha's life is not just something in a historical past, with us left behind and lost here. The Buddha is not meant to be envisioned as a presence whom we will encounter in some world in the future. We should, rather, make the Buddha immediate for ourselves. We should connect ourselves to the Buddha's immediate presence in our minds, intentions, and actions. We do not just aim to emulate or admire the Buddha, the ancient saints, and bodhisattvas. We aim to become buddhas today, saints today, bodhisattvas today, at our level of ability.

THE JEWEL TREE MEDITATION

Now, before we meditate on anything that we want to understand deeply, we have to visualize the setting and focus our minds. In this practice, throughout the book, we will create the wish-fulfilling jewel tree, the wish-granting gem tree. As you read the text here, read it meditatively, that is, just try to see the images as the words go along. Don't grasp for the physics or mechanics behind it or try to analyze it. Don't get frustrated and feel it's complicated. Just go with it. Think of the images as creating a huge, wish-granting jewel tree right there before you, as if suddenly you were Jack before the Beanstalk—you came around the corner, and there was this giant beanstalk reaching up into infinite space, except this is a tree, it is made of jewels, and it bears jewel fruit.

We create a foundation for this celestial setting by visualizing ourselves giving away the universe. We say "OM" to invoke the universal, divine energy of all buddhas and gods and deities and teachers and prophets and saviors of all traditions throughout the universe. "OM" invokes their presence and their energy and their blessing. "AH" celebrates that this permeates us through and through, and radiates through our invocation to all beings everywhere. And "HUM" integrates this energy in this moment, in this situation in which we currently are. So, "OM AH HUM" is like "Amen," from the cosmic vibration of divine energy in the universe. If you're a Jew or Christian or Muslim, you can say "Amen," or the Arabic or the Hebrew version of "Amen."

The ancient text of the *Mentor Devotion* says:

Primal wisdom in reality appear as inner offering and individual offerings and works to create the distinctive bliss-void wisdom in the fields of the six senses, extending outer, inner, and secret clouds of offering, totally filling earth, sky, and all of space with inconceivable visions and sacred substances.

This means, just think of everything that you can think of, every beautiful thing that you know of, not only your own possessions but things you've admired in museums or seen in advertisements or seen in movies—any beautiful gems, flowers and gardens, landscapes and planets—all of it. And think of giving it all away to the enlightened beings, to the savior beings in the universe. This is a way of giving up your ordinary perception. To make offering is to give up your possession and perception of things that get in your way and can keep you from seeing clearly, and to turn them over to the pure perception of the enlightened being, of the divine being to whom it never looks imperfect, who can see beauty in everything, can see all joy and bliss in everything, in reality. So, you're giving it away, giving it up, giving over your perception to a higher perception.

So, always in your meditative practice, you begin by visualizing yourself as giving away the world, entrusting it to the care of more enlightened beings and so giving yourself permission not to worry about it for a while, turning your focus inward to your own spiritual unfolding. We'll come back to this point again and again.

If you are doing this practice in the context of another tradition, in place of the mentor that I visualize in the crown of the jewel tree as indivisible from His Holiness the Dalai Lama, or Buddha, you can visualize Jesus, Mother Mary, Muhammad, al-Khidr, Moses, Krishna, or Socrates. You put there whatever mentor you have, whatever teacher you know whose immediate presence inspires you most deeply. And you don't have to have just one.

Now, here's the description from our *Mentor Devotion* text:

In the middle of the all-good offering clouds arranged in the vast heavens of bliss-void indivisible; in the crown of the miraculous, wish-granting gem tree, radiantly beautiful with leaves, flowers, and fruits; on a sparkling jewel lion throne on cushions of spreading lotus sun and moon sits my thrice-kind root mentor, the actuality of all enlightened beings.

His form is of a fulfilled mendicant with one face, two arms smiling radiantly, right hand in the Dharma-teaching gesture, left hand flat in meditation, holding a bowl of elixir. He wears the three robes glowing saffron color, head beautiful with the yellow scholar's hat. At his heart sits the omnipresent lord Vajradhara, with one face, two arms, sapphire blue in color, holding vajra and bell, embracing Lady Vajradhatu Ishvaree, goddess of the diamond realm; both partners ecstatic in the play of bliss and void, resplendent with multifaceted jewel ornaments, draped with divinely wrought silken clothes, adorned with the signs and marks of perfection, surrounded by halos of five-colored rainbows, shining like the sun.

He, my lama mentor, sits in the cross-legged vajra posture. His five body-mind systems are really the five bliss-lords; his four elements, the four buddha-ladies; his sense media, nerves, muscles, and joints, the eight bodhisattvas. His body hairs are the 21,000 immortal saints. His limbs are the fierce lords. His light rays are protectors and fierce spirits, and the worldly gods lie beneath him. Around him sit in rows an ocean of live and ancestral mentors, archetypal deities and divine mandala hosts, buddhas, bodhisattvas, angels, and defenders of the Dharma [Christs, prophets, gods, goddesses, teachers of every variety and every tradition on all planets in all universes].

The three doors of all these deities' body, speech, and mind are marked by the three vajras: OM on the crown, AH at the throat, and HUM at the heart. The iron-hook tractor beams of light rays from their heart HUMs draw wisdom-hero spiritual duplicates of all deities from their natural abodes. Wisdom heroes and visualized heroes become indivisible and substantially present.

The jeweled lion throne is in the central crown of the jewel tree, which is this vast tree that rises before us from our position on a hill high above earth, out of an island in a jewel lake that sits below us on the top of the world. And this vast tree rises there, shining radiantly, filling us with rainbow light.

And at each branch and on each leaf, there sits another heavenly angel. Whatever beings it makes you feel good to imagine—your parents, your teachers, whoever it may be for you—are your heavenly host. They are not my heavenly host—I am, of course, visualizing my own version, following the *Mentor Devotion,* but you should visualize your own heavenly host. The host could be she, it could be he, it could be Buddhist, it could be Christian, it could be Jewish, it could be secular humanist. Whatever you want. Taoist, Confucian, Hindu, Jain, or all of them together—the vast perennial host of enlightened beings. And from them, light rays sparkle and flow down to us, melting our sense of ordinariness, our ordinary self-image, our ordinary self-identity, our ordinary feeling of being just Joe or Jeff or Jim or Bob or Ann or Nena, in an ordinary world, in an ordinary building. We temporarily suspend that whole thing. We're in a sacred shrine space, a force field, filled with rainbow energy, with luminous solar light, intense, blazing, powerful, buoyant energy.

We're enfolded in communion with the mentor lama because of that energy. We're lifted out of our normal perspective, our normal self-limiting self-image, and our potential is unfolded. We're capable of understanding any new thing. We're capable of seeing more deeply any old thing. We're capable of being close to Christ, close to Muhammad, close to Buddha, close to God, close to Mary, close to Goddess.

We're not far away from them. There they are in this giant jewel tree, fulfilling all our wishes for happiness. Light flows from them as if it were liquid elixir, jewelline, flowing, brilliant, radiant light, filling us in every pore, pouring into the crown of our head, driving away all doubt and anxiety and self-concern, as if they were only shadowy, flickering things in our heart and mind and body. They're just washed out of us and flow away. We're in this magical environment in front of Lake Manasarovar, the highest lake in the world, the most crystal lake in the world, with the magical island and the magical world tree, wish-fulfilling gem tree, growing out of that lake with all the heavenly beings shining on all the Hindu gurus, Krishna, Shiva, Uma, Radha, Rama, Sita, Hanuman, Saint Teresa, Hildegard of Bingen, St. Francis, Thomas Merton, all together there. They are looking particularly happy, chatting with each other, sitting on their branches of this jeweled, jingling tree in this radiant light. And they are happy because we are meditating on something beneficial.

We are in our retreat space. We are visualizing ourselves in this space of all potential, space of all fruition. And we're going to turn our mind to a path of evolution, accelerating evolution for the sake of all beings. We want to join their being to those beings who have become a refuge for others, being free and blissful themselves. And now, we imagine that around us on this bluff, sloping down toward the lake, are all the beings that we know, all the beings that we're barely acquainted with, and all the beings that we don't know, all in human form. If you talk to animals and animals can talk to you, you can have some animals, too. And they're all around us, but they don't see that jewel tree at the moment. But they see us, and they're looking at us, and as we fill up with light as it flows down for us in blessings from the jewel tree, and from the mentor deity in the jewel tree, the mentor beings, the savior beings, the goddesses, the gods, as it flows down to us, we fill up with that light, and it reflects out from us to the beings around us, and so we feel, "Well, they're not seeing those mentor beings and the jewel divine tree, but they're seeing us."

And as much as we find communion and we become luminous, to that extent they will receive that blessing through us. So, we are accomplishing this understanding for them. And we look at them, and we think of our loved ones there, and, of course, we want any benefit we have in our mind, any opening, any joy, any happiness, immediately to be shared with them.

We're doing it for them. Even those we don't know, they could be our intimates. They could be our loved ones. They have been in previous lives, they will be in future lives. And they could be in this life, we could get to know them. So, we send them the same loving blessing, see them as equal to our loved ones. Then, there are the beings that don't like us, and we don't like them, and even thinking of them being there is almost offensive, because we can't stand them. But we must put them there anyway. And we radiate and we bless them and we reflect that, actually, they were our loved ones in previous time. They certainly were; they will be again. We will find out, because enemy becomes friend, friend becomes enemy. Both friend and enemy become unknown. Unknown become both friend and enemy.

All these keep changing in their roles and relationships to us, again and again. So, we must try to feel equally positive toward all of the beings around us, and equal love and blessing and affection, equal commitment to opening their minds and hearts as our minds and hearts open.

And when they see this light from us, even the ones who don't like us, they're kind of intrigued by it. They send back a vibration—in the case of the loved ones, of gratitude; of the unknown ones, of interest; of the unloved ones, a kind of challenge. But all of it is energy, and it comes back to us in the form of more encouragement and energy. And then we send the light back, our gratitude and our offering, our feeling of turning over the world to the enlightened beings in the refuge jewel tree. We create a kind of figure eight of positive energy, positive reinforcement between us and the jewel tree and all the beings around us. We sit at this nexus point of energy for all of our meditations. And all of our meditations and reflections in the future sessions will be within the context of this environment. Even though we may not be able to see it in any detail, we may not be able to visualize it clearly at first, or hold it firmly, we shouldn't feel frustrated or worry about it—we should just know it's there.

We can grow used to this great image, like a familiar room or favorite place in nature. We automatically can imagine that we have come into this luminous realm at the beginning of any meditation session. We can enclose all of our life and especially spiritual practices within the environment of this wish-fulfilling jewel tree, so that we're not in the space of our ordinary, limited, frustrating, and disappointing reality. We're in a space of infinite potential, infinite possibility, infinite luminosity, infinite openness, and endless friendliness.

We feel at home in this. We develop a feeling of being at home here in this space. We can spend time visualizing specific branches or the whole tree or the lion throne or individual figures whom we know, even the glowing face of our most beloved mentor lama, Jesus, Mary, the Great Goddess, Krishna, or Buddha. The beings above us feel really happy when we do this, when we enter this connection with them.

The *Mentor Devotion* has us bring our actual mentors into our visualizations:

> *The three doors of all these deities' body, speech, and mind are marked by the three vajras: OM on the crown, AH at the throat, and HUM at the heart. The iron-hook tractor beams of light rays from their heart HUMs draw wisdom-hero spiritual duplicates of all deities from their natural abodes. Wisdom heroes and visualized heroes become indivisible and substantially present.*

We see on the crown of every single one of the beings a diamond OM letter, could be in Sanskrit or English, OMs on the crowns of their heads, all of them, ruby red AHs standing at the throats of all of them, and deep blue sapphire HUMs standing at the hearts of all of them, glowing and radiating and sparkling. Once we feel the mentor deities are really there, we salute them, make offerings to them, invite them, and then receive their blessings. We'll look at the salutations and offerings in the next chapter, but the *Mentor Devotion* here formulates the invitation and the blessing:

> *You are mentor! You are archetypal deity! You are angel and protector!*
> *From now until enlightenment, I seek no other savior!*
> *With compassion's iron goad, please take care of me,*
> *In this life, the between, and future lives!*
> *Save me from the dangers of both life and liberation!*
> *Grant me all accomplishments!*
> *Be my eternal friend! Protect me from all harm!*
>
> *By the power of thus praying three times, the vital points of the mentor's body, speech, and mind emit white, red, and blue elixir light rays, first one by one and*

then all together, which dissolve into my own. . . . A duplicate of the mentor melts in delight and blesses me completely.

And from the white OM, diamond light rays flow to a white OM on top of our head and merge with our body, and our body becomes living diamond in substance and blessed by them, and one with them, and we feel very blessed in our body, healed. And then, the white OM, that white diamond light, goes out to all the bodies of the beings around us. It reflects out from us, and they feel healed, and their bodies feel empowered. And then, next, the ruby red AHs at their throats radiate ruby rays, and they flow to us, like liquid red jewel elixir, and fill the ruby red AHs at our throat, and bless our speech. And our speech becomes one with their speech, and then, this red AH reflects out from our throat, goes to the throats of all beings around us, which become marked by red AHs, and their speech is blessed. And then, the blue HUMs radiate liquid sapphire light rays that flow down to us, to the blue HUMs in our heart, and fill our heart with the mind of all buddhas, the oneness with the reality of all buddhas, deep, sapphire blue. And this blue then reflects out from our heart to the hearts of all the beings around us, and they are bound by a deep blue, sapphire blue, in total communion with us.

Then, finally, the white, the red, and the blue all simultaneously radiate from all the divine beings, all our mentors and all their attendants and all the ocean of angels and all the heavenly host of beings and Socrateses and Marys and Buddhas and St. Teresas, and flow to us simultaneously in three brilliant jewel rays of white, red, and blue, and fill our body, speech, and mind with the body, speech, and mind of all buddhas. And the mentor beings are so delighted that we're visualizing this, they flow into us, they melt and dissolve into us.

And we no longer can see the jewel tree, and it flows into us, and it becomes one with us, it enters and merges with us. And our heart becomes one with the jewel tree and with all the mentor beings, and Socrates and Buddha and Jesus all become one and become present and manifest in our heart. And then we feel so delighted and charged and buoyant and energized by this that we want to dedicate the merit of our meditation and our reflection to all the beings around us, and we dissolve into pure jewel light and flow into all of them, and they become charged with light, and our being merges with each one of them, infinite numbers of them. We become one with them. We dissolve and disappear.

And everything becomes a vast, great bliss state, great bliss-void-indivisible jewel state. And then, the beings around us on their own think, "Where did we go in the ordinary mind? What happened? So-and-so was sitting there, shining out upon me." The moment they think that, we think, "Where are we?" Then we're back in our ordinary mind at the conclusion of that meditation.

This is our first encounter with the wish-granting jewel tree of Tibet.

OM AAH HUUM

TWO

THE FIRST LEVEL OF THE PATH
The Transcendent Attitude, Compassion for Yourself,
and Taking a Break

Now we have learned a little about "Buddhism" and the Tibetan past, and we have learned a bit about how to visualize the wish-fulfilling gem tree field. We'll soon return to that field, and even elaborate it a bit further, but first, we will think through the root verses for this next stage.

My liberty and opportunity found just this once,
Understanding how hard they are to get and how quickly lost,
Bless me not to waste it in the pointless business of this life,
But take its essence and make it count!

Fearing the fires of suffering in hellish states,
I heartily take refuge in the Three Jewels;
Bless me to intensify my joyous efforts
To give up sins and achieve a mass of virtue!

Tossed by fierce waves of evolution and addiction,
Crushed by the sea monsters of the three sufferings,
Bless me to intensify my will to liberation
From this terrifying, boundless ocean of existence!

As for this egoistic life cycle, intolerable prison,
I give up my delusion that it's a garden of delight,
Bless me to educate myself in ethics, meditation, and wisdom,
The treasuries of the jewels of noble beings,
And raise aloft the victory banner of true liberation!

The name of this stage, transcendence (Tibetan, *nges-'byung*), is often rendered as "renunciation," which is not incorrect but in English connotes self-denial, asceticism, the hardship of giving things up, even self-negation. I used to think it was about that. When I became a monk in my twenties, I even felt righteous about "renouncing" pleasures, mortifying myself, being hard on myself, thinking I was really getting somewhere. It actually took me about thirty years to realize that this step of moving into an initial level of freedom, breaking out of all kinds of habitual bondages and addictive preoccupations, is the beginning of the experience of *real pleasure*, pleasure that comes from within.

In the usual approach to happiness, we concede to an inability to feel any inner well-being. We constantly seek little breaks of relief from the stress of our pursuit of lasting satisfaction and our relentless failure to achieve it. The transcendent attitude that we want to develop, however, offers us a procedure to change our habits, to break free from our futile preoccupations. We can achieve a feeling of inner freedom that opens us to the more fruitful pursuit of our opportunities and a realistic enjoyment of them. *This transcendent attitude in fact is the achievement of real compassion for ourselves.* Having compassion for ourselves means opening up to really feeling our own pain and becoming determined to overcome it. We do this by analyzing its sources and understanding how to prevent them, and then by moving creatively to do so.

We develop the transcendent attitude by following specific steps of thought. First, we reevaluate our self-image by looking critically at our sense of our reality. "What am I?" we must ask. When we do ask this and reflect deeply on it, we realize we have been taught that we are not really very important, not very meaningful. The theories of physics, biology, and psychology that we are taught in school tell us we are material entities randomly present for no reason, that we came out of material complexity into consciousness and will subside back into matter and spiritual nothingness at death. We must change this incorrect sense of self.

We come to a happier, healthier, more realistic sense of self by understanding our spiritual purpose, by recognizing how rare and precious each of us is and what a great opportunity our human life is for us. We *can* attain freedom, we *can* understand our true nature and that of the world. We must come to a realistic self-esteem, a new kind of appreciation of ourselves.

Second, we must realize how impermanent we are, confront our inevitable death, imagine that at some unknown point we will cease to exist in this embodied form, *"how quickly lost."* We do this mentally and regularly to intensify our energy to take advantage of every moment for positive development.

Third, we concentrate on our evolutionary causality, which means that we commit to understanding the causes and conditions of things and events. We accept that nothing is random, nothing is purposeless, everything has evolutionary momentum and impact. This acceptance intensifies our mindfulness about everything around us and everything we do, say, and think. Nothing is insignificant. Everything has an effect, for good or ill. So we'd better make it good.

Fourth, we confront our habitual egoistic mental process. This means that we make the effort to notice how we are bound in a circle of self-preoccupation that dooms us to anxiety, dissatisfaction, and frustration. We recognize that we are never content with what we are or have, that we always want more or something else. Instead of finding the treasures in our moments, we are lost in memories or fantasies, comparing the seemingly inadequate present to romanticized past events, or unrealistically anticipated futures. This fourth thought step frees us from an amazing pile of self-imposed ideas, ambitions, judgments, expectations. With these four thought steps, we slowly but surely move from the anxious, fearful, discontented, mundane outlook up into the realm of the transcendent attitude. We feel compassion for ourselves, and we decide to allow ourselves to find our true purpose in life, our true fulfillment.

When you achieve the full transcendent attitude, you are like a man whose hair and clothes have caught fire—you can think of nothing but how to get into some water to put out the flames. Ordinary pleasures and pursuits seem absolutely trivial, and you want none of them. You want to learn, reflect, meditate, realize, and transform yourself from a helpless, driven being to a free person. You feel on the one hand a great relief, and on the other an intense focus on the infinity of the now. You want to enter the refuge of the Buddha, the protected reality (Dharma) he teaches us about, and the Community that helps us live it. Then you want to *be* that refuge.

When I had my first hints of transcendence, I was gripped by this exquisite ambiguity of peaceful release and intense determination. I felt free of all habitual ambitions, and I was determined to become a monk. My wise teacher told me it was good I was living with such a determined focus, but that I should not formalize my monkhood because I would change my mind about that later. I did not believe that to be possible, so I went ahead to formal ordination anyway. It is wonderful that a Buddhist, enlightenment-oriented society accepts and honors the renunciate and supports her or him to stay alive while pursuing the ultimate. But our productivity-obsessed society is not that developed, not truly supportive of the individual's will to freedom. So, in time, my wise teacher was proved right. Eventually, I couldn't live as a transcendent anymore, and I had to return to society. When I did, I attempted to focus on the transcendent attitude and still support myself and others. This attempt has ups and downs, of course, but the joy and relief of transcendence energize the love that makes it all possible and worthwhile.

THE JEWEL TREE MEDITATION: SECOND ROUND

Now, move into your meditative space before the jewel tree.

Dissolve yourself into the sacred space. Let your ordinary personality and your mental worries and your thoughts and your self-image and your sense of the environment around you—the room, the building, the town, the planet—let them all melt away. Arise from this spacious, skylike space, find yourself at the roof of the world, overlooking Lake Manasarovar, not far from the holy mountain, looking down from a grassy bluff, where you are comfortably and softly sitting, looking down on a jewel crystal lake. And the jewel crystal lake has a little lovely garden of an island sparkling there in front of you, and from this island springs a giant jewel tree made of agate and sapphire and ruby and emerald and diamond substance, and in that tree high up above you, above where your forehead is, sits the Lama Mentor, the being who to you represents the highest possible enlightenment, the greatest possible spiritual power, whether it be Buddha or God or Jesus or Muhammad, or the Goddess, or St. Teresa, or St. Francis, or Milarepa, or Tsong Khapa, or Padmasambhava, or Krishna, or Lao-tzu, or Socrates. Whoever it may be . . .

All the teachers who ever taught you are around you, as are all those whom you ever found inspiring in your life, and all the angelic beings you can imagine, the deities you can imagine. You can see God himself on his throne if it pleases you to meditate on that, or Goddess herself on her throne. Or you can see all these beings up on the branches of this giant jewel tree, sitting there glowing, sending down jewel-toned, laserlike, coherent light rays that flow to you like liquid elixir, flowing crystalline. The light tumbles down like a waterfall, a cascade of uplifting energy falling upon you and merging into you . . . this elixir of immortality, this buoyant, vibrant energy of wisdom. All these beings are smiling and glowing and happily greeting you there in your new meditation space, and as you fill up with their light, you no longer feel incapable, you no longer feel confused, you no longer feel depressed or anxious. Your habitual cycling thoughts waft out of you, and you feel buoyant and you feel luminous and you begin to share the luminosity of the refuge tree, and then you reflect on the beings around you—your loved ones, your neutral ones, your unloved ones. You reflect this light back out to them, and they feel aglow in your light, and they send you back grateful encouragement, and you send your gratitude back up to the refuge tree.

For now, we're in this special space, and we're our meditative self, our spiritually awakened and quickened self. So, now let's link up more powerfully with the jewel tree before turning our mind to the path of enlightenment itself.

There are said to be seven limbs of communion, seven ways of connecting yourself with this jewel refuge tree. The first is the limb of saluting, where you salute your enlightened beings. You say, "All hail, Socrates. You who were said by the Delphic oracle to be the most enlightened person in the Hellenic world but felt that you knew nothing, so you went to inquire from others who said they were enlightened what they knew, and you found that it was all vain and hollow. And through that inquiry, then, you brought yourself and your whole culture as recorded by Plato toward enlightenment. Thank you very much. Keep working through your teachings to us today."

And, "O Buddha, thank you very much for your great accomplishment of turning your heart inside out and seeing the world in a new way, from a nonegocentric perspective."

And, "Thank you, Jesus, for showing the power of love and compassion, and how you could actually let hatred and prejudice take your body and put it on the cross and wrench it into bits and still arise from death and show that the power of love and wisdom is more powerful than even physical death."

And, "Thank you, Krishna, for doing your *rasa leela*, your dance of adoration and your conquest of the evil king and your restoring of the world to sanity and to liberty."

And, "Thank you, Lao-tzu, for revealing the Tao and introducing us to its wondrous ways."

And, "Thank you" to anyone else of whom you may think.

The *Mentor Devotion* text says:

Mentor like a gem embodied, diamond bolt,
Live compassion from the great bliss element,
You bestow in the fraction of a second
The supreme exaltation of the three buddha-bodies—
I bow to the lotus of your feet!

Primal wisdom of all victors of the buddhaverses,
Supreme artist, creating whatever tames each being,
Performer in the dance of upholding the monastic form—
I bow to your feet, O holy savior!

Eradicating all evil along with instincts,
Treasure of a measureless jewel mass of good,
Sole door to the source of all joy and benefit—
I bow to your feet, O holy mentor!

Teacher of humans and gods, reality of all buddhas,
Origin of the eighty-four thousand holy teachings,
Shining axis of the entire host of noble beings—
I bow to all you kindly mentors!

To the mentors in all times and places,
And all worthy forms of the Three Jewels,
With faith and devotion and oceans of praise,
I bow with bodies as many as atoms in the universe!

That's the limb of salutation. Next, we extend the limb of offering. You offer the world to the noble beings. You give away everything, even your own mind and body and thoughts. Give them away. Just give them up, let them go. Give them over to the beings of enlightenment.

To the noble mentor savior with your retinue,
I offer an ocean of various offering clouds;
From these well-arranged bright, broad jewel vessels
Four streams of purifying nectars flow.

Earth and sky are filled with graceful goddesses,
With beautiful flowers, garlands, and showering petals,
Delicious incense smoke adorns the heavens
With summer rain clouds of sapphire blue,

Masses of lamps lit by suns, moons, and radiant gems,
Shine ecstatic light rays to illumine the billion worlds;
Boundless oceans of fragrant waters swirl around,
Scented with camphor, sandalwood, and saffron.

Himalayas of human and divine food heap up,
Wholesome food and drink with a hundred savors;
The three realms resound with sweet melodies
From infinite specific varieties of music.

The outer and inner sensory goddesses
Pervade all quarters and present the glorious beauty
Of form and color, sounds, scents, tastes, and textures.

Going beyond these limited offerings, you move to give the entire world to the enlightened beings in the jewel tree. Picture yourself picking up the planet in your hand, as if you're a gentle, giant, spacious being seeing a beautiful green planet with the vision of the astronauts. You see the continents—North and South America, Africa, Europe, and Asia, Australia and the Polynesian Islands, the North Pole, the South Pole—the entire beautiful, glowing planet. Visualize that you take this planet reverently in your hands, and you hold it up and you offer the planet to the entire galaxy full of enlightened beings, to the wise, those who know the reality of the planet and of you and of themselves, and visualize that you hold it there.

By giving away the whole world, you offer it to the buddhas and bodhisattvas and to the enlightened beings and saviors and Jesus and Moses and Krishna. You stop worrying and nagging in your mind about the world, because after all, the world that you think you know, you know only from your perspective of being unenlightened, of being deluded, of seeing it from your narrow, egocentric perspective. So you give away whatever you know from that perspective, whatever you possess, whatever you feel you connect to, you give away the entire cosmos to the beings who see it from multiple perspectives, who see it in the enlightened way. That is a tremendous relief. Let them worry about it, this giving away.

• • •

The *Mentor Devotion* text says:

> *These hundred trillion four-continent, planet-mountain worlds,*
> *With the seven major and seven minor jewel ornaments,*
> *Perfect realms of beings and things that create great joy,*
> *Great treasures of delight enjoyed by gods and humans—*
> *O Savior, mercy-treasure, supreme field of offering,*
> *My heart full of faith, I offer it all to you!*

Next, we come to the limb of repentance. Because we have been afraid of this and that at times, because we have coveted this and that, and worried about this and that, we have done harmful things. We took something from someone, we injured a neighbor in some way, we spoke harshly to a friend, we spoke unskillfully, meaninglessly, or frivolously to a loved one. We were untrue with someone. All of the negative things that you have done—think about not doing them again. Lay them down. No longer defend and pretend, "Well, I might have done this and I might have done that, but, well, there was this excuse and that excuse." Simply embrace that you did these improper things and set them down and resolve not to do them again. Lay them out in front of enlightened beings who are aware of them anyway . . . all the infinite angels who watch over us and seek to help us in our lives. Set them down, all these negative things, and resolve never again to return to them. Don't just sit remorsefully and grind yourself in guilt about them. See through them. Let them disappear. Let go of them, but resolve nevermore to connect with them.

> *From beginningless time, whatever sinful acts*
> *I did, had done, or rejoiced at others' doing,*

I repent before you, O Compassionate Ones,
Confess and solemnly swear never to do again!

Now, we come to the fourth limb, of rejoicing and congratulating. Think about the good things that you've done, and also the good things, especially, that others do, and their achievements, accomplishments, and enlightenments. Allow yourself to notice that when others do good things, you normally feel a little envious, a little left out. We think, "Why didn't I do it? How come they did it? How come they had that success?" And whenever you think that, correct that thought, that envious thought that separates you from someone's good deed. Instead, rejoice in that good deed and think how great it is that that person did that. Think how good it is that at least one person has done it, at least she had that success, or at least he had that achievement. And genuinely rejoice from the depth of your heart at all the good things that other people do. Whenever you are rejoicing, you, too, share in the merit and the virtue and the glory and the pleasure of it.

Though things are naturally free from signs,
I heartily rejoice in all the dreamlike
Perfect virtues of ordinary and noble beings
That bring them all their happiness and joy!

And now we come to the fifth limb, of thinking about the beings above us. And we think, "They have knowledge, they know their reality and our reality, and this knowledge enables us to take refuge in them. Knowing our reality and their reality, they can teach us methods appropriate to ourselves to travel the path of enlightenment and the stages from wherever we are developing in whatever way we need. Through that teaching, we can come to a knowledge of ourselves." So, we request that the rain of Dharma fall from these enlightened beings. Think again of them there in the great jewel refuge tree that is all aglow and that lights us up in its radiance. You don't have to visualize every branch and every leaf and every flower and every precious person, or even the exact details of the face of the beloved mentor, your main teacher. Don't worry. Just know that they're all there, and request them, "Please, give the teachings, make the teachings come alive in my mind, make me able to practice and perform them."

The sixth limb is when you remember that these beings don't need you. They don't even need you to become enlightened. They know only that you need to become enlightened. But they are utterly transcendent. Their bliss is beyond everything. Even your state of unenlightenment is transparent to them; they are truly transcendent. They don't even need to manifest a body to you. They're not there doing that for their own pleasure or benefit or glory. They are absolutely aware of the uncreated, of the absolute, of Nirvana. And they do not even need to be present in this world. So, therefore, you should ask them to be present.

So you say, "Hey, Jesus, God, Buddha, Mary, as you sit there in your transcendent absolute state, be involved in the particulars of my relationality and my suffering and my confusion and my distortion and my isolation and my alienation, and manifest to me. Always stay with me. Be my friend. Be my protector. Be my teacher." In this way, you ask them to stay with you, all these spiritual beings and angels and deities and teachers, these enlightened teachers.

Though your diamond body knows no birth or death,
You treasure chest of buddhas self-controlled in union,
Fulfill my prayers until the end of time—
Please stay forever without entering Nirvana!

Finally, the seventh limb is the limb of dedication. Remember that everything you do, even thinking or visualizing being in the wish-granting gem tree field, is all done for more than your own sake. Because you are totally interconnected with all other beings, who are your mothers, in a sense, you're doing everything for everyone else. Any change in your mind, positive or negative, affects all others. The wish-granting gem tree is a morphic resonance field. The energy of one contains within it the energy of all. Every action affects all other actions. Whenever you turn your mind toward the wish-granting gems, everyone else's mind is turned in that way, too. The planet's mind turns with your mind. If you let your mind go in some negative, paranoid, self-indulgent, distracted way, the planet's mind turns in that way. You're totally interconnected with everything.

> *The mass of perfect virtue thus created,*
> *I dedicate to stay with you, my Mentor, life after life,*
> *To be cultivated by your threefold kindness,*
> *To attain the supreme union of Vajradhara!*

So, whenever you do anything or accomplish anything or gain a vision or have a little sparkle in your mind, don't appropriate it and think, How great, I've got this sparkle in my own mind. Dedicate it to others. Immediately share it with them. Just as the light flows in and fills you up from the gem tree of the deity beings, the divine mentors of the gem tree, it immediately reflects out from you as it fills you up. It flows from you to all the beings around you. And they fill up with the same light. You immediately share it and dedicate it to them.

Those are the seven limbs of interconnecting with the jewel tree and all its noble beings, energies, and intentions. It feels really good when you enter the refuge in this way. You can even do this in about two or three minutes. No matter how long it takes you, it is crucially important to help you prepare for the path. Each of us is a kind of Atlas, the poor demigod who had to hold up the whole planet Earth on his shoulders, his neck crunched uncomfortably under it. He's very strong, but he's holding up the world and so must be tired and in pain. All of us all the time are holding up the world like that. Even when you sit quietly, and for a moment don't think of any thoughts in your mind, you still have a subliminal, cosmological pattern in your mind that you're on planet Earth, that you're in such-and-such a town, that you're in such-and-such a building. Up is up and down is down. You have such-and-such a body, you have such-and-such a name, you're forty years old, and so-and-so is in the White House, so-and-so is in the UN. All these different terrible things have happened. Your parents are hither and thither. Your ancestors are hither and thither, your friends, your exes, your lovers. Everybody's all over the place.

As you're holding the huge world picture in your mind, you have a picture of yourself. You can see yourself as half-baked, you sometimes do right, you sometimes do wrong. Sometimes you feel good, sometimes you feel bad. You sort of know your limitations, you draw your lines, you can do this, you can't do that. You don't understand certain complicated things. This world picture fills and affects you.

So, the beginning of all meditations tries to loosen and lighten that world picture. Let it dissolve into space. Realize that any particular part of it, if you really investigate, you can't really verify. And so, you let it sort of float away. Let it melt. Let it ease up. You don't have to sustain it and support it. And, in fact, since you're seeking self-transformation, you can certainly decide that anything you see around you in the world may be your delusion. It may not be this way and that way. It may not be World War V. It may not be this or that or the other disaster area. It's just your own delusion creating that, to some extent. Let it go.

And now, borrow from the Tibetans' vision of the wish-granting gem tree and allow your own wish-granting gem field to grow. Visualize it. Imagine it. And if you can't visualize it in detail because you feel you can't visualize, hold a simple, stable picture in your mind. Just run over to it, to your tree. Remind yourself it's there. You're at the top of the world, looking at the lake. A tree springs out of the lake, a Jack and the Beanstalk type of tree, all made of jewels, with every mentor and angel on it, all radiating floods of light to you, buoying you up, and filling you up in that light, and around you all the beings of the light flowing out to them. Know that you're in that vortex. And suddenly, you're not your normal self. Suddenly, you're rising to the occasion. You're rising to the challenge. And the challenge is: Make some degree of transformation in your mind, because that will transform all the beings around you. That will please the enlightened beings, and they will feel relieved that you feel this relief.

So now, we come out of the jewel refuge visualization but not out of the field. You must continue to feel you're in the wish-granting gem tree field, luminously wound by skeins of luminous light rays, rainbow light rays. Always think of liquid gems, of emerald and ruby and diamond and topaz and sapphire, and just being wound with these beautiful strands of light that also fill up your mind and body. But as we go forward in this chapter, you don't have to sit in a formal way, or rigidly, or tire yourself. Try to stay awake, to think, because now we are on the first level of the path, taking the first steps of thought that we need to develop the transcendent attitude.

The first thing we must transform is our self-image, our view of what we are as human beings. How we live our life is determined by what we think of ourselves as human beings. What is it that we are? Not only *who* am I—am I John Doe, or Jane Doe?—but *what* am I? What is my human life-form? What is a human being?

THE BUDDHIST VIEW OF HUMAN EVOLUTION

We were taught in school that we're made of cells, and those cells are made of atoms and energies, and that we're sort of randomly created by how our genes have developed from the genes of our parents. We're taught that all of this randomly mutated some time back, out of a sea of lifeless gases, that our genes came from the genes of apes and other beings, and we personally showed up here when the two seeds of our parents joined at our conception, and then we were born. Since then, we've been running around and, when our body stops, and our brain stops, and when our cells no longer function, then we die, and we cease to exist. This is what we think we are, at least in one side of our mind.

If we have some religious affiliation or spiritual tendency, we may think we have a soul that is a fixed thing, or one that is temporarily trapped here in this physical process. We may think that our soul gets taken away at our body's death by a deity or some other force and put in a nice place. In the West, even some of our wisest teachers normally think that that soul began with our birth into this life.

Now the Buddha's vision of the life process was very vast, huge. The Buddha saw, like Darwin, that we come out of a great ocean of evolutionary life-forms. Unlike Darwin, proponents of the big bang, or creationists, however, the Buddha didn't believe it was possible to say that there was any *first* beginning in one particular big bang, or an initial cosmic creation point, at which the world was created out of nothing. To him, that seemed senseless, illogical. It's meaningless to say that things were created out of nothing. Nothing is nothing, therefore it has nothing from which you can take something out. It is simply meaningless to say that something is created out of nothing. Things are created out of other things. This is our universal experience. From the Buddhist view, it is simply an incoherent use of language to say that something comes out of nothing.

Therefore, the Buddha saw that life was beginningless, the world was beginningless. It had always been going on. Things have always been something else and come from something else.

Why does a thing become a certain type of something? Why have we become human beings, embodied with body, mind, and speech? How did we get to be the way we are, from this beginningless time? Well, the Buddha looked, and he saw, as Darwin did, an evolutionary pattern. He saw that we adapt to our environment. He saw that we behave in a certain way: We reach in a certain direction, pick up a certain fruit, and begin to get a certain type of hand, a hand that is skillful at picking up the fruit. Darwin wrote that those who survive because of this adaptation pass on the trait genetically. The individual with the gene that gives the instructions to the cells to form into a certain type of hand that can pick up a certain fruit eats more of the fruits, gets stronger, and that strength favors that development within the species. The individuals are just examples of a species. They have no individuality, really; they are just carrying the genes of a species, according to Darwin.

The Buddha saw the same kind of evolutionary interrelationship with causation, but then he said, "For the individual who is experiencing himself as the giraffe, there's a reason why he personally feels that he is a giraffe. His personal feeling about himself, his individual continuity, is part of reality. Therefore, the giraffe didn't come from nothing. It cannot possibly have come from nothing. It has its own previous continuity. So, the mind has an infinite and beginningless continuity, as does the body." Mind is always interwoven with body, but mind is somehow experienced as irreducible to body, and therefore, in its own stream of continuity, it is beginningless as well.

The Buddha developed a more complicated view of evolution than the materialist view. The Buddha saw that we personally have been embodied in various life-forms, life after life, from beginningless time. And we personally will continue to be embodied, in various life-forms, life after life, until endless time. The fact that we now are a particular form, in a human body, with a human intellect, and a human embodiment, is because we gravitated toward that form. We are attracted to that form, because we go toward what we are attracted to, because of our acts in previous lives, because of our evolutionary experience. Just like the giraffe gets the long neck, just in that way we humans got to *like* being with certain senses, with eyeballs up on a skull, and ears flapping out on the sides of the skull, and nostrils in the middle of the skull, and a little mouth going *munch, munch,* and a tongue flapping around inside, two hands and feet, with little digits, fingers and toes, and different kinds of joints and things, capable of moving in this and that way, and skin that isn't very hard or armored but sort of light and permeable.

When we became mammals, we were able to understand the permeability of the boundary of self and other, because we grow our young within our bodies, and we unite with each other to create them. When we saw the permeability of inside and outside of the body, we developed the ability to imagine. We developed all these extra folds in our hard disk, or wet disk, or sloppy disk, our brain. With all these extra folds, we could envision an image, and imagine. In our imagining, we began to develop the ability to imagine what the other feels. We could empathize with other beings, and imagine being those other beings. We began to loosen ourselves from experiencing the world only through our own sense organs, from our own egocentric point of view, and we became able mentally to imagine and experience the world from others' points of view. Initially, our sensitivity would unfold for only the beloved, only the members of our species, only the child, the infant for whom we were caring. We would identify with them. But we became capable of imagining all of the beings, and representing all of them. Finally, we became able to become enlightened, feeling the feelings of all the other beings by means of a vastly expanded empathy.

We became human beings through developing these compassionate qualities, not through being successful aggressors. A successful
aggressor, like the dinosaur or the tiger, is so successful within a certain structure of relation between self and other, and self and environment, that he doesn't have any impulse to transform himself. He
sticks at that point to that place, eating what is in front of his face.
Therefore, he is not so adaptable if the environment drastically
changes. Yet because we couldn't compete with the tigers, mam-
moths, or rhinos, we had to go hide in a cave and figure out some
multiple options. Somehow, actually *because* of our weakness, we figured out how to be more gentle. We began to chat with each other
about our different miseries, and how we were being eaten by certain
animals. And then we began to think, "Well, gee, if we all got together, maybe we could surround the animal."

We began to coordinate our activities, to develop technologies,
and then we did become powerful aggressors—potentially destructive, in fact. Yet even though we are potentially aggressive, we didn't
achieve that ability through *being* aggressive, we achieved it by adapt-
ing to *failing* at aggression, from the Buddhist view. The human being
develops to be human by generosity, by sensitivity to others, ethical
sensitivity. This human, humane sensitivity expresses itself as tolerance, patience, and the ability not to react lethally to injury from
others but to tolerate that, and then to sort of work it out with the
others rather than just chomping them down.

From tolerance and patience grew our creativity, our imagination, our concentration, and our wisdom and broader knowledge of
reality. These qualities are what we have as human beings. As human
beings, we personally earned our "human being–hood." Yes, our
parents helped us by providing genes, but we were attracted to the
form of our parents. We were able to be in love with our parents before we were born, because they did look beautiful to us, and they
looked beautiful to us because we had developed the weird idea that

it's a wonderful way to be, to be a creature with a funny kind of a spine, and a head bobbing around with a bunch of slimeware in it, and senses, eyeballs and ears, and hands that can run around and do things with opposable thumbs. Our idea of a lovely way to be would not at all appeal to other life-forms—the lizard, for instance, wouldn't think it was cute. But somehow we figured that our way was a playful, friendly, funny way to be. And, therefore, we were able to fall in love with those parents. So, we personally have earned this human life-form, by acts of generosity, ethical sensitivity, and empathy with others, primarily, and also by intelligence, concentration, and creativity.

When you inherit a bunch of stuff, easy come, easy go, you don't necessarily pay attention to it; you take it for granted. But if you earn it, if you make it, if you build it yourself, then you really like it, you really appreciate it, because you made it yourself. You don't want it to be taken away easily. Similarly, if you realize that you made your own body, you made your own body-mind complex, you created your own special human sensitivity, and you did so through these self-transcending actions, like not immediately eating the first person you met, not immediately using someone else in some egocentric drive but learning to communicate with him, giving and conceiving something with him, getting along with her, communicating—if you realize this, you value your life even more.

To get to this life, you gave things away to others. You didn't grab everything for yourself. When others were a little harsh on you, you didn't freak out; you remained tolerant and patient—all self-transcending actions, which are difficult even though they are what makes us human. It is easier to follow those immediate impulses, greed and anger, of the self-centered instinct. Yet you developed the ability to stop that when you were a different type of animal. As an animal who sat there, and flicked your tongue, and grabbed a fly, you were instinctual. But to think, "Oh, that's a cute fly, I'll let that one go," that's transcendence. You didn't have the words to think about it as an animal; you weren't thinking about Buddha, or liberty, or evolving; you were just fascinated by the fly, how beautiful it was, and then you let one go without flicking that tongue to trap it. When you are a tongue-flicking lizard, it's not easy to get such an inspiration. And yet, we have all done that billions of times to have gotten here in this precious human embodiment that we have all earned. Even some great Western teachers have realized this. Herbert Spencer wrote, "Soul is the form and doth the body make."

When you think in this way, you can begin to be critical of all those meaningless cosmologies. You can't immediately just suspend your worldview and have a different one, but you begin to look at the boundaries of the worldview that you do have. Does it really make sense that mind came from nothing, or came from a cell at a certain moment, the way the materialists try to say that the illusion of sensitivity, the illusion of mind, just arises with a certain complexity of cells? You may as well say the mind just came from a table, or a stone, or a piece of dirt. Instead, we stand up for our awareness, and we say awareness always comes from awareness, and our awareness is something, it is who we are, and it is precious.

We can experience the most exquisite things. We have a special type of human embodiment. Of course, our awareness is also vulnerable, and we can suffer because of it. Look at the people who we know today live on this planet. How many of them are starving to death right now, in some terrible ecological catastrophe inflicted by postcolonial, postimperialist exploitation of the planet, climate change, tribal dementia, prejudice, hatred, or disease? How many have no thought of liberation, except liberation from this immediate agony in front of them, or within them, or around them, and for their loved ones around them? How many beings are in that state? How many beings live in cultures where they are told just to follow the routine, fit in with the spirit, do what the collective wants them to do, what the witch doctor tells them, what the chief tells them, go out and kill their neighbor, with no thought of liberation? Maybe one shaman, or one person, goes somewhere else, but most of the people just fit in. How many beings even in a supposedly educated modern society just work in a factory from dawn to dusk, get a very poor education, have no job, and then commit a crime and go to prison until death? How many beings are there who are working endlessly in fields, eking out a living, or living as hunters in some vast snowy waste, just thinking about getting the next seal, with no time to reflect on liberation?

In India, before Buddha's time, in the time of the Vedas, there was no mention of liberation. People wanted power, wealth, duty, pleasure, progeny. Even the ancient songs of the Vedic people, for example, never talk of liberation. They just did what God wanted them to do, which meant then what the priests and the kings wanted them to do. Even today, many of us in our modern society just live mechanically, go to school, get our grades, graduate, go out, make money, have a family, pay taxes, do our duty, serve in the military, retire, then live in Florida and die. And that's it. They have nice lawns, and they hope that their heirs do better than they did. There's no meaning to that sort of lifelong pattern, finally, because that life ends. And even the different religions tend to annihilate your sense of personal spiritual continuity, inviting you to be a bland holy angel, waiting on God.

Why would you seek to transform yourself in life, in a really deep way, if there's no continuity? If you're a person who has sought her whole life long to transform herself, to become enlightened, do you have the same nothing at death as the person who has only sought to indulge himself his whole life long? If the person who does evil and gets away with it receives the same nothing at death as the person who does good and even suffers for it, why would you bother?

The modern world lives in a deep cosmology of meaninglessness. All of the traditional religions have really failed to control this general feeling of meaninglessness. They do provide some spiritual meaning when they say God wants you to do something, or God is doing this something for a reason, when they fit you under the inscrutable authority of God's will. But the operative, life-controlling idea is that reality is just material and basically meaningless. If you think you are basically meaningless, what do you really care for yourself? You will let yourself live your life, just making money, for example, saving it and hoarding it, and trying to be a big shot, dying with that, putting your whole life toward investing in something that you will lose.

Yet the supercomputer that is your brain is capable of realizing the kingdom of God within you, capable of realizing the great bliss state within you, according to the Buddha and all the awakened and enlightened teachers, including Jesus. But instead of turning your attention to that kind of total fulfillment of all of your wishes, and developing the ability to fulfill the wishes of others for an infinite future of enlightened living—instead of that, you just waste your life on some ephemeral thing that will not ever satisfy you and will just leave you at death. Who is satisfied with wealth when they accumulate it? No one, ever. They have $100 billion, they want $200 billion.

THE ENLIGHTENING STEPS OF THOUGHT

So, now that we know we have a meaningful view of life and can see its continuity and endlessness, we also come to the preciousness of our human life, which is endowed with liberty and opportunity. We cancel those views of meaninglessness; we just suspend them. We are critical of worldviews that say, "This is the law of nature, this is the law of reality, and that's where you fit, and that's all you can do." We don't necessarily accept that. If we have an instinct or an intuition that we have something in us that can flower, that we could really be fulfilled, that we could achieve a kind of bliss that would be deep and upwelling from within and that would be a reservoir of joy for others as well, we let that come out. We realize, this lifetime is the time that we can do that.

> *My liberty and opportunity found just this once,*
> *Understanding how hard they are to get and how quickly lost,*
> *Bless me not to waste it in the pointless business of this life,*
> *But take its essence and make it count!*

The liberty that we have is the liberty from immediate suffering and an oppressive environment. The Buddha taught us the eight liberties and the ten opportunities,* the most important of which are having freedom to pursue your own spiritual evolution consciously and having access to enlightened beings, to great saviors, to great spiritual leaders, to great saints, who can inspire you to fulfill yourself in this life, as a human being. And the jewel tree is one of the teachings that gives you that access.

When we reflect on this preciousness of our human life, endowed with liberty and opportunity, we find a new level of appreciation of ourselves. At this very point, we start on the Buddhist path, on the path to enlightenment, the Tibetan path, with the realization that our life is precious. All enlightened discourses—Burmese, Sri Lankan, Zen—describe how precious you are, you, a human being, because you can become enlightened. Reflect on this, and then think

---

* The eight liberties are the liberties of being free from birth in hells, birth as a hungry ghost, birth as an animal, birth as a long-lived god, birth as a human with false worldviews, in a country with no Buddha Teaching, as an idiot, or in uncivilized societies. The ten opportunities are being human, living in a Dharma country, having your faculties intact, not having committed serious crimes, having basic faith, having the presence of a Buddha, and his teaching, having them endure, and people who practice them, and living among kind and loving people.

about yourself and how you spend your life. How much do you do that is valuable for you? What do you have to do that is just dishing something out to make a living? If you could combine some generous gesture toward others with that dishing out to make a living, some cheerfulness that you convey with the food you give, or service you provide, however you interact with others, then you're doing something for yourself and for them in the process of making your livelihood. And that is wonderful.

Anything that you do just to earn money, however, keeps you from your true self and happiness. You spend that money on a house, then you get greedy and want a bigger house, and you have to spend more, and waste more time, and you sleep half the time anyway. How much of this precious quality time that you have, evolutionarily speaking, as a human being, with a human intelligence, do you spend on using that human intelligence to understand yourself, to understand your world, to understand others, to understand reality, so that you can transform yourself and find your true happiness? How many minutes out of a twenty-four-hour day do you invest in yourself in that way? You'll be shocked if you actually take inventory. I am shocked, constantly, by how much time I waste, with this precious body that I have, whose time is running out. That's the first thing. True self-appreciation, not a fake self-love, that is, "I'm great because I'm rich, I'm great because I'm beautiful, I'm great because I went to Harvard, I'm great because I'm American, I'm great because I'm male, or I'm great because I'm female." All these superficial identities, the kind of false pride in them, are not real self-love, because in them we are really not appreciating our own vastness.

Each of us is potentially an infinite being. Each of us has been an infinite being, has an infinite past experience, evolutionarily speaking. Each of us has been a god, actually. And now, as humans, we have the opportunity to become more than humans or gods. We can become perfectly enlightened beings, the summit, the peak of evolution. That form of life, at the end of all possible culmination of evolution, that is perfect compassion, meaning the perfect ability to feel others' feelings, and perfect wisdom, to help them feel better, knowledge of our self and others' reality, so that we can help them feel better. This is what we can become: bliss indivisible.

That is the first step of thought on the path of enlightenment. Once you begin to cultivate a deeper sense of self-appreciation, cherish yourself and take care of yourself every moment, expand your understanding and intelligence, and use this time of infinite malleability that is the human form, the human lifetime, to its maximum meaningfulness, then you have to reflect realistically on where you are headed.

Here, for the second thought step on the path of enlightenment, we turn to something that at first may seem disturbing but in fact is vastly liberating. We turn to the topic of death. It's a big note. And you have three vibrations within this note of reflecting on death. In the first you reflect on the surety, the certainty, the absolute certainty you can have that you personally will die.

My liberty and opportunity found just this once,
Understanding how hard they are to get and how quickly lost,
Bless me not to waste it in the pointless business of this life,
But take its essence and make it count!

At first you may think, "Well, why do I do this? Everyone knows that he will die." But if you really reflect and meditate on death, you will realize that you are carrying on as if you are going to be here forever. I know I do. Bob Thurman, this body, a slowly decaying form of this body, but still basically this body, with this mentality, personality, education, background, brain, body limbs, senses. It will always be like that, so I can go and meditate tomorrow, next year. When I retire, I'll really take this seriously, and transform myself, control my temper, control my obsessions, later, because I will be here forever, basically. I'm sort of assuming that it will always go on like this. So, when I begin to reflect that I am going to die, I realize that I will *not* go on like this.

Now, that doesn't mean that something will not go on, some continuity of consciousness. Certainly I know that the body will go on, and it will become fertilizer. Or it will become fuel, if it is cremated, and then heat waves in the atmosphere. So, the body will go on, in some continuity. And consciousness will go on, it seems sensible to declare, because just as something cannot come from nothing, it makes no sense for something to go into nothing. Something will always transform into another realm and become something else. Something cannot become nothing and sort of blank out. Everything that we've seen—all of our experience in nature and rational theories, even according to the law of conservation of energy in physics, for example—indicates that something never becomes nothing. It always becomes something else.

But the point is that I, as I am conceiving myself, as a body-mind complex, Bob Thurman, that will cease, that will die. Even Buddha died, in his form as Shakyamuni. Jesus died. Jesus rose from the dead, was resurrected, but he died on earth as a human being. Even gods die, in the Buddhist perspective, insofar as you see the god as some sort of embodiment. A transcendent, absolute body, what they call *dharmakaya* or truth body in Buddhism, doesn't die; or absolute godhead, as they may say in Christian theology; or the nameless, absolute as they may say in Judaic theology; Nirguna Brahman, unqualified Brahman, as they would say in Hindu theology; the absolute Tao, as they would say in Chinese theology—that form doesn't die, but neither does it live in the normal sense that we understand vitality. As an embodiment, it's beyond all embodiment, and uncreated, and uncompounded, and therefore can be eternal, like space. But anything creative, such as an embodiment made of parts and pieces that are separated from the rest of the world, will dissolve again. The pieces come together, and they go apart.

So reflect on the fact that you will die. It is a good thing to do. Western thinkers as well as Eastern sages have realized this. E. M. Forster, for instance, wrote, "Death destroys a man, but the idea of death saves him." You can do it as a kind of subtraction meditation; there you are, you have your relationships, and your friends, and your possessions, and your house, and your property, and even your knowledge, and your memories. But then, these are all lost. Look how we cannot remember our previous lives, can't even remember many things that happened in this life. It all gets lost. We will die, so in our meditation we sort of subtract our self, the self-image or identity that we're pushing forward in the world. We do this now because it will get subtracted. It gives up, it loses control, it dies, we die, you die, I die.

The second root consideration is when we think, "Well, when will I die?" And then, we realize there is no knowing when we die. Just as we definitely know that we will die, we definitely know that we *don't* know *when* we will die. We could die anytime. When we connect this uncertainty about when we will die with this certainty that we will die, it gives a great sense of intensity to the moment. We realize that this moment could be the last, any moment could be the last. This means that we should savor, we should seek the vastness in this moment. It's useless to scheme and plan, "Oh, when I do this, I'll have the other." If I'm expending a lot of energy, anxiety, and expectation on some temporal, temporary thing, it is useless, because I could die. Being healthy, young, and rich are no guarantees—well people can die before sick people. Young people die before old people. Rich people die before poor people. People who live in a secure, safe surrounding can have an accident and die before people who live in a dangerous place. So, there is no certainty about when and where death will come and claim us. We cannot feel certain about it, if we are reasonable and realistic.

The third root consideration about death is that, when we do die, only the Dharma will help us, only truth will help us, only reality will help us, only our knowledge and incorporation of the nature of reality will help us. Now that we have become aware of what the dying process is like, we realize that when we do die, only those qualities of generosity, ethical sensitivity, tolerance, creativity, concentration, meditation, wisdom, and intelligence that we have integrated into our soul will go with us. These qualities do not go with us, however, if we treat them as something we can acquire from a rote formula in which we just repeat some words. These qualities are not some sort of accomplishment or some laurels upon which we can rest. We create these qualities by having been generous, by having been sensitive to others, by having been tolerant, by having been creative, by having been focused and concentrated, by having been wise and intelligent. We turn them into a code in our soul, into a spiritual gene that will go with us to build another embodiment.

That spiritual genetic pattern will be attracted to another lifeform, but that is the only thing that goes with us at death. Nothing else is of benefit. Our possessions are not of any benefit. We cannot take our bank account, our car, our house, our land. Our physical body cannot go with us. Our relationships, our loved ones, our friends, cannot go with us. Fame, status, power, authority cannot go with us. All of that is left behind. Any investment that we have made, that is all gone at death. It comes to nothing. Only the investment we make in the deepest inner quality of our being goes with us. This means, of course, that any good act that we did goes with us. For example, if we give a generous gift, that giving benefits us—not because we gave a hundred dollars to such-and-such, but because we liked that hundred dollars, we wanted to keep it, but we let go of it and we gave it over to someone. That habit of giving it over, and finding even pleasure in that giving over, creates a sort of loosening, a lightening of the soul in the subtle mind, the seed mind. And that seed mind is the seed of our future life.

You don't have to go to an astrologer or soothsayer to find out what your future life is going to be. "Will I be born a yogini? Will I be in Tibet? Will I be in heaven?" To find out where you will be in your future life, look at the seed of your mind today. What is the deepest inner part of your mind, when you get away from all of your surface distractions? What is down inside there? Is it a joyful, happy spirit? Is it an open and loving spirit? Is it a bubbling well of positive energy? If it is, then that is the place where you will be in the future. You will dwell in the well of positive energy. However, if you find in there a little lump of fear, of paranoia, of anxiety, of unconcern, a withered, neglected sort of thing that doesn't know this from that, that is confused and terrified, and hiding, then, unfortunately, you will be in a realm of confusion, terror, and fear. In short, changing this deepest inner quality should be the main focus of our life.

These are the three root thoughts that help us through death and help our next existence: the certainty of death; the uncertainty of the time of death; and the certainty that when we die, it is this inner seed that is all-important. When we follow these three root thoughts, we will rise to what is called awareness of the immediacy of death. Far from being morbid, far from being depressed and paranoid, we become transcendent. We become deeply intense about this moment. We recognize that this moment is everything. The seed of our being, all our future states, the product of all our past states, infinity stretching in both directions, infinite expanses in both directions, is now here in this moment, and this moment begins to become more and more infinite. We find more and more fruition in this moment, especially when we know already how deeply wonderful the human life is. We see what a great opportunity for freedom this life is, especially since each moment of it could be the last.

What is essential in each moment is the quintessential experience of that moment. When we know this in the deepest part of the soul, then we begin to have a soul life. We begin to have soul intensity in life.

THE TRUTH OF KARMA

We've gone through the first two steps of the path: the recognition of the preciousness of human life, which is endowed with liberty and opportunity, and the awareness of the immediacy of death. As you go on in your lifelong retreat, you can spend days, months, and years reflecting on each one of these. You can bring them into your study of biology, history, and natural history, into your experience of life. So, you want to meditate on them at all times, not only in times of retreat.

Now we move to the third step of thought on the path of enlightenment, which is the theme of the inexorability of the cause and effect of evolutionary action. In this one, we increase still more our sense of intensity, immediacy, and infinity of the moment. We sense the preciousness of the moment, in order to invest in our deepest inner spiritual transformation.

> *Fearing the fires of suffering in hellish states,*
> *I heartily take refuge in the Three Jewels,*
> *Bless me to intensify my joyous efforts*
> *To give up sins and achieve a mass of virtue!*

We are being developed by what we have done, and what we do, not only physically and verbally, but mentally also. What we now do in mind and speech and body will determine how we will become.

The different forms and idiosyncrasies of all beings and all things—all worlds in fact—depend on this inexorable causality of evolutionary action, or karma. Karma is not mysterious. *Karma* doesn't mean "fate," although in a way it occupies the place of fate. *Karma* means "evolution, evolutionary causality."

For example, if you have killed many beings in past lives, then you get a shorter life, you get a difficult existence, you end up in subhuman states of existence, of fear and crystallized paranoia, and agony and killing and destruction. If you have taken what is not given, you get a very spare and sparse environment, you suffer and you starve, and you're poor, and you never have sufficiency in quantity, because you took away from others in previous lives. If you commit sexual misconduct, you become ugly, and you become out of control, you lose control of yourself, and you're exploited and abused by others, and so forth in other lives. If you tell untruths, then in your future life you become someone whom no one believes or trusts; what you do and say is felt to have hidden motives, to be exploitive of others; you're always confused, and you don't know what is true and what is untrue.

This ethical law in Buddhism is like a law of nature, like a law of biology. For instance, if you train as a runner and you run five miles a day, then your legs become strong. That doesn't happen because somebody rewards you with strong legs. The running itself changes the structure of the muscle, the leg, and you become stronger and stronger. No pain, no gain. That's the cause and effect that we understand in material reality. In a karmic or evolutionary reality, whatever we do and what we say and what we think affects how we become. Ethics is actually a way of maneuvering through the causation of life toward better forms of life. Negative ethics, or doing bad things, is a way of maneuvering backward, regressing, and degenerating our form of life.

We do not kill other beings, for example, not just because someone orders us not to kill beings, although if a reliable person ordered us not to, it would be all right to follow his or her orders. However, if you don't do something only because you're obeying someone, in some situations you might do it because you think you can get away with it; you disobey and do it because you think you can. But if you don't do it out of inner restraint, because you know that the act is going to transform your being in a negative way, you will never want to do it in any situation. If you do not take others' lives, you yourself will have a vaster existence, a more generous, more open existence. If you prolong other beings' lives, you will have a longer life. If you act out of such understanding, enlightened self-interest combines with your ethical sensitivity, and they reinforce each other. Learning about the inexorability of ethical action, the law of karmic evolution, resembles the study of biology.

If I have a happy moment in my life today, it is because I did a positive thing in a previous life, or a previous time in this life. If I have a miserable moment today, it is because I did some miserable thing to someone else, or to myself, in a previous time. Understanding this dynamic, we develop a very minute sense of responsibility, of how we behave, of what we do, and we don't blame others for the negative events that happen to us. We accept responsibility ourselves. This acceptance doesn't result in self-laceration, or self-belittling, but rather gives us responsibility and the power to do something about it. If something happens to us, even an accident, and we just sit and bewail our fate, then we're only heightening our sense of powerlessness. Instead, when an accident occurs, we should think, Well, I was in the way of that accident, and thus put our focus on what we can do.

Many people think, Well, I didn't exist before I was born, and I won't exist after I die, because material science says that when there's no brain function, there's no awareness. But actually, if you were to accept those views that a vast infinite past is nothing and an infinite future is nothing, then that would mean that right now there is also nothing. Take this as an example: Say you are an ardent materialist who thinks that at death you will not exist; you will be undifferentiated, nonindividuated oblivion. If you come to a moment of great agony in the present, if the now suddenly is filled with immense agony—because you have a cancer, or because you have broken something or have been disgraced, or because you're on fire—then it would be rational for you to take a bullet and blow your brains out. And as the bullet goes through the brain, you would be thinking that the essence of the present moment will be revealed as nothing. You think that the essence of this present is a black hole, it is a nothing, it is a radical singularity of a black hole. For you, caught in that view, the "now" is nothing but being a nothing.

However, if you face the fact that nothing is nothing only, and therefore is not an object of experience, it's not a location where you can be, it's not a place where you can hide. If you are experiencing what you are thinking is nothing as nothing, then you're really experiencing a "realm" of nothingness that you mentally have conjured. You have made something out of nothing. You made it, and you are dwelling in it, so it is a mental fabrication, not a nothing.

It is very powerful to become minutely and deeply aware of the causal processes of evolution, because thereby we become more and more aware of the interconnectedness of ourselves with everything else. Everything we do is infinitely ramified and interconnected with everything else. And everything else becomes infinitely connected and ramified with us. This realization is crucial to our positive development.

The title of *Be Here Now*, the book written by our beloved Baba Ram Dass, has become a motto that resounds through our culture.

"Being here now" challenges our culture's tendency to defer gratification to retirement or life after death. Instead, get something out of
your life now. Be present to reality now. Enjoy and appreciate things
now, because now is where you live.

But we must be careful here. If you really integrate in your mind
the preciousness of life and the immediacy of death, really understand them, and gain insight into them, you will be here now, totally,
intensely. But, then, how will you define the now? If the now is just a
nothingness, essentially, because you have an image in your mind
that you didn't exist before you were born, and because you have a
picture in your mind that you will cease to exist after you die, then
the essence of the now is that you are nothing. If you reduce everything to what is its deepest essence now, that deep essence will be revealed as nothing. Your awareness will be revealed as an illusion,
some sort of surface consciousness. And the deeper consciousness
will just be nothing, oblivion. It's what's called a realm of nothingness.

So, what is the now that you're being here? What is the here? It's
nothing. The now is nothing. So, what do you have? Nothing.

But if you connect this with the inexorability of causation, of
evolution, you couple this with the vast ocean of interrelationships,
and everything is a vast surface of interconnections, you and all beings infinitely interwoven in an infinite fabric of life, then the moment is as infinite as you can expand your awareness to encompass.
For example, right now, if you have a very tiny little flicker of
thought, of the wish-fulfilling gem tree reality, of the predominate
power within relationality of love and compassion, and light and luminosity, and jewel tenderness, and intimacy, the tiniest imaginative
flicker of that vision can expand infinitely to become that, in billions
of worlds, resonating in billions of consciousnesses of other beings.

By contrast, if you have an infinite flicker of mind of darkness and fear, harshness, and hardness, and nothingness, then that can lead you to such realms of darkness, and you can drag many beings with you, and imprison yourself in a nothingness realm for infinity or aeons. So, this moment is infinity. The energy that you have to turn away critically, to see through the delusion of anything negative in this moment, and create a positive in this moment, even in the minutest way, has infinite consequence. The moment and your positive action are, in a way, infinite.

A famous verse from the *Royal Samadhi Discourse* (a *sutra* or sacred scripture of the Buddhists) says that one who understands causality understands emptiness. One who understands emptiness understands freedom. And one who understands freedom understands the importance of the minute, and is mindful of the most minute detail.

We tend to think that there is some ultimate state that we hope to achieve to get away from all this suffering, that there will be someplace outside the world, some sort of vast infinity that will not have any differentiations. But we'll be there and then nothing can harm us, and we'll be secure and safe, and we can ignore every kind of minute thing because we will become vast and infinite. In our escapism, in our fear, we reify states such as that as being states of liberation and enlightenment.

But when we really realize the ultimate as the void, we gain the absolute freedom of the realization of the void. That freedom is also free from itself as a separated state. That freedom is free to be invested in the most minute infinities, the infinity in a grain of sand, the infinity in a petal of a flower, the infinity in the tip of a hair, the infinity of the tone and the timbre of the tiniest gentleness that can be extended to another, that can alleviate his tension, her suffering the tiniest bit, that can open another's happiness the tiniest bit. Compassion infinity, not just wisdom infinity, invests in every being's happiness.

• • •

So, that is the third step of thought on the path—the interconnection of all our thoughts and actions and their infinite effect. The first step is the preciousness of our human life, endowed with liberty and opportunity, and the second is the immediacy of death. And in this third step, the intensity of every moment of that human life and the fruitionality of every moment get linked with the infinity of time and space. Instead of our being isolated in some sort of a dull, disconnected moment, in a sort of solipsistic hiding in some form and some place apart from others, we are connected to an infinite past and an infinite future. There is no beginning or end to our being here. This makes our *now* of infinite significance. The way we are here now with other beings is optimal and positive. It is leading to happiness, satisfaction, and freedom, not to bondage, misery, frustration, or suffering.

HAPPINESS COMES FROM REALIZING
YOU ARE NOT "THE ONE"

These three steps of thought, the preciousness of human life endowed with liberty and opportunity; the immediacy of death, and therefore, the intensity of the moment; and the interconnectedness of cause and effect of evolutionary action, the interwovenness of all things, the infinite past, present, and future—all bring us, finally, to the fourth step of thought on the path, the overall suffering of egocentric or unenlightened existence.

> *Tossed by fierce waves of evolution and addiction,*
> *Crushed by the sea monsters of the three sufferings,*
> *Bless me to intensify my will to liberation*
> *From this terrifying, boundless ocean of existence!*

Here we come up against what the Buddha called the First Noble Truth, the truth of suffering. People who misunderstand this truth think of Buddhism as pessimistic or gloomy and of the Buddha as a killjoy, some guy who comes up when you're slurping down a delicious vanilla fudge ice cream and says, "All this is suffering." We don't like to hear this when we're slurping down that ice cream. But, we have to understand it.

When the Buddha said, "All this is suffering," what he meant— and did say in many other contexts in which he was being more elaborate—is that all this unenlightened living is bound to be suffering compared to enlightened living, which is infinite bliss. If the Buddha had thought that this suffering was inevitable—that all of life would only and always be suffering—he would have kept silent. Why would you tell someone who is imprisoned for life how horrible his situation is, if there's no chance of his gaining any freedom? Buddha was actually saying, "You're imprisoned under this-and-that confusion," so that we would seek to understand what's imprisoning us, so that we can become free.

The Buddha's good news, the Buddha's great insight, is the Third Noble Truth, that there is freedom from suffering. There is an end to suffering. Everyone knows that there is suffering, so the First Noble Truth is not really news. What is news is that there is an end to suffering that we can realize, that it is only the *unenlightened* life that is suffering.

We can easily understand suffering. What is the cause of suffering, as the Buddha saw it? It is our attachment, the Second Noble Truth, to absolute beliefs. Everyone, here and now, thinks that he or she here and now is it. I think I'm it. As my great old Mongolian teacher used to say, everyone secretly thinks, "I am the one." He and she may claim to be very friendly and cooperative, selfless and altruistic, but inside they really think, "I am the one." Actually, everyone *is* the one. But when you think you are the only *real* one, you immediately are paranoid, because you immediately know that nobody else agrees with you. In fact, you think they are so messed up, all those foolish other people, they all think *they* are the one. And you know that's for sure wrong, just as they know you are for sure wrong. But knowing that they think you're for sure wrong makes you paranoid.

Descartes, remember, was certain that he was sitting there thinking and doubting. That was the absolute foundation of certainty for him, he couldn't question that. He doubted everything else, that he had a body, that the world had definite qualities, but he was there thinking, he did not doubt that. And we all feel that way.

When you think your self is the most absolute thing, the one irreducible thing, what sort of situation does that put you in? I, myself, all alone, am the only one. The whole world disagrees with me. All the other people think they are the one. I'm just grist for their mill, fodder for their meal. Naturally, I'm in conflict with all of them. And, besides being in conflict with them, I am also in conflict with time itself. Time comes to me eventually in the form of death, and says, "You're not the one, you're dead." It comes to me in the form of sickness, says, "You're not the one, you're sick. You don't know what you are." It comes to us in the form of old age, when we change; it comes when we don't even know who we are, in Alzheimer's.

Everything is against my feeling of "I'm so it. I'm the universe." My whole universe is I, but the universe doesn't agree. So, everything I do is doomed to failure. Pit yourself in a struggle against the universe, and who will win? You will lose. That is what Buddha is saying to us when he says that all this is suffering. He means this struggle of the egocentric person who thinks he is in conflict with the world, and his certainty of identity is suffering. With such an absolutized foundation of egocentrism, his progression through the world will always be suffering. Other people won't agree with him, he'll lose his loved ones, he'll meet his hated ones. He'll be tortured by others. Death and birth will torture him. He'll face sickness and old age.

Now, if this were the only way we could be, Buddha wouldn't have brought it to our attention. He would have said that we have to make the best of it; we have to figure out how to bear with this suffering. If he had gone through his time, and his investigation of self, and of the world, and his deep insight, and his deep concentration, his scientific exploration, if he had decided, "Well, that's just the way beings are, there's no way of getting out of that wiring, we're hardwired to think we're the one, and so we're inevitably pitted against the world, and it against us, no way out of it"—he would not have created the enlightened path. If he had thought, "We have to resign ourselves to our lack of freedom or modulate it by palliative measures," then there would be no such thing as Nirvana. There would be no Buddhadharma, Buddha teaching, Buddha path, enlightenment path. There would be no freedom.

But Buddha did look, and he saw through the suffering, and he took up the challenge. He said, "Well, if I'm the one, and I put my absolute effort of being the absolute one into finding my absolute self, then I should find it, because absolute is not to be obstructed, absolute is what is real. Reality will come through if it puts itself out to do so." So, he looked for himself as "the one." He put laser-like, diamondlike, nuclear fission–like energy into finding himself. And you know what? He failed to find himself. He didn't find anyone. He also didn't find a failure to find. He didn't find "nothing" as the one. He didn't find that what the one was reduced to was a nothing. He saw through the delusion of nothing, the escape hatch of nothing. He dived right through it and realized that nothing was itself just like a pane of glass, just transparent, because it couldn't obstruct everything. So, he didn't find the failure to find and he didn't find the self. And the not finding of the self, courageously sustained, became the realization of the transparent openness of the self, the emptiness of the self, and the infinity of the self. The self, the sense of "the one," became diffused over the entire, infinite universe, and he realized that he was all of the beings being "the one." He suddenly felt himself as the universe.

Now, there is a difference between what the Buddha felt and the feeling you can get that you and the universe are all dissolved in some big nothing. The latter is a fake, mystical, irrational state, even though you can experience it. But it's not the absolute. The Buddha rejected again and again that kind of altered state or *samadhi* as being the absolute. He rejected it because it's not the absolute, because it's a state you go into, in which you are isolated from other beings of the world. In that state, you cross a boundary between a place out of which you came and the state in which you are. A state that has a boundary is therefore not an absolute. It is a state that didn't exist before and later comes to exist; therefore, it is created by cognitive effort, so it is not an absolute.

The absolute, by definition, is infinity, but you could not go now from being in a finite realm into infinity, because infinity could not be excluded from the finite realm in which you once were. Infinity is infinite, therefore nothing can limit it, it has no boundary, so it has to be everywhere. All the "somethings" also have to be infinity, actually. Finitude and interconnectedness are, in fact, the surface of infinity; they're the surface texture of infinity. Similarly, in the world of interrelationships of others and selves, as all interrelated and inconceivably intertwined, relativity is the absolute, is the freedom, is the emptiness. This is what the Buddha realized.

When you are in the Buddha's feeling of being the universe, suddenly you realize you are not against the universe, you *are* the universe. Your universe is specifically other people in the universe. Therefore, when they think they are the one and they have happiness, that's your happiness. You and they are one being, you identify with all of them. You feel their feelings as your feelings, and they're not against you, and your bliss radiates into them as their bliss, and when many of them become blissful it radiates back from them, into a much greater bliss than you individually could even conceive. When we're imprisoned within the self-enclosure of self-preoccupation and egotism, and seeing the world only from my—the one— perspective, and feeling alienated from the universe and separated from it, any state of existence that we have controlled by that per- spective, controlled by that imprisonment of self-preoccupation, will be suffering.

The purpose of this theme, the fourth thought step on the path, is to free ourselves from ambition for any self-centered state as a de- sirable state, an ultimately desirable state. In other words, we give up the ambition to become a god, which we define as a being that is greater than the universe, and different from the universe, and still, therefore, in a sense, finite in relation to an infinite universe. Because even the vastest god, in relation to a particular galaxy or universe, in relation to the infinite multiverse, the infiniverse, is still like a firefly, like a mosquito, like a tiny grain of dust. Even a god is crushed, nothing but a subatomic particle in the toenail of another god in a different dimension. Even a god who is born into heaven based on generosity and love and joy, which the heavenly realms are made of, because the god enters that state at a certain time, he or she will lose that state at another time. Without realizing it in their giddiness of pleasure and joy, the gods roll over and crush a couple of universes in between bouts of lovemaking; and in crushing those universes, they create a negative karma, a negative evolutionary impetus, very, very subtly, that attaches itself to their souls, and eventually that's the seed of their downfall from the heavens. And they become human beings again or subhuman beings, and they suffer in the future.

Any egocentric being, from the hells to the heavens, is pitted against the infinite, and he or she always loses in the end. So here we meditate on this, and we inventory all possible conceivable forms of self-centered existence. Take the social world, being president of the United States, being a superstar in Hollywood, being a great artist and performer, Picasso, being Jackson Pollock, being whatever you can think of as an ambition you could have about a worldly state in the human realm. Reflect, look at the president of the United States, what a suffering. Look at a great performer, a great violinist as his or her fingers become arthritic, what a suffering. And, the most difficult, look at the gods, the pleasures of the gods, which in the Indian imagination, the Indo-Tibetan imagination, are incredibly delicious from a human sensory perspective, but nevertheless, if you see time, if you see the passing of an aeon as like a moment, when you come to death, after even a 150-year life, it's like the whole thing has been a dream, over in a flash. At the end of it, although it may have seemed long and laborious at times along the way, it's as if you had just awakened from a dream. All of life is like a moment.

So, even if you live a billion aeons, like a god's life, at the end it's like a momentary thing, and you fall. And they say that the gods become clairvoyant a few god-weeks or god-months before they die, which is like a billion years in our time, because the god time is very slow compared to ours, very vast, and the agony they experience in those few god-months, which are a billion aeons of our time, makes the whole trillions and quadzillions of years they lived as gods meaningless. It's hard for us, as pleasure-oriented people, to think of heaven as a suffering, but it's necessary, to free ourselves from longing for paradise.

There's an old Buddhist wisdom story about a man who was born blind with a film over his eyes. This man would argue with his friends about whether light or colors, or even the sun, moon, and stars existed, because he had never seen them. His friends argued that they had seen these things, so he should believe in their existence, but he was unmoved and argued back that if colors or light really existed, he would be able to touch them just as he could touch other things that he knew to exist. He told his friends that what they saw had to be illusions because they couldn't be touched. Then one day, a physician visited the blind man, mixed four medicines, and put them on the man's eyes. The medicines melted the film, curing his blindness, so that he could see reality in all its forms and colors. It is taught that the Buddha is the physician to all of us; the man's blindness is the illusion, and the four medicines are the Four Noble Truths.

These are four themes that we have gone through, in the very briefest detail: one, the preciousness of human life endowed with liberty and opportunity; two, the immediacy of death and the spontaneity and intensity of the moment; three, the inexorable, causal interconnectedness of our infinite past and future with our present evolutionary involvement; and four, the unsatisfactory quality of all egocentric states of existence, even the most seemingly vast and glorious and expanded.

When we really accept these four themes and gain insight into our life and others' as you now are doing by tasting just the tiniest drop of them all together, we feel tremendous relief. Far from being depressed, far from feeling morbid or discouraged, we feel terrific relief. Why? When you no longer desire to be a god, or the president, or a billionaire, or a star, or whatever it is, when you realize the sufferings of all of those conditions by thinking them over carefully, then you won't waste your time trying to become them. You won't invest in those futile, vain ambitions or goals. You will realize they will not bring you happiness. You realize that happiness comes from knowing your true nature, from feeling your inner bliss of freedom.

As for this egoistic life cycle, intolerable prison,
I give up my delusion that it's a garden of delight;
Bless me to educate myself in ethics, meditation, and wisdom,
The treasuries of the jewels of noble beings,
And raise aloft the victory banner of true liberation!

You realize that your precious moments of human life, each one of which has infinite effects, and each one of which is never lost in its impact, because of the inexorable causality of everything, you realize that you may as well be free in mind now. You should orient, and reorient, and restructure your life. To be free, you drop out, in a way. You become "transcendental." You renounce the conventional, routine egocentric cosmology and living in the uneasy truce with all the other egocentric beings. You leave that society as your home. You abandon it. You abandon that world, and you enter the world of the wish-granting gem tree, the world of individual liberation, the world of individual fulfillment. You put the full energy of every moment, bit by bit, as much as you can, into the transformation of your soul, the opening of your soul. The chrysalis, butterfly expansion and flight-taking of your soul—that is where you put the focus of your life. You declare to yourself, "I don't know what the meaning of life is, perhaps, yet. I don't know fully what reality is yet, but I'm encouraged enough by the alternatives that I have heard from the karmic evolutionary scientific tradition, from the enlightenment psychology tradition, that I will determine to make my life meaningful, whether so-and-so says it's meaningful or not. It will become meaningful for me. I will create the meaning. And that meaning will be love. It will be joy. It will be infinite positivity. It will be the meaning for me, and for all other beings. That is the meaning that I will make for it. And I give up getting a million bucks. I give up being a big shot. I give up being controlling of the world. I give up possessions, all of these things. I give that up. I don't mean that I want to fling myself into the street. Then I would be a burden on others, and I wouldn't have a chance to study." Actually, in ancient India and Tibet, I could have just flung myself in the street, but when I really reached this "warrior's abandon," as Carlos Castaneda's Don Juan would have called it, when I reached "transcendent renunciation," as the Tibetans call it, the determination to transcend, I could just go out and yell, "Eureka, I am released, I am not after any of this. You guys keep all of it, except please share a little lunch with me once a day." You have a begging bowl. You live as a mendicant. You're shining with relief.

In the enlightenment-oriented civilizations, the monastic male and female monk and nun, the vacationing mendicants, are considered to have received a great boon, a great happiness. The word for ordination is not *ordination,* it is *graduation, liberation, escape.* You gain insight and say, "Okay, I'm going to put my whole life toward transforming my soul, and as much as my soul transforms, it will resonate with yours and everybody's soul. And when I become fully transformed as a buddha, I even will be able to intervene directly in the confusions of others, and help them become more aware." You can proclaim that, and walk into the street, and people will knock each other out to be the first to give you lunch. They wouldn't feel you had conned them, or you weren't pulling your weight, or you weren't justifying your existence. They would feel honored to support you. You have become a true child of the universe, and doing the universe's most essential work, the work of freedom and bliss, the work of discovering of the universe itself, discovering its own reality.

Time and again, the enlightened eleventh- to twelfth-century yogin Milarepa demonstrated the ecstasy of the full-blown transcendent attitude by living stark naked in Himalayan caves throughout the harsh winters. In his youth, he had killed thirty-five people during a family feud, and he repented when he realized the evolutionary consequences of such a deed. He allowed himself to feel the terror of the prospects of the hellish effects of killing, and he used his transcendent mindset for a relentless effort toward real freedom. He would meet people who would think him mad and would compare their mundane states of comfort and security with his superhumanly ascetical lifestyle, but he would turn his poetic gifts to the vivid rendering of the supreme comforts he enjoyed. The worldly person may sleep in a downy bed, carelessly unconscious of the effects of his evolutionary actions, unaware of the horrors awaiting him at the end of his life. But Milarepa saw the downy embrace as an evolutionary trap and felt the touch of his pillow of stone as even softer, as it kept him alert and awake so that he could investigate and purge his deepest instincts of delusion, hatred, and lust. The stone cushioned him against the dreadful spikes of hell that wait in the future of the passion-driven human, and Mila's warmth came from his inner heat of wisdom, the fire of transcendent insight.

Now we have completed the first four themes on the actual path of transformation toward enlightenment in the jewel refuge tree. Each time we work one of these themes, we gain a little corner of insight into it, we deepen the insight we already have, or we even imagine the insight we need to gain.

Let's close this chapter by reinvoking our jewel tree: As they see us working on this in our meditation, the beings in the jewel refuge tree above us, in the heavenly choir, in the heavenly host, they flip out, they become so happy. They shine, they glow, and they glee and they giggle, and they send more intense light rays down to us, and we glow more with their blessings of light rays, as well as glowing with the blessings of our inner insight. And then, our glowing shines out to the beings around us, who feel pleasure, warmth, security, and refuge in the power of that glow. And we subliminally send the little seeds, the little pattern of our own new insights about the preciousness of our human life endowed with liberty and opportunity, with the rays of our glowing, as it reflects to them. We send our realization of the immediacy of death, making each moment infinitely valuable and precious; and the inexorability of causality, making each moment extend everywhere so that we can find all fruition in this moment, and bring to bear all fruition in all future moments. And we acknowledge the vanity and the inadequacy and the suffering of all mundane states that we experience as self-centered people, so we excuse ourselves from all superficial motivation and ambition. Our transcendent attitude then resonates everywhere, and freedom rings everywhere.

And as we do that, the mentor beings in the wish-granting jewel tree, high above the jeweline branches of the tree, are so pleased, they radiate, they dissolve, the tree dissolves, the lake dissolves, the high top of the world dissolves, and it all pours and floods into us in the form of rainbow light, of white diamond, of red ruby, of blue sapphire, of yellow topaz, and of green emerald. We fill up with that light, and then we dedicate the merit of that meditation to all of the beings around us, infinite numbers of beings in the vast infinite field around us; and then we dissolve into light, and we become one with them. And we and the refuge field become one with all the mother beings around us. We experience this dissolving as a flood of bliss, and we rest in that union.

And then, somebody thinks, "Hey, where did everybody go?" And we come back to our conventional site on planet Earth and go out into the world.

❧

THREE

BEING HERE NOW IN LOVE AND COMPASSION
The Spirit of Enlightenment

Let's begin by visualizing our jewel tree again. Let your habitual identity and self-image go into a sort of meditation mode. When I say this, I don't mean that you're supposed to be sitting rigidly without moving and getting aches and pains. When I say, "Meditate together" in this book, sometimes I'll lead you into a meditation, but mostly we're learning, we're thinking, and we're in this presence of the wish-granting jewel tree and its radiation and its beautiful, luminous, rainbowlike jewel energies. You can be relaxed. Shift around, change your position if something aches. Don't worry about it. Close your eyes or partially close them, sit in a balanced posture, breathe evenly and gently. Open up a field of vision above your forehead, not looking with the eyes but looking up into the center of your forehead, where the third eye would be if you were a fierce deity. Looking up that way, sit comfortably, let yourself feel vast and spacious, calm. Let the world dissolve around you. Whatever you identify as your town, home, or apartment building, era, country, continent, and planet . . . let these all dissolve from your awareness. Let yourself be sort of unsure where you are. Let yourself feel a kind of gentle, spacious voidness, a feeling of freedom floating . . .

And then, arise from that with your mind to find yourself on top

of the world on a grassy bluff looking down over Lake Manasarovar, the giant crystal lake. You can barely see its far shores.
You're at fifteen thousand feet. The air is pure and clear, there are
fluffy clouds in the sky. In front of you is an island, a jewel island
with all kinds of mythic creatures prancing around its gardens. The
center of the island is a giant tree that springs out of the earth like a
Jack and the Beanstalk type of thing, going way up into the heavens,
out of sight.

This giant tree is glistening, made of a jewel substance, luminous
like a Christmas tree, except in place of the Christmas ornaments
there are flowers, thrones, and in all these flowers and on all these
thrones are seated enlightened beings, human and divine. Whoever
you want to see is there. You can have Buddha. If you're a Tibetan
Buddhist, you would have your own personal lama or mentor, who
would be dressed in the form of Lama Tsong Khapa, Milarepa,
Karmapa Lama, or His Holiness the Dalai Lama. In the mentor's
heart would be the Shakyamuni Buddha, the historical Buddha of
twenty-five hundred years ago, and in Shakyamuni Buddha's heart
would be a little Vajradhara with his consort, the divine buddha
form, male and female in union.

If you are a Christian, you may have Jesus there. Perhaps in his
heart God would be on his throne. Perhaps Mary would be there,
perhaps in her heart would be Jesus and within his heart God. If
you're a Muslim, you could imagine Muhammad being there, not as
an icon, but as he was historically, or in your own imagination. If
you're Jewish, you can think of Moses or one of the great rabbis,
Rabbi Akiva. If you're Hindu, you can have Krishna or Rama or
Sita, Radha, the goddess Shakti, or Shiva. If you're a Taoist, you can
have Lao-tzu there, or Chuang-tzu. Or as a humanist, you can have
Plato, Socrates, Pythagoras. Or you could have all of them there. To
the entire pantheon of great teachers, you could add your teachers
of this lifetime, your third-grade French teacher, your history

teacher, your civics teacher—whoever was meaningful to you, who opened your eyes, taught you the alphabet, made you understand something new about your life, about yourself. Your parents could be there.

In the presence of these people, you feel secure. You feel they have a knowledge superior to yours. You feel that you have learned from them or could learn from them. I myself think of His Holiness the Dalai Lama, indivisible from all the teachers I've ever had, very kind teachers, Geshe Wangyal, Ling Rinpoche, Serkhong Rinpoche, Tara Tulku, Locho Rinpoche, Yeshe Dhonden. I see my own personal history, all the teachers, fused into one being who looks like His Holiness the Dalai Lama. I have thought of all of them as his emanations, and he is fused with Tsong Khapa, then Atisha, then Guru Rinpoche, then Nagarjuna, then Shakyamuni Buddha, and then fused with Vajradhara.

I refer to these great teachers often, so here is some background on them. Tsong Khapa attained full enlightenment in 1398 and then taught for twenty-one years in such an intelligent, energetic, and charismatic way that his movement transformed the whole of Tibet and brought it into a genuine renaissance regarding its embodiment of the Dharma. Some credit him with keeping the traditions in bloom for five hundred years longer than they had been expected to last. The first Dalai Lama was his disciple, as was the first Panchen Lama, though their reincarnation lines were not called by those names for another few centuries. Atisha was a Bengali prince who renounced his kingdom and revived the teaching of the spirit of enlightenment of love and compassion for India itself, and then moved up at the end of his life into Tibet, where he renewed the Dharma with his inspiring example and eloquent wisdom.

Guru Rinpoche is more or less the supernatural emanation of Amitabha Buddha, the Boundless Light Buddha who presides over the Blissful Heaven in the Western direction, the destination of the hundreds of millions of followers of Buddhism's Pure Land school, currently flourishing in China, Korea, Vietnam, and Japan. He was invited to Tibet by the emperor Trisong Detsen in the eighth century; there he tamed the bloodthirsty mountain warrior deities of the Tibetan military empire and began the millennium-long process of making Tibet safe for the Dharma.

Nagarjuna was a great doctor, philosopher, and adept of India, credited with rediscovering the Mahayana—universal vehicle— teachings with the help of the dragon kings from under the ocean, teaching the profound teaching of voidness and relativity in an un- rivaled way, serving as personal preceptor of several south Indian kings, then voyaging to America on a dragon's back and teaching there for several centuries before returning to India to kindle the Unexcelled Yoga Tantras of esoteric practice and attainment—he is believed to have lived around six hundred years.

Shakyamuni Buddha is the buddha of our historical era, born an Indian prince more than twenty-five hundred years ago. After living it up for twenty-nine years, he achieved the transcendent attitude and departed for the jungle to discover the meaning of life. After six years of ascetic meditation and deep critical inquiry into himself and the world, he opened into a complete understanding of every- thing, and then he spent the next forty-five years teaching men and women from all nations and all walks of life, inventing the monastic community or Sangha to give them shelter and stipends to support them during their own study and practice.

Finally, Vajradhara is the divine, sapphire blue, rather sexy (often appearing in union with an exquisite sapphire blue or ruby red con- sort, in fact indivisible from himself/herself) buddha who is the es- oteric emanation of all buddhas whose pleasure is to teach the Unexcelled Yoga Tantras, such as the *Esoteric Communion* and the *Su- perbliss Wheel* Tantras. These Tantras are the superhigh technologies of spiritual development that bodhisattvas use to accelerate their evolutionary progress to full buddhahood by learning to control their extremely subtle dreamlike minds and bodies in order to compress countless lifetimes of evolution into a single or at least several lifetimes—sort of like psychoneurogenetic engineering technologies of spirit and body, of wisdom and compassion.

That's my own pantheon, and don't worry if you do not recognize some of them. There are countless hosts of such historical and legendary beings in the jewel tree field, all of them so realized, so at one with "the force" that they can appear in light body or "astral" form anywhere to help anybody at any time, just as Obi-Wan would appear in transparent emanations at important moments in the *Star Wars* universe.

For your own jewel tree, you install your own pantheon so that you feel you're in the presence of your highest mentors. And then you feel that they really are there. You don't just think you're having an unstable vision of them. You think of them as really being there in this wish-fulfilling jewel tree, a giant tree that fills the whole space in front of you, radiates jewel lights to flood you with positive energy.

These beings *are* there, and they're looking at you, and they're saying, "How nice. So-and-so is just meditating there. He's trying to pick himself up by his own bootstraps, trying to contemplate, becoming more aware. She's traveling the path to enlightenment. What a wonderful thing." And they smile down at you.

From their glistening smiles, light rays radiate and flow toward you, and those light rays are diamond, crystal, coherent light, laser, liquid, gentle though flowing, ruby, emerald, topaz, sapphire, the whole spectrum flowing toward you. Amethyst liquid jewel light flowing into you, filling you up with light, making you feel energetic and buoyant, lifting you from your sense of heaviness, driving out of your mind your usual worries about your own self-identity and self-image, such as "I'm so-and-so. I understand only this much." You are lifted out of your own self-imposed limitations, the inner voice that talks to you and inhibits you.

These thoughts and habitual monologues inside are washed away by a Niagara of jewel light that flows down from this gem tree and fills you up in a glowing, glistening being. And you become your whole potential. Any sense that you have of "Well, I'm going to learn this teaching, I'm going to meditate, but of course it's going to be me doing it. I'll come out of it afterward and then maybe I'll go back later, but I'll be the same old me"—that whole attitude dissolves, just floats out of you in the form of dark, shadowy, little scuttling thoughts. You just sort of drop your thoughts and embrace the light. You feel good in it, feel everything is possible, feel open to new understanding, feel open to seeing your own faults in a new way and rising above them and using them to bring yourself into new, virtuous qualities.

Then you notice in the field around you on this bluff that's looking over the lake out of which the great giant gem tree springs, you notice that all beings are around you, all in human form, and toward your left are the beings that you like and to whom you feel attachment. In front of you are the beings that you don't know and you have a kind of ignorant disinterest in, and to the right of you a little bit are the beings that you don't like and you're quite aware that they don't like you. In fact, just thinking of them being there makes you feel nervous and ill at ease and sort of restless and paranoid at first. You feel aversion, even anger and hatred toward the beings to the right; you feel ignorance and disinterest toward the beings straight in front; and you feel attachment and fondness toward the beings to the left.

And you immediately think, "Why am I reacting like this to these beings? The ones I like now, I like because they're nice to me and they're friendly and I get along with them and they do nice things for me. If they started being nasty to me over a regular period, I would

pretty soon move them over to the right-hand category and put
them with beings I don't want to see, beings I don't like. So, in fact,
my liking them is just because they're nice to me. The beings in front
of me, I simply don't know them. They may be the nicest, most
beautiful people with great qualities, and I may become very attached to them if I get to know them. And the beings to the right of
me, whom I don't like, they're just mean to me. Maybe I was mean to
them. Maybe they're getting revenge. In fact, I know now that some
of the beings in the 'like' category have been in the 'not like' category,
and some of the beings in the 'most not liked' category were very
dearly liked in the past. So there's nothing intrinsic in these beings
that makes them that inherently likable or inherently unlikable. It's
just my attachment and aversion and my ignorance that separate
these three beings into these three categories."

So you try to equalize, be a little less attached to the loved ones,
be a little less averse to the disliked ones, and take a little interest in
the unknown ones, realizing all of the great potential that they have.
And these beings, all of them, all three groups of them, are looking
at you, and they're seeing you begin to glow. They're noticing that
your usual form changes a little bit and you start to radiate and you
start to luminesce and then the light flows out toward them as it
overflows from you.

They don't see the refuge gem tree; they're not looking at it.
They're looking at you. But, in fact, the light of the wish-granting
gem tree from you flows to them, and they feel happy, those who like
you. They feel interested and intrigued, those who don't know you.
And they feel annoyed and competitive, those who know you and
dislike you, but that gives them a little stimulus, and they feel challenged and quickened and awakened.

And so, back from them comes a kind of stimulating energy,
whether it's competition or whether it's interest or whether it's fondness and love and gratitude. This energy loop comes back to you as

encouragement, just as you send to your mentors energy of feeling loving and secure and friendly and peaceful and grateful for their blessing.

This jewel tree landscape is the setting for our path of meditation for each of our chapters and for all of the themes in our practice, the steps of thought toward enlightenment that we are undertaking. We can sometimes even keep this sense of refuge alive in our daily life, and retain a feeling of this heavenly host there in the sky. The whole of Tibetan culture became like this, after many centuries, with people visioning their mentors, Guru Rinpoche or Milarepa or Tsong Khapa, in their meditation sky. They visioned such beings as looking after their welfare, as concerned for them, especially Tara and Avalokiteshvara, the female and male Buddhist archetypes of compassion, the angels of compassion. And they began to feel that these beings were always present in the space around them. To symbolize the noble beings' presence, the people went into the mountains, and they carved *Om Mani Padme Hum,* the mantra of great compassion, plastering these letters all over the mountains. And they carved giant buddhas and bodhisattvas and angels and mentors and lamas and deities in all the hills and mountains. As you would ride around Tibet, you would be reminded all the time of the presence of all the enlightened beings shining about you and lifting you up out of your ordinary negative habits and putting you into the mode of seeking your own evolutionary fulfillment, of seeking happiness, of seeking to fulfill your deeper wishes for yourself and for all beings. They created this wonderful culture in which everything became a way of reminding you of your highest aim in life as a human being.

This is the beneficent environment that we're dwelling in during this retreat. We're setting up the pantheon of teachers and deities around us in the jewel tree. And we have withdrawn from the other environment, where stealth bombers fly overhead; where satellite dishes of the big corporations radiate consumer sitcoms; politicians control the White House; hungry, starving people are all over the planet; religious and ethnic violence and hatred are everywhere; the earth is being polluted, the ozone layer depleted, and a future seemingly lost. We drop out of that environment and into this different realm, where all the bodhisattvas are hovering in the starship of the wish-fulfilling gem tree and radiating their light around us, making everything possible for us in this context.

Now that we're in this environment, we turn to the next steps on the path to enlightenment.

THE MOTIVATION OF COMPASSION

Whenever we meditate or practice or learn something or even as we go through the day, we should always think about our motivation. Why am I here giving this meditation? Is it just because this is my job? Is it because I want to become rich and famous? Is it because I want to be healthy or have more fun? Is it some sort of self-centered purpose like that? Is there something I want to get out of it right now in this life?

Or is it because I care for all beings? Is it because I want to become enlightened and awakened for the sake of every being? Is it because I'm not content anymore to be temporarily happy myself as an egocentric, separated person, but I want to have the real, deep happiness that comes from knowing that others I love are happy, and also from finally knowing that everyone is happy?

This motivation, our main topic in this chapter, the motivation of the bodhisattva, is known as *bodhichitta*, the will to enlightenment. *Bodhichitta* is the spirit of becoming perfectly awakened and perfectly wise, perfectly compassionate and loving, so that we are capable of helping all other beings become perfectly happy and perfectly wise themselves. This is really the motivation with which I should do whatever it is that I do, every day. I should remind myself of the fundamental opportunity of every human being to find the teaching of freedom. I should be motivated in everything I do toward that for myself and for others.

Inevitably, however, more selfish types of motivation do creep into our attitudes. Unfortunately, that motivation condemns whatever we do to yielding a lower result.

When we're learning, we should always try to avoid the faults of prideful thinking, such as I already know it all anyway. Even if we've heard something a thousand times, we should think, "I'm going to learn something new this time from this. I'm going to see more deeply. I don't really know what it is all about; I just heard the words." We don't want to have the flaw of the covered vessel: however much you try to put in a covered vessel, no matter how big and beautiful the vessel is, it just falls off, splashes on the floor, and spills because the vessel's lid prevents anything from going in.

A second potential flaw in learning that we should avoid is that of the leaky vessel. If we do not exercise mindfulness and memory, we hear something with one ear and it goes out the other. When our mind is wandering and we're paying no attention, just as whenever the best elixir is poured into a cracked vessel, it leaks right out.

The third flaw we should avoid is that of the poison vessel. It doesn't leak and its lid is open, but inside it are mixed the poisons of egocentric greed, delusion, and hatred. This is like when we're doing or learning something in order to gain power, revenge, or profit, so we're mixing our mind and learning with greed. We're doing something to confirm or rationalize our existing ignorance.

We want to avoid all these things and be receptive, attentive, and mindful, motivated by learning, realizing the aim of our human life, which is to become free and wise and loving.

With that thought in mind, let's review the stages of the path as if it were a kind of arpeggio, a scale of notes to run through on the piano of the mind. And so, the first set of notes that we learned in the last chapter leads up to the mind of transcendence. There are four main notes in that arpeggio, and the first is appreciating our precious human embodiment endowed with liberty and opportunity. What a wonderful life we do have, with access to the great teachings of liberation, omniscience, and awakening, with the time and the understanding and the assistance and the community that help us put these into practice. So remember that note. Quickly play it in your mind and resonate with it.

The second note is the immediacy of death. Remember that we shouldn't go on acting like we're going to be here forever, as we habitually do. You should recognize that you definitely will die. Reflect on who you are without the body-mind complex to which you attach your name. Subtract yourself from the relationships you're in, realize that you will die out of them. Possessions, friends, loved ones, name, fame, superficial knowledge—all will be gone. Play that note of mindfulness with the first.

As you play that second note, reflect on the certainty that you don't know when you will die, and you could die at any time. Every moment could be your last. And when you do die, only the Dharma—reality itself or knowledge of that reality—and how you have incorporated those teachings of the nature of reality into your life by means of openness and generosity and patience, only those subtle innermost qualities of your soul will benefit you.

To play the third note, you interconnect that infinite moment of the present with the cause and effect of karma. As you sound the third note, you see that everything about your current moment is determined by all of your past actions of body, speech, and mind, and that everything positive about it came from your positive actions, and everything negative about it from your negative actions. Every action that we take now, even the subtlest thought or mental action, every word and physical action leads to an infinite result in the future, either positive or negative. Each little tiny thing in the present moment is infinite in its effects. There is tremendous intensity in this awareness, tremendous mindfulness of even the subtlest element in our being.

When we sound the fourth note in this arpeggio of the mind, we remember the inadequacy of all egocentric life states, including being a god, king, billionaire, star, whatever it is we think it would be great to be. Even if we think of being a buddha as being a big shot, that is an egocentric state, although to be a buddha, of course, is to be totally selfless. We have such notions of a buddha as being powerful, the "go-to guy," because we can't imagine a selfless being. It's virtually impossible for us to think of how we could be here and yet at the same time be all the other people who are here. As a buddha, we could be all the other people in the town, and all the other people in the city, and all the other people in the country, state, and universe at the same time that we are responsibly who we are here. Such a vast, cloudlike being is inconceivable to us.

So, naturally, we are beings that are enclosed in our own little envelopes of our senses—our eyes, ears, nose, tongue, and skin. With our mind, we imagine things beyond what we sense, but still we're basically enclosed inside this sheet of skin and five senses. So we imagine all other beings are like that, too, but then we sound the fourth note in the scale, the inadequacy of all states of such a being. And we recognize that our individual struggle with the rest of the world and all the other beings will always be a losing struggle. It will always lead to suffering. Samsara is the suffering cycle of life based on self versus other, on the false habit of absolutizing the self, thinking, "I'm it, I'm the one." So the fourth note is the deep acknowledgment that all states, even the seemingly highest states, are inadequate, are fundamentally suffering compared to the happiness of enlightenment and the wisdom of selflessness.

Once we sound these four notes—the preciousness of our human life endowed with liberty and opportunity; the immediacy of death and the essentiality of the soul at death; our interconnection through cause and effect of evolutionary action of everything infinitely; and the suffering and frustrating inadequacy of all relative states of the egocentric being—we gain a great relief. We feel a wonderful, buoyant energy of transcendence. We excuse ourselves from all paltry ambitions, to be rich or famous or powerful or muscular or beautiful or whatever temporal, temporary state or even divine state we have imagined. We give up any ambition toward any of that. So, therefore, we free ourselves from all of the things that we do to make money, to be famous, to be powerful, to have possessions, to be liked by many people, all of this anxious activity that we nervously and expectantly do all the time based on ephemeral goals that are ultimately worthless and ultimately unsatisfying.

It is a tremendous thing to be free of all of that. That is why monks and nuns are actually always smiling and cheerful, why they have a kind of presence. People like to hang out with them because they don't have the same set of wants and desires as people who are seething with worldly ambitions. This is the mind of transcendence, the transcendent attitude.

Now you can conceive of yourself as a free person spending your free time reading this teaching. You're not reading it because you're getting a material benefit. You're reading it because you're free and you're enjoying the prospect of greater and greater freedom. You feel happy, you feel relieved. When you think of your ambitious friends studying, working and strutting and saving and investing and nervously looking at the Internet, you realize that they're caught on a treadmill, like ants rushing in and out of an anthill, grabbing something and rushing over to the other place. You realize the worthlessness of all of those aims.

You feel relief, and you feel pleased because you really respect yourself now. You really respect your human embodiment, the evolutionary achievement that you are, the awareness you have of the suffering nature of any sort of habitual state, and the sense of interconnection with its enduring optimism that nothing you do gets lost, even if the planet does get destroyed next week. If you are in a positive frame of mind, if you are aiming at the positive, you go on infinitely. You'll be reborn in another life, and you'll be in a better state because you'll be more generous, more loving, more wise, more open.

So you feel really cool. And then you begin to look around, and now we come to the stage of the path that we're focusing on in this chapter: the spirit of enlightenment of love and compassion. But it cannot be developed without the transcendent attitude at heart. Compassion for others relies on compassion for oneself as a foundation.

True self-appreciation is, "Why would I waste my human brain playing a video game? I have this fantastic engine of freedom and openness and awakeness, why would I waste that by not meditating on ultimate freedom, by not cultivating love and compassion, not being transcendent and dropping out?" Being a monk or a nun—or being like a monk or a nun—is not mere denial, it is being good to yourself, avoiding many common sufferings, anxieties, and preoccupations. In fact, it is fabulous to be a monk or a nun. It is one of the great things you can do for the world, to be a monk or a nun, and for yourself. A person who really loves himself recognizes, "I'm so fabulous a being that I'm going to protect myself against wasting any of my time just habitually making money, paying mortgages, producing children, growing food, any sort of involuntary thing. I'm not going to waste my time doing any of that. I'm going to just beg some food from people who like to give food—there are some who do, who don't think that there's any other thing they can do, although eventually I'm going to disabuse them of that. Even as they're feeding me, I'm going to say, 'Well, you really shouldn't be working to earn the money to make this food to feed me. You should join me and just drop out and be on vacation and seek freedom, because that's what the human life is for, seeking freedom.' Of course, many people will not do that anyway, even though I urge them to, but they'll still feel a little more free because I'm seeking freedom."

Buddha not only taught the great teachings of love and compassion, he taught whatever specific beings need to become liberated. He is not the founder of a dogmatic religious institution but he is instead the ultimate teacher, the ultimate educator, who, having realized that beings can only find their freedom and make their lives fulfilling and achieve their happiness by learning, by cultivating their understanding, was forced to be an educator. He couldn't just be a prophet, although he did prophesy. He couldn't just be a founder of institutions, although he did found institutions. He couldn't be giving orders from God, because he found out that God didn't really know what to do. The gods asked him what should they do, they were his disciples. All of Buddha's vehicles were for everyone.

Now, we come to the heart of the Buddhadharma, to compassion. If you wanted to say in one word what is the essence of Buddha's teaching, of the enlightenment teaching, it would be compassion. The statement of Nagarjuna, the great master of two thousand years ago in India, crystallized this. He said, "Voidness is the womb of compassion." In Sanskrit this reads, *shunyata karuna garbham;* in Tibetan, *tong nyid nying jey nying po jen,* which may be the most beautiful phrase ever in Tibetan, too. By the void, he means freedom, our realization that reality is totally relational, which we realized in our first four-step meditation. When we discover our freedom, this discovery flows immediately into universal compassion for all beings. When we *feel in our hearts* complete oneness with others, we feel completely relieved and fully blissful ourselves, but we can no longer bear for them to suffer. Freedom is the womb of compassion. If there's anything that might serve as the motto of Buddha's revelation, of Buddha's gospel, his good news, it is "freedom, the womb of compassion."

IS NOTHING SACRED? THE TRUTH ABOUT EMPTINESS

Too many people think that all Buddha realized under the bodhi tree was that the world sucks, that everything is horrible, life is horrible. People, myself included, feel frightened of all the pains and sufferings of life. Yet we can get even more fearful of our future when we go beyond the modern materialistic view that we suffer only in this one life and then become nothing, and we realize that our awareness has an infinite continuity, and *we can never get away from our awareness.* Therefore, there's the danger that we'll suffer in infinite future lives. We become so frightened of that idea on a deep, subliminal level that we long for obliteration, we long for oblivion.

Selfishly, we think there's nothing we can really do for others except just mention the appeal of oblivion to them—"Hey, why don't you get oblivion, too, because we're just all going to suffer together. There's nothing we can do for you. So let's jump into the oblivion; it's good enough for us, and we'll just be gone." We meditate, or we do this or that practice, and basically we think that Buddhism is some kind of marvelous yogic meditative technology for achieving an altered state. We can call it awakening, we can call it enlightenment, or many other grand things, but we basically are waiting for the day when we will be obliterated. We talk about vast empty space, and we think we're going to leave the problems of life, of interconnection, of bumping into beings and things and stubbing our toes, and having obligations and complications, and we think, "Wow!

Wham! I go into infinite space! I reach infinite solitude, infinite quiet. Nobody bugs me forever. What a great thing."

I tease people in some Dharma schools when they tell me they had a great meditation session. I say, "You really were into it, and you stopped your mind and you stopped your body, and then the only big letdown was the end, when . . . darn it, *you were still here.*" You had to get up and wash the dishes, change your underwear. So you felt you hadn't made it, you hadn't succeeded. You hadn't achieved that enlightenment you view as an absolute obliteration, freedom, or minimalist Nirvana.

This view of enlightenment as oblivion is completely wrong. It is foolish. It is breaking the basic law of the Buddhist worldview of interconnectedness, which was Buddha's great revelation. This interconnection is freeing; it can free us from suffering. There is no noninterconnected thing. There is no nothing. That is the simple hub of his teaching. There is no such thing as nothing. *Nothing* is the word for that which does not exist. Therefore, no one is going to become nothing. You cannot become nothing. It is impossible. It is a misexpression, it is a mistake. It is misknowledge.

To get a sense of the distorted working of our mind in our unenlightened state, think about how deeply you feel there is such a thing as "nothing." We want to meditate on "nothing." We can have experiences as if we're in a realm of nothing, really concrete, and we can become convinced that nothing is a real thing in a place, and no one can convince us it isn't. Our mind is set. It's very difficult to transcend this conviction once we gain that experience. It reminds me of the Gahan Wilson cartoon that depicts people bowing before an ornate throne that is labeled "Nothing." Our minds try to make "nothing" sacred.

But logically, you can understand there is no such nothing, and therefore, any experience you are having is the experience of your mental picture of such a thing. Your picture of nothing is a sort of dark, empty space. The fact that you can make a concrete picture of something that in principle could not be pictured proves that you are living in a world of your own imagination. It does not prove that the world really is what you are imagining it to be.

So, there is no nothingness Nirvana. Emptiness is not nothingness. It is voidness—knowledge of which is freedom. These terms refer to the fact that there is no absolute thing-in-itself within anything that is its substantial, independent essence. This supports the fact that all things are totally interrelated. There's no independent thing in us that is not related to other things—no mind that is not related, no speech, no body, no physical thing, no soul that is not related. That does not mean they all do not exist. It just means that there is no thing in anything that is not related to everything else.

That's what emptiness means. We are empty of any isolated essence, of any nonconnected essence. We are free of any such nonconnected, isolated, alienated essence. That is what it means. Enlightenment is realizing that freedom at the deepest level. And therefore, enlightenment is realizing our inexorable interconnectedness. The vast space of reality is nothing but the surface of the interrelations of all things. All of the interconnected things are the reality of emptiness. Therefore emptiness, voidness, freedom are the womb of compassion, the sensitivity and will that refuses to accept anyone's suffering, that automatically wills everyone's happiness.

"Emptiness is the womb of compassion" means that in realizing emptiness, we are free of the illusion that we have carried from the beginning of time that "I am the one." We accept there is no absolute one thing in us that's apart from everything, no essential, real us, no irreducible part that we can sort of get back into and withdraw into and get away from all of the burdens of connections and obligations. When we get rid of that absolutized place of self, we break through nothing, which is our last reification, the last made-up thing we impose on reality. We break through it, and we find we are face-to-face with everything.

Being face-to-face with everything, we are most compelled to pay all of our attention to other living beings, especially the ignorant ones who are suffering, who think of themselves as isolated from the rest of the world and are therefore struggling with the rest of the world, who don't know their own emptiness, who don't know their own reality and freedom, and who think they're bound in their struggle to get away from their bondage of connection into some absolute self-center that is apart from everything. They attract our attention because they are points of agony and suffering. Our mind through emptiness expands vastly and embraces them as if they are us. Their suffering is ours at that point, although fortunately, because we know reality, because we don't leave emptiness, because freedom is infinite, we're solidly within that emptiness. We solidly are that emptiness. Therefore, we can bear being aware of their theaters of agony as if they were virtual realities. We see them with a kind of binary double vision. We see them as suffering, realizing how awful it is for them, and therefore we completely dedicate ourselves to compassion, to helping them become free. Yet we're not dragged into their suffering because we also see a deeper reality of sheer bliss within them, as well as in everything else.

So you see, enlightenment is not an escape. Enlightenment is not some sort of obliteration. Enlightenment is fully being here now, but the now is of infinite duration and the "here" is of infinite extension. It is not a here and now that is an isolated, private moment of my own. It is a here and now that includes all the vast sky full of mother living beings. Each moment is *shunyata*, voidness or freedom, the womb of compassion. How can we refine that compassion, develop it to the point where it is *bodhichitta*, the will to enlightenment, or as I prefer to call it, the spirit of enlightenment? Some people call it the "mind" of enlightenment, but I like "spirit."

BECOMING A BUDDHA

There are two kinds of spirit of enlightenment. One is called the "aspiring" spirit of enlightenment, and the other is called the "venturing" spirit of enlightenment. The first, "I wish I could be a buddha, a perfectly enlightened being, perfectly blissful and perfectly aware so that I could help all other beings become perfectly blissful and perfectly aware; I want to be happy, and I want to be happy in such a way that I can make all other beings happy," is based on the acknowledgment that if anybody else is unhappy, I can't really be happy, not perfectly happy. The venturing spirit of enlightenment begins from the moment the aspiring spirit engages all your gears, the rubber hits the road, and you take the vow of the bodhisattva to become a perfect buddha yourself to deliver all other beings from suffering and help them become buddhas themselves. We'll talk about this view shortly, but there's a wonderful story about the great sage Asanga that illustrates the drive to enlightenment. Asanga meditated for twelve years in the attempt to see Maitreya Buddha. After six years he was about to give up, when he saw a rock grooved out by generations of birds building nests on a ledge. The soft brushing of the rock by their wing tips had gradually worn a hospitable home for them and their offspring. Seeing the effect of such subtle persistence, he was renewed in his determination.

The aspiring mind can be called the "will to enlightenment," but the venturing mind is more of a "spirit" than a "will," since here you are already fully engaged in the transcendent virtues, you are activated in the work of inclusion of all beings into bliss, and even without consciously willing anything, your very atmosphere, your morphic field of resonance, is simply filled with the orientation toward freedom and enlightenment for all. Your spirit is then one with the spirit of all enlightened beings, it is the pure force, the infinite energy of love, the ocean of energy that insists on and sustains the happiness of all sensitive beings.

This is of course something mysterious and ultimately inexplicable—though that won't stop me from explaining it as much as possible. When you are realized in freedom, you can feel the sea of bliss that is reality engulfing all others, but you don't ignore that their unhappiness still is their unhappiness to them, and you are they; and therefore your happiness is incomplete. No one is completely happy until everyone is completely happy. Therefore, the buddhas are compelled to be inexhaustibly present to all of us. They will not be perfectly happy until all beings are perfectly happy. "You're not excused, Buddha. You still have to worry about me." You can think that way. The bodhisattvas don't mind.

In a way, however, you do escape unhappiness, because you have that other, deeper vision where you see you're already there. You see all moments of time as interpresent in the enlightened vision. This moment contains every instant of past, present, and future of all beings. The future is here now. The past is still here now. So, in a sense you have escaped. You are really free. Nirvana is embodied in a present that seems to be caught in a specific flow of time and space with specific limited beings. That is truly the miracle of what is known as the "Nirmanakaya," the emanation body of the buddhas. When you become a buddha, not only do you not have an end of life, you have infinite life; you become able to become present, to manifest presence as emanation, as incarnation, to infinite numbers of beings simultaneously. Your will or spirit of perfect compassion of that time can be perfectly present to everyone. The best way, of course, to be present to all for their sake is as a teacher, because the best way that they achieve happiness is not just by some salve, some palliative applied from without, but by their own understanding opening them from within to their actual own reality, so they have their independent freedom themselves.

In a lovely statement in Maitreyanatha's *Universal Vehicle Discourse Literature*, the future buddha says, "There is not one buddha and there are not many buddhas. Buddhas are neither one nor many." You can't say there are many buddhas because all buddhas are one in the body of reality. They share the same body of reality, which is infinite and absolute. But you can't say there is only one buddha, because each individual being evolves to buddhahood and enjoys her or his own communion with all other buddhas in oneness. Each enjoys it individually, so in their form bodies, in their beatific bodies, all buddhas are distinct, so that your buddhahood does not somehow subsume my buddhahood. Shakyamuni's buddhahood doesn't prevent us from the joy of our own buddhahood, even though when we achieve our own buddhahood we realize we are one with Shakyamuni. We are the same being as Shakyamuni, yet we individually enjoy being the same being, each of us. Isn't that lovely?

THE ELEVEN STEPS TO COMPASSION, LOVE, AND HAPPINESS

How do we get this compassion, this *bodhichitta,* the spirit of enlightenment? How do we give birth within ourselves to a new spirit, a quantum leap in our evolutionary process, a guarantee of positive progress life after life, almost like a shining new soul, a soul of enlightenment? The *Mentor Devotion* puts forward these amazing verses, which reveal the soul of Tibet, the heart of its friendliness and charm:

> *As I think how these sorry beings were all my mothers,*
> *How over and over they kindly cared for me—*
> *Bless me to conceive the genuine compassion*
> *That a loving mother feels for her precious babe!*

Not accepting even their slightest suffering,
Never being satisfied with whatever happiness,
I make no distinction between self and other—
Bless me to find joy in others' happiness!

As I see my chronic disease of cherishing myself,
As the cause that brings me unwanted suffering,
I resent it and hold it responsible—
Bless me to conquer this great devil of self-addiction!

As I see that cherishing my mothers makes the blissful mind,
And opens the door for developing infinite abilities,
Though all beings should rise up as bitter enemies—
Bless me to hold them dearer than my life!

In short, the fool works only in self-interest,
The Buddha works only to realize others' aims;
As I keep in mind these costs and benefits,
Bless me to equally exchange self and other!

Self-cherishing is the door of all frustration,
Other-cherishing, the ground of all excellence—
Bless me to put into essential practice
The yoga of exchange of self and other!

There are two major precepts for conceiving the spirit of enlightenment in the Tibetan tradition, both coming from the Buddha. One comes via Maitreya and Asanga and is called "The Sevenfold Cause-and-Effect Precept of Mother Recognition." And the other comes via Manjushri and Shantideva and is called "The Exchange of Self and Other." The person in our generation who is the main holder of this second precept of practice is His Holiness the Dalai Lama.

The teaching of Shantideva animates His Holiness the Dalai Lama's "common human religion of kindness," as he calls it, the basic human religion, not any particular religion, but the basic love that is beyond religion. The Panchen Lama put the teachings of the two precepts together in an eleven-step process, which we'll embark on next.

The first of the eleven steps is called the "meditation of equanimity," which we do every time we enter the refuge field. Remember where you are, before your jewel tree with its pantheon of enlightened beings.

In a certain sense, all beings are equal from the Buddhist point of view, because all beings have the buddha-soul. Not that there's some little fixed golden-and-platinum buddha sitting in a little vacuum chamber in each one's heart, but in the sense that they're all free. Freedom is their real nature, their very reality. So, they are all free from being fixated on any particular structure, ignorance, and suffering; they have the evolutionary potential to achieve buddhahood, the perfection of evolution, the full opening of all of their abilities, compassionate and intelligent abilities. Given the infinite time that we all have to spend here in life, since we can never get away from our awareness and its continuity, we all will inevitably become buddhas sooner or later. It's just a matter of when, in your own time line, in your own perception of time.

In Buddha's perception of time, since our future moment is ever present, we already have all attained enlightenment. But he's aware also that it makes a huge difference to us in our time lines whether we do so sooner or later. Therefore, the buddhas make tremendous effort, even in their blissful leisure, to help beings accelerate their progress in their evolution toward buddhahood.

Remember the beings around us on the bluff, overlooking the crystal lake, who are looking at us. The ones we love now are those who are nice to us now, who are kind to us, who do things for us and make us happy. Therefore, we love them. If they started being nasty to us, we would not like them so much, and sooner or later, we could become their enemies. We hate other beings, because they're nasty to us, because they are mean, they have hurt us, they've injured us, insulted us, or deprived us, they've been ungrateful to us, so we paranoidly invest them with a notion of real implacable evil.

In fact, those whom we now hate have been our loved ones in the past. Those whom we now love have been our enemies in the past. Those whom we don't know have been both enemies and loved ones. If we truly loved all of them, and if we truly understood the full vastness of each being—that each being (including ourselves) is capable of malevolence as well as benevolence, and each being has been that way in many previous lives—then we would realize that they're all equally related beings. Because we've all been connected with all beings infinite numbers of times, we may as well positively think of them all as beings that we care about.

After all, if even our worst enemy were really happy—not happy by achieving vengeance on somebody, which is never satisfying because he would have to get more vengeance on the next one—but if he were really contented and happy, he'd be nice to us. He'd stop being our enemy. So we really want him to be happy. We want our enemies to be satisfied and happy, because then they'll leave us alone, and they may even be nice to us. And the ones we don't know, we certainly want them to be happy so they won't become enemies. They'll be happy and therefore be nice, share their happiness. And the loved ones, we already want them to be happy.

Equanimity is the foundation of the spirit of enlightenment. The great love or compassion that we are seeking to conceive, the new soul we seek to give birth to, must be universal. It must orient itself toward all beings. We cannot leave a single one out, even Hitler,

Genghis Khan, Saddam Hussein, or even Lucifer or any demon. Any person you think of as the most evil person, you want him to be happy. You want him to be a buddha, really, or you won't have the great love and you won't have the great compassion. You can't get it if you exclude anyone. So, the first step of the eleven-step process is the step of perfect equanimity.

The second step, which is also very powerful and profound, is called the step of "mother recognition." It is based on coming into an awareness of the infinity of life. This insight came to the Buddha on the night of his final enlightenment, as he sat under the bodhi tree. As he deepened his diamondlike concentration on the nature of reality, his mind drilled far into the past and he remembered millions and countless trillions of his previous lives, each one in total detail. It is not usually mentioned in the basic description of that amazing *samadhi* of his, but of course, when he remembered a particular life, he clearly remembered his mother in that life, whether animal, divine, or human. The next insight he achieved was the insight into all the previous lives and all the future destinies of other beings. He therefore remembered being mothered by countless trillions of beings. Indeed, as his unstoppable gaze went past the event horizon into the infinity of the past, he recalled having been the child of the infinity of beings. And he remembered just who his mother was in countless instances. He achieved the recognition of all beings as his mother.

While we may not expect to achieve such a vision right away, we can move in that direction and feel a sense of remembrance of a few previous lives, from which we can infer a beginningless past full of them. At the very least, it is essential to have the vision of the continuity of life. You don't have to have a precise vision of transmigration or reincarnation. Buddhism is not dogmatic in its verbal formulations about relative reality. It's always open to further development because freedom means that all descriptions of relative reality are hypotheses awaiting further evidence, to be proven or disproven. They're not dogmatic laws. But the law of the infinite connectedness of everything is as close as you can get to a law of nature.

And compassion depends upon it. Everything is interconnected infinitely, and therefore, we have been here infinitely, we will be here infinitely. You and I have been living here together in this world, and in other worlds, since beginningless time. That means infinitely. You and I have been related to each other in every single conceivable way. And *you* means all of you, all you infinite numbers of beings. You, the microbe who's crawling around my intestine now, as an egocentrically driven being, a delusion-driven being, you have infinitely been that; I have infinitely been that. I was a microbe in your intestine. But we also were human beings together, infinite times; we were enemies, infinite times. We killed each other, infinite times. We fought with each other. We didn't know each other, infinite times. We were related intimately, infinite times.

The most altruistic way in which we relate to each other in normal biology is when I was your mother, or you were mine. At that time, I let you live inside my body. I fed you with my blood and my vitamins and my calcium. And then I gave birth to you with great labor. And then I fed you from my breast with my milk, and I did that for you an infinite number of times. You did the same for me an infinite number of times. All of you did. Infinite numbers of times you gave me human life, just like you sacrificed your life for me, which is the most altruistic thing in our normal, egocentric, self-versus-other universe that someone can do for another, give his or her life for another person. Then you're reborn again, off, back into whirlpool.

But the mother gives her life as a daily investment. We all did that for each other, an infinite number of times. This is the meditation of mother recognition. It's impossible to do this meditation if you identify only yourself, even your continuity self, your relative self, as birth to death, that's the end of it. If it were so, of course, you would not have been related to all beings—you would have had only one mother. You will find it hard to recognize the mother in all beings.

Please, meditate deeply on this. And take your recognition of universal motherhood into connection with your mother of this life. If you had trouble with your mother of this life, try to go back to remembering when you were at the warm breast, held in the loving cradle of her arms, and then try to see all the beings as your mother.

I did this mother meditation and really melted down. I got to the point where I would really have trouble in the subway, because I got this weird déjà vu feeling with people. When you meditate on the mother recognition, when you see a person, and he looks like you've met him, you don't want to look away in case you do know him, and you don't want to be rude. You also don't want to seem to be coming on to him, if you don't know him, because then he'll think you're weird. It can be sort of hard to get through the sea of faces, because everyone looks "familiar." Every living being becomes familiar—like a member of your family—through the recognition of the mother in each of them.

The third step is remembering the kindness of the mother. Even if you had trouble with your mother, even if your mother handed you over to a nanny or an au pair, it doesn't matter. Even if you were not breast-fed (I wasn't, apparently, my mother and I both imprisoned by forties' medical theories!), this really works. However difficult your family, you wouldn't be alive today if they hadn't cleaned you, fed you, cared for you, kept your blanket on, cured your colds. You would not be alive. Even though maybe you're a little demented because they were harsh with you, you still are alive, and that took effort, and they gave you that effort. The point is, in your meditative state, go back and remember your childhood. In the wish-granting gem tree's luminous energy, in the radiant jewel light field, you can quickly remember your infancy. Tears will come to your eyes. Hairs on the back of your neck will rise. You'll feel so sentimental. How kind my mother was to me! And then you'll diffuse that sentimental feeling of the dependency of the small child to every being as giving you the couchy-coo and delighting in you, looking at you with loving eyes, and seeking your happiness and your comfort and your satisfaction and your pleasure—that is all they are living for.

After we get the sentimental feeling and tears come to our eyes, we move to the fourth step, which is the step of repayment of kindness—gratitude. We've had equanimity, mother recognition, remembering of kindness, and now gratitude for the kindness, the wish to repay it. Here we reflect on how we want to repay all these mother beings' kindness, how we want them to be happy and comfortable and not to suffer. We know that the real way not to suffer is to achieve enlightenment and realize selflessness and true reality and freedom, and to achieve the deep, upwelling inner bliss of freedom. And that's what we want. We want to be their mother of enlightenment now, the mother of all mothers. We want all others to be free. That is how we will repay their infinite kindness. And that is, therefore, the fourth step, of gratitude in repaying their kindness.

This then leads to the fifth step in this special system from the great teacher Tsong Khapa and the Panchen Lama, the equal exchange of self and other. In this step, we ask, "What do all beings want?" We think of our equality with them, and we think that they want happiness, just as we want happiness. None of us wants to suffer. My enemy, a person unknown to me, my friend—all want to be happy, and that's what I want.

Suddenly I realize there are so many more of them than there are of me. And I also realize that I have been looking for my own happiness since beginningless time, and I have remained this egocentric being seeking my own happiness, preoccupied with my own state of what can I do, what can I get, how great am I, how much have I got, how happy am I? And it's never been satisfactory, all this time.

If I think back to when I have thought of others' happiness, however, I realize that then, temporarily at least, I didn't worry about how unhappy I was. At that time, I realized that their happiness is more germane to me than my happiness. So, I realize I'm going to try something new here. I'm going to switch my self-preoccupation for being preoccupied with them. I'm going to extend my mother gratitude repayment to them by being their mother, thinking only of their happiness, like a mother does. I'm going to adopt them as my children, all beings. And, most importantly, I'm going to exchange self-preoccupation for other-preoccupation. It won't hurt me at this point to recognize that the self-preoccupation I have been engaged in since beginningless time has not produced self-satisfaction, certainly not a lasting one.

Being human is a marvelous state of existence relative to so many other life-forms, and being endowed with liberty and opportunity is the most wonderful evolutionary moment in a being's career. Still, having human life is not really satisfying in and of itself. I'm never satisfied. I'm restlessly dissatisfied at all times in pursuing the wish to be self-satisfied. That drive of self-preoccupation has let me down every single time, and all I do is slave for my self-preoccupation. I try to go out and get what my self-preoccupation tells me I need and want, and it's never good. It's never enough. And it never satisfies for more than a second. And it doesn't even satisfy a second when I'm thinking of how much it satisfies.

So, it doesn't hurt to put a little enlightened self-interest into your creation of altruism at this point, and to exchange self for other. Become other rather than self. Become preoccupied with others, and cherish the happiness of others rather than obsessing over the happiness of self.

Now we move on to the sixth step, which is the step of universal love. In this step, I will all my happiness to my mother beings. I visualize them as having happiness and the cause of happiness. And I look at all my mothers from the point of view of seeing them through to happiness. And when I see all the beings as happy, and I look for their happiness, they look so lovely and beautiful to me, because beings that are happy are beautiful. Beauty in a being, in fact, is happiness in that being. A being that is unhappy is not beautiful. Even if objectively a person has certain alluring endowments, high cheekbones, or abundant hair, unhappiness makes him or her dull and downcast and keeps that person from being beautiful. When angry, even the most well-proportioned person looks ugly. The beauty in a being is the being's happiness, and so, when I look at the mother beings' happiness, they look beautiful.

When I visualize all my mother beings as happy and beautiful, in a way, I let myself fall in love with them. Being in love with someone is wanting his or her happiness. It is not wanting to possess him or her for our happiness. That's possessiveness and desire for control. But when we're really in love with others, we want only their happiness. We forget about our happiness, and then, therefore, ironically, we get very happy, because we temporarily stop worrying about how happy we are. *When we forget about how happy we are, we become happy.* That's why people like to be in love, because when they're in love, they focus only on the beauty and the happiness of the beloved other. The moments when they stop to think whether or not their love is requited, that's when they feel dissatisfied. That's when they feel unhappy. This sixth step is the step of great love, of universal love.

The seventh step is universal compassion, which involves looking at the beings, having been in love with them, and getting over this being in love with them a little bit. We have seen them as lovely and happy, in the previous rosy view of the lover, seeing the happiness and the beauty of the beloved. Now we become more like the doctor, who looks at the health of the beloved, and who sees how unhappy the beloved really is. We look at them and realize they don't all have minds of transcendence: They are too preoccupied with their own self-fulfillment; they are chasing illusions of being happy; they are filled with the paranoid feeling of "being the one," the one that is unappreciated by the universe; they're struggling with the universe; they are born infinitely again and again in unhappy lives and suffering; they're being eaten by other beings, consumed, exploited, and abused by them. Even when they eventually become gods, they just indulge themselves and waste their time, and then they're terrified when it comes time for them to die as gods.

Remember the previous meditation on the suffering of all the different states of egocentric life in the universe, and see that your mothers are always falling into those states endlessly. They wish for their own happiness, but they act only to develop their own unhappiness. They're selfish, self-centered, and confused. They're angry and impatient and irritated, and they never really have happiness. You see that, in fact, all your beloved mothers are not happy. And when you feel that, then you feel, "This is intolerable. They must be free of this suffering that they have, and they must have the cause of the freedom from that suffering." When you feel that way deeply and intensely, this is universal compassion.

Love and compassion are like two sides of a coin. My love wants to reach out and give my happiness to them, make them happy from my happiness. The compassion wants to reach out and take away their suffering from them, and bring their suffering away from them and back upon me. Once you really see the beings as your mother, you feel a kinship and familiarity with them, your way of connecting is through love, and you will your happiness to them. Through compassion, you will their suffering to come to you. And you turn it into bliss and send it back as happiness. This is how you have the connection of love and compassion.

The eighth step is thinking of the disadvantages of cherishing the self as opposed to cherishing others, and how this self-cherishing habit and self-preoccupation habit has led one endlessly and beginninglessly into samsaric, egocentric life states of endless frustration, endless unfulfillment, and constant struggle with the universe.

All the lamas in the jewel tree in harmonious accord describe self-cherishing as the constant inner desire to gain happiness for ourselves, the preoccupation with our own comfort and pleasure. This preoccupation has caused people to commit all the ten deeds that have negative evolutionary effects, such as killing others, taking their possessions, and so on. These deeds are the cause of all our suffering. It is ironic but no less true: It is the very desire for your own happiness that produces your ceaseless unhappiness.

As I see my chronic disease of cherishing myself,
As the cause that brings me unwanted suffering,
I resent it and hold it fully responsible—
Bless me to conquer this great devil of self-addiction!

The ninth stage is the stage of thinking of the advantages of other-cherishing, and realizing how others really are the source of all of one's happiness.

For example, whenever someone is really happy, it is because of the love of others. Whenever someone does something for someone else and gives to others, he or she feels happy. Whenever someone develops higher ethical sensitivity, it is because she or he thinks of others. Whenever one develops the greater strength of tolerance and patience, it's when others irritate her and she learns to overcome that. Think about a ring that you love—and the connections it gives you to others. Somebody else made it, somebody else found the stone and mined it, and somebody else fashioned it into a beautiful ring. Your clothes come from fabric that someone else created, some mother living being. Wool came from mother beings who grow it on their bodies as their fur; then it was shorn from them. Then spinners and weavers made the cloth, and others sewed it into its shape as a garment. When you have food, it's because some farmers grew and cared for it, and somebody shipped it in a truck, and drove it, staying awake in the truck, and somebody cooked it.

Everything good in our life comes from others. If we enjoy poetry and words, it is because of language, and language comes from others who communicated in previous generations. Even our body comes from others, from the cells of parents who developed genes over billions of life experiences, from billions and billions of other beings. Our mind comes from others, our speech comes from others.

Others make it possible for us also to become buddhas. Without others to feel compassion for, we couldn't have compassion. Without others' suffering, we would never feel compassion. Without developing compassion, we couldn't evolve to the state of buddhahood. Wisdom alone would leave us too quiescent and too complacent. If it weren't for our communion with others, we would never evolve the magnificent embodiment, the great giant multiple butterfly embodiment of buddhahood, the infinite bliss of buddhahood.

Therefore, there's a tremendous advantage to living fully aware that the real source of our happiness lies in other people and their happiness. We usually think of a wish-fulfilling gem tree as being populated by exalted other beings, our mentors, the Buddha, the bodhisattvas, Jesus, Mary, the Goddess, the gods. We think of them as powerful and happy and able to make us happy. But actually, you can consider ordinary living beings to be wish-granting gem trees, too. We become wealthy, for example, karmically and evolutionarily, only by giving gifts, and if there were no one to receive the gifts, we would not be able to develop generosity, and we would not be able to evolve wealth and substance. We become ethical only by thinking of others, and thinking how our acts affect them, and imagining how they are, and developing empathy and sensitivity, and therefore, through ethics, we develop the human life-form. And without patience, which is the root, the true source of beauty, we couldn't develop beauty. Being beautiful or handsome comes from being patient in many, many lives, and you could never be patient if there weren't others who make you irritated, who injure you and harm you. Therefore, people who bug you are also like wish-granting gems.

We couldn't have creativity and effort and enterprise if there weren't others to spur us on to do these wonderful things, like become buddhas for their sake. We couldn't have meditation and concentration, even, because we wouldn't have others to distract us, and from whom we wanted to move away to develop concentration. Finally, we couldn't have wisdom or selflessness without others, because no one would be there to teach us of selflessness, those like Nagarjuna and Buddha, and others who had realized the great teaching of selflessness.

And, so, the ninth step is the stage in which we reflect on the advantages of our thinking only of the happiness of others. Only when we focus on the happiness of others, and accomplish the happiness of others, do we really feel happy. When we are lifted out of ourselves, and exalted in some way in our orientation toward others, then we're really happy. Whenever we are preoccupied, we are really unhappy. As soon as I think, "How happy am I?" I feel unhappy, because it's never enough. And when I'm thinking only, "How happy are they? Oh, it's great, they're a little happy," I ignore my unhappiness, I forget about my little aches and wounds and pains, and I feel perfectly happy, directly or indirectly. So, that's the ninth stage, which the *Mentor Devotion* describes in these words, worth reflecting on, over and over:

As I see that cherishing my mothers makes the blissful mind,
And opens the door for developing infinite abilities,
Though all beings should rise up as bitter enemies—
Bless me to hold them dearer than my life!

In short, the fool works only in self-interest, ·
The Buddha works only to realize others' aims;
As I keep in mind these costs and benefits—
Bless me to equally exchange self and other!

Self-cherishing is the door of all frustration,
Other-cherishing, the ground of all excellence—
Bless me to put into essential practice
The yoga of exchange of self and other!

And, now we come to the tenth step, which I call "messianic resolution," or high resolve, overflowing mind, overflowing inspiration.
In this stage, we basically cultivate the messiah complex, or the
"messiess" complex, the feminine, and realize that we can't bear for
these mothers to suffer. I am preoccupied only with their happiness.
I must accomplish their happiness. How can I accomplish their happiness?

The buddhas who are already buddhas, and have already accom-
plished buddhahood, should supposedly be accomplishing these
beings' happiness. Maybe on some level that will come to pass. Who
am I to say? But it looks to me as if these beings are still not happy,
and therefore, I can't just rest content thinking, "Well, there are
some other buddhas out there who will take care of it." I myself
must help them become happy. I myself must help them become
free of suffering. It is my job to make them free of suffering and
help them achieve happiness. It is my job to do it. I will be the one to

save them. I vow to be the one to save them. I will not rest in all my future lives until I save them.

Here you have to have the sense of the infinite future, so you'll have time to do this. You have to cultivate a sense of time past the next big crunch, the next big bang, and feel as if your spirit and the energies will go on, and in some sense you will be you. Because if you think of death as an automatic obliteration, death as a self-centered, negative Nirvana, you can't develop this messianic resolution. You would think that the messianic vow to save all beings from suffering is insane because you wouldn't have time. But if you see yourself as intertwined with all beings in the matter of the universe, or in the Buddhist sense as intertwined with the lives of the living individual beings, the souls of the beings intertwined, going on infinitely into the future, then you'll see we will be interacting with each other again and again. We'll be in each other's faces again and again. Sooner or later, I will be there in such a way, and I will interact with you in such a way, and I will love you in such a way, and I will be compassionate with you in such a way that I will enable you to achieve happiness and the cause of happiness. I will become a buddha who will be able to help you do that. I have infinite time. We're going to be locked together in this infinite universe, me with all my infinite mother beings, you with all yours, and therefore, I may as well optimize our infinite interconnectedness. Why not? If you're going to be infinitely there with people, you can't get away from them, why not be there with them in the best possible way, where you and they are totally focused on each other's happiness, rather than totally in conflict with each other? And therefore, you optimize that situation. You become a buddha, they become buddhas.

There are three ways of becoming a buddha. It is said that we can become a buddha like a shepherd, like a pilot of a ferry, or like a king or a queen. The buddha-shepherd is the one who herds the flock into the pasture, then comes in last and closes the gate. In this attitude, you make the vow that you will not become free of suffering in enlightenment until you've helped all beings become free. When you are the second, the buddha-ferryman, you'll all arrive at the other shore of freedom from suffering together with all beings, although you're piloting the ship. As the third one, the buddha king or queen, you actually will be crowned, you will take the responsibility of ruling and serving; you will first become a buddha, and then as a buddha, you will establish everyone else in buddhahood. Of these three analogies, it is said that, emotionally, the bodhisattva prefers the first, where he or she goes last into permanent bliss, into exquisite, constantly transforming, but eternal bliss. Second best is to be the ferry pilot, and third best is to be the king or queen; practically, the last option is the most effective.

Finally, the eleventh step on the road to compassion is the recognition that it takes a buddha to help other beings become free and enlightened. Without being fully free and enlightened myself, how could I possibly help others become fully free and enlightened effectively through the last stages of the process, at least? I may help them, inspire them, share with them some inspiration. But to really help them accomplish it, I'd have to be a buddha myself. Therefore, the eleventh step is, I will become a buddha for the sake of all living beings, out of my preoccupation with their happiness, because being a buddha is the only way effectively to assure the accomplishment of their happiness.

Western psychology considers the tenth step, the step of messianic resolution, to be a form of dementia, because we in the West believe in a limited length of life of the individual, and the obliteration of the individual at death. When you meditate on the messianic resolution, the magnificent intention to save all beings, you *should* feel an intensity like that of a mad person, that of a person who can't bear the conventional wisdom, "Well, *later* they'll get enlightened.

Well, *sometime* there'll be Shambhala; it will come in the future. Heaven or New Jerusalem will come later."

No. The messianic resolution is like an apocalyptic madness where *now* we have to achieve buddhahood to be able to help all beings become free of suffering and the cause of suffering *now*. I can't bear my mothers dwelling in this suffering. I can't bear my mothers having fallen into the hells of hunger and thirst. I can't bear them having fallen into the animal realm of one eating another. I can't bear them having fallen into the human realms of mutual conflict, mutual exploitation, mutual destruction. I can't bear them wasting their time idling in the heavenly realms of self-indulgence and idle pursuits of ultimately unsatisfactory pleasures. I must help them become buddhas now, become free of suffering, so that they may have the cause of freedom from suffering now.

That intense madness, that high intention, gets channeled into the vow to become a buddha for the sake of others. It comes by remembering that many beings, in fact, infinite numbers of beings, already are buddhas and have already felt this kind of messianic intolerance of the suffering of others, and have gone to that intensity, and that determinedness, and have become buddhas for the sake of all beings, and are doing maximum efforts for their sake. And so it's not that they're still in an infinite frame of reference. There's always more to be added to maximum. There's no finite maximum. So I will add mine to that. And I will bring those beings to whom I have karmic connection to happiness, and I will accelerate their progress to enlightenment by becoming a buddha myself.

When we reflect this way, the buddhas and the bodhisattvas and the prophets and the gods and the goddesses and the angels and Jesus and Mary and Muhammad and Lao-tzu and Confucious, and Krishna, and Sita and Raga, and Uma and Shiva, and Rama, and Plato and Socrates, Pythagoras, Newton, Descartes, Galileo—all of them shine happily in the refuge tree, glistening and glowing. Because we have had even the simulation, even the imagination of this magnificent new outlook on life, this new will, this new spirit, they radiate more diamond, ruby, sapphire, topaz, emerald, jewel light rays to us. We fill up and glow with this light energy that radiates from us to all the beings around us in a burst of fabulous connection and dedication and gratitude and encouragement.

It is said that there are twenty-two similes of this moment in our evolutionary life, this moment of conceiving the spirit of enlightenment. This moment is like the earth, because it sustains the growth of the crop of enlightened evolutionary qualities. It is like pure gold, incorruptible. It is like a waxing moon, because it causes your positive qualities always to increase. It is like a great fire, because it consumes all obstructions to happiness. It is like an inexhaustible treasure, when expressed as transcendent generosity. It is like a jewel mine, when expressed as transcendent justness. It is like the ocean, when expressed as transcendent patience. It is like a thunderbolt, when expressed as transcendent creativity. It is like a mountain, when expressed as transcendent contemplation. It is like a supreme physician, when expressed as transcendent wisdom. It is like a good friend, a wish-granting gem, a shining sun, celestial music, a good king, a treasury, a highway, a divine genius, a shout of joy, a river, a rain cloud, a bridge, pure butter, a great tree, the elixir of immortality. Actually, twenty-two may not be enough—there are limitless ways we can contemplate our determination to practice compassion and save all beings.

You may have already achieved this spiritual conception in previous lives, when you conceived the spirit of enlightenment, gave birth to the spirit of enlightenment, which this eleven-step process is designed to help you do. The eleventh step will infallibly enable you to conceive this spirit, if you do each step carefully and thoroughly. It is a moment in your evolution that is like a birth—a second birth in Buddhism. You are born again in the family of the buddhas as a child, or a daughter, or a son of the buddhas. I like to say it's like suddenly having your heart turned inside out. You're wearing your heart on your sleeve, as we say in English—but it's sort of an inside-out heart on your sleeve. Normally, the heart is closed in on itself. My heart beats for my own self, my own blood, oxygen, life, pleasure, profit, and fame. Habitual self-preoccupation drives my life and seems to drive the lives of all beings. Our culture even says that's natural, and theories of biology say that it's inevitable and no one cannot be like that, there is no such state beyond that. But buddha-biology, buddha-evolution, the Buddhist science of biology, claims that is completely false.

In buddha-biology, the human being is the being whose heart is naturally inside-outside because of her or his empathy. We bear our young within our bodies, and we realize that the boundary of self and other is permeable. Our speech enables us to inhabit each other's minds. We can think in each other's minds by talking to each other. We can embrace the minds of others in our mind by listening to what they say, by communicating. Our communication is a way of entering each other's minds. Our strength as humans, our social strength, in fact, is that we can live in others, and through others. We daily overcome the boundaries between self and other.

Opportunity comes from our natural empathy. When we conceive the will to enlightenment and activate the spirit of enlightenment, that is when we fulfill our humanness to its ultimate extent. Because then we actually acknowledge that we live empathetically. And we live cherishing the happiness of others, whether they're our family, our community, our nation, our race, our species, all living beings, all sensitive beings on all planets. This outlook changes completely all of our future lives. Our vast, infinite future instantly and infinitely changes when we adopt this orientation.

Suddenly, we *are* all the beings, at least in spirit. We imitate the actual awareness of a perfect buddha in which she or he feels herself or himself at the same time to be all the other beings. We feel every bit as much as they do within their own skins. In fact, buddhas get so much into this cloudlike multiple embodiment possibility that they can be many beings simultaneously and still feel themselves as the other beings that are not they. Even though all other beings are buddhas, a buddha honors their sense of alienation. The Buddha doesn't force them and say, "You gotta be me!" They are they. But they will be really happy only when they also feel they are all other beings, when they also become buddhas.

So, the spirit of enlightenment is not just some sentimental wish: "Oh, I want to save all beings." If you actually believe that it's impossible, you cannot do it. No one can take a bodhisattva vow authentically without the infinite sense of the infinite continuity of life, an infinite connectedness of life. Because you can't mean that you're going to save all beings if you have only a short time until your death, a death that is the absolute end of you. You can't mean it. You can say it in a Zen center. You can say it in a Dharma center. You can say it in church. But you can't mean it as a matter of fact, because you don't believe it's possible.

This turning inside out of the heart is called at this stage a "spirit of enlightenment," because it isn't enlightenment, it's a vow. It's a matter of will and spirit. It's not yet a matter of full awareness, of full realization, but it is *a* realization. Even now, we can have that new spirit if we think it's possible, if we have the sense of the continuity of life, and the vastness of it, and if we can suspend disbelief that it is possible. And then we have that inspiration, actually. We have the spirit of enlightenment as an inspiration.

The functioning or venturing spirit of enlightenment is engaged when we actually take the bodhisattva vow. Once we have that, even when we're not thinking that way, we are getting the benefit as if we think in that way. We make a vow. We actually, take the vow: "I *will* become a Buddha for the sake of all beings, to establish them in happiness, and to provide them with the causes of happiness." And we can do that in a formal ceremony, so that it becomes a real promise and a vow.

But we shouldn't do that, of course, until we're sure we can keep the vow. And that's where we will begin in the next chapter. We will look at that issue of taking that vow, of really embarking on the whole new infinity of life: life as a bodhisattva, life within the buddha family, life as a child, as a son or daughter of the Buddha, of all the buddhas—which is our new clan, our new family, our new race, the buddha race, you can say. We join other buddhas in this second birth through conceiving the spirit of enlightenment, combining the exchange of self and other teaching with the sevenfold mother recognition teaching and implementing it and practicing it, and then, finally, performing it as we have done together in this chapter.

Remember that you could spend a month, a year, a lifetime on each one of these eleven steps, although bodhisattvas would be unhappy to waste much time. We've done them all in a single chapter so that you can begin the process or refresh your commitment to the process.

Now that we have gone through the eleven steps on the path to compassion, the beings in the wish-granting gem tree refuge field are so overjoyed they can't stand it anymore, and they melt totally into light. The whole refuge field just becomes a splash of light, of diamond, emerald, ruby, sapphire, topaz light that flows down from the refuge tree. And the refuge tree itself melts into light, and the lake at the top of the world melts into light. And the island and the bluff and all of it dissolves into us, and we become one with the refuge field, with all the mentor beings, enlightened beings. And we feel really terrific and buoyant and illuminated and insightful and inspired and enthusiastic, and we dedicate all of that benefit and merit from contemplating this to all living beings. We right away invest the merit and the virtue of it with them. We give it away to them. We give this happiness to them, and we melt into light, and as light we merge, one by one, individually in every way with all of these beings, and become indivisible from all of the living beings, friends, enemies, and unknown beings.

And at a certain moment, the beings all wonder, "Where on earth did they all go?" And then we arrive again from our meditative retreat space back in our ordinary self, our ordinary body-mind complex, and our ordinary environment, having concluded the third chapter of Tibet's wish-granting jewel tree retreat.

FOUR

MIND TRANSFORMATION

Becoming the Engine of Happiness for All

To begin this chapter, let's again open to the space for meditative reading. Sit in a balanced way and breathe gently. Let your ordinary reality, your sense of body and location as well as the cosmos, continent, planet, era—let it all dissolve. Don't think about anything. Feel that you're just a vast empty space floating there nicely, no division of self and other. No worries, just pure, sheer, lucid voidness, vast space of freedom itself.

And then, arise from that, suddenly in your most alert, perky, luminous form, your meditative self on the roof of the world, on a bluff overlooking Lake Manasarovar, the highest lake in the world, to the south of a great sacred mountain. As ever, you see an island in the middle of the lake, and out of it grows a giant tree made of jewels, agate and coral, diamond and emerald, ruby and sapphire and topaz. Lights radiate from it everywhere. Its crown is in the heavens, with fluffy clouds, and on the branches of the tree instead of the Christmas ornaments are the glistening lotuses, and on the buds of the lotuses sit the holy mentors, the enlightened beings, the great teachers, the saints, the saviors, the goddesses, the gods, your whole pantheon of enlightened beings, sitting and looking down at you, happily blessing you, radiating light rays to you.

You fill up with the light rays, you glow and you energize with them, your self-doubt and your self-limitation and your self-defeating attitudes melting away, flowing out from you, and then you become so glowing with light that the light reflects to all the beings sitting around you on the greensward. Those who don't know to look at the tree, they don't see the tree, they see just an empty lake. So they're looking at you, wondering what you are looking at and why it is that you're starting to glow. You hum, feeling so good as you're levitating in your energy field.

Now, let the visualization just stay there, in that field; you're filled up with this rainbow of jewel light rays. Salute the beings: "Hail, enlightened ones, thank you for coming. Please bless me to realize the teachings and sustain me. Bless all beings to realize the teachings, and bless me to help them realize the teachings."

Chant three times,

Namo gurubhyoh. Namo buddhaya. Namo dharmaya. Namo sanghaya.
Namo gurubhyoh. Namo buddhaya. Namo dharmaya. Namo sanghaya.
Namo gurubhyoh. Namo buddhaya. Namo dharmaya. Namo sanghaya.

Then make your offering: Give the whole world to them, pick up the planet in your hands, hold it out to them, say, "Here, you take the world, we're messing it up, polluting it, filling it with too many people, destroying too many species. You take it. Have the universe." And you feel relieved of the burden. You put the responsibility for the universe on the enlightened beings.

Now, think about your own actions, your negative actions taking lives, taking what is not given, inappropriate sexuality, telling lies, making divisions between people, speaking harshly, speaking frivolously and meaninglessly, holding greedy thoughts, holding malicious thoughts, and holding unrealistic worldviews. Think about those negative acts of body, speech, and mind through all your different lives, and say, "I sincerely repent. I'm sorry I wronged you all,

I let you down. I apologize to the mentor beings, Three Jewels, enlightened beings, for not living up to your standards. All ordinary beings, I'm sorry I wronged you, I harmed you, I misled you, I failed to attain enlightenment to help you. I'm really sorry I did that, I won't do it anymore.

"Now, I'm going to do the opposite. I'm going to do virtuous, wonderful things. I'm going to save lives, I'm going to give gifts, I'm going to be sexually correct and helpful and sensitive. I'm going to tell the truth, I'm going to speak reconcilingly, to make peace. I'm going to speak sweetly. I'm going to speak meaningfully. I'm going to hold generous thoughts and detached thoughts. I'm going to hold loving thoughts and patient thoughts. I'm going to hold realistic views of the cause and effect of evolution and turn them toward the transformation of enlightenment.

"I'm going to rejoice in front of you. O mentor beings, let us rejoice in all the good deeds of all beings throughout the universe. Let us not feel a drop of envy, of competitiveness or contempt, but let us sincerely congratulate every single one from the depth of our hearts, and rejoice with their good deeds and well-being.

"O enlightened ones, please bring your teaching, make the Dharma rain the teaching of enlightenment upon me and upon all beings, so that we can gain the understanding to be free of suffering and the cause of suffering and can achieve happiness and the cause of happiness.

"O enlightened ones, don't be beyond and aloof from us out there in the truth body. Don't just stick to your great bliss-void vision, but see our suffering. Help us, stay with us forever.

"Anything we do that's good here, let us dedicate it, not for personal fame or profit or gain but for buddhahood. Let us dedicate ourselves to total enlightenment for the sake of the happiness of all beings."

These are the seven limbs of propitiation, by which we connect ourselves more tightly to the jewel tree refuge field. After we invoke these, we turn our minds to the four steps of thought that reinforce our transcendent attitude, our feeling of true self-appreciation, our feeling of wanting to drop out of the rat race of the world and pursue spiritual quests and retreats in our lifelong attempt to achieve transcendence. These are the themes of the preciousness of the human life endowed with liberty and opportunity; the immediacy of death and the infinite blessing of each moment; the inexorability of causal connectedness of the infinite continuity of life and the specific shaping of positive and negative experiences in life based on positive and negative evolutionary actions; and the universal suffering inherent in every aspect of egocentric existence.

These four themes liberate us from any ambition for anything short of total enlightenment, total liberation, total freedom. No mundane or egocentric state of power or pleasure or even knowledge is worthwhile. Nothing about the egocentric life cycle is satisfactory. When we realize these four themes—the preciousness of life, the immediacy of death, the infinite connectivity of causation, and the suffering of the egocentric life cycle—we achieve mental transcendence, we feel tremendous relief. We excuse ourselves from all kinds of boring routine duties and obligations and refocus upon the true meaning of our life, which is to attain perfect freedom, perfect awareness, and perfect love and compassion—perfect enlightenment. Contemplate this.

Then, we remember that we are interconnected with all beings, and that all beings need the same relief, freedom, and enlightenment. Since we are indelibly interconnected with them, until they also have relief, our relief will not be absolutely perfect. And so, we resolve to conceive, cultivate, and develop the spirit of enlightenment in our mindstream. So we contemplate the eleven-step process. We create the ground of equanimity, the sense of equal dedication and commitment and connection to all beings, with no partiality, no special enemies, and no special friends. Upon that ground, we recognize all beings as having been our mothers in the infinite life. With that sense of kinship and familiarity, we remember the kindness of the mother of this life and, therefore, all the mothers of all the lives. With that sense of deep affection, deep appreciation for the mothers, we then develop gratitude and a wish to repay their kindness by making them truly happy.

We decide to exchange self and others, to give up our self-preoccupation, and to cultivate preoccupation with others, adopt all of them as our children in a way, so that we are the mothers of all of them. We recognize that each one seeks happiness and seeks to avoid suffering just like we do, that self-preoccupation has gotten us into trouble and kept us in an unsatisfactory state since beginningless time, and other-preoccupation is the doorway to happiness for both self and others.

We recognize the advantages of cherishing others, how all of them are dear to us. They are the jewel mind of our potential virtue, of our own buddhahood. Without them, we couldn't become buddhas and have perfect bliss. We feel totally loving toward all of them; we see them in their happiness; we visualize their happiness; we determine that they should have happiness and the cause of happiness. We appraise their condition of suffering and develop great compassion for them. We wish them to become free of that suffering and the cause of that suffering.

We realize that we must take responsibility for all of them. We develop the magnificent, messianic resolution that we'll be that one more buddha who will see to it that all of the beings we are aware of in the universe achieve freedom from suffering and gain the permanent and total fulfillment of enlightenment. Finally, we recognize that infinite numbers of other beings already have become buddhas before us. They are doing the utmost they can for all beings, and we must join their number to become buddhas for the sake of all these beings.

Through all of these steps, we conceived a mind that aspires to become a buddha for the sake of all beings. Our mind then turns the heart into a purposeful engine of evolution. We become determined that, through the continuum of future existences, whether through the system of reincarnation, or transmigration, or the law of conservation of energy, every atom of our consciousness, or whatever it is that goes forward, will not rest until we have become the engine of the liberation and the freedom and the happiness of all beings.

Now, staying within the luminous energy field of the jewel tree, let's focus our contemplation on the practice of mind reform, which can also be called in English "mind-training" or "mind-transformation," in Tibetan *lojong*. I like *reform* because it is less behavioristic than *training*, which makes me think of training dogs, horses, and soldiers, and because it is more practical and methodical than *transformation*, although it certainly is both training and transforming.

THE PRACTICE OF MIND REFORM

The *Mentor Devotion* urges us onward here:

> *Therefore, O Compassionate Holy Mentor,*
> *Bless all beings to obtain happiness,*
> *Letting my mothers' sins, blocks, and sufferings*
> *Entirely take effect upon me now,*
> *And giving them all my joy and virtue!*

With this we begin the mind reform practice, preparing for difficulties ahead of time by bringing them on ourselves voluntarily.

Other-preoccupation means foreseeing others' troubles and resolving to take them upon yourself, just as you habitually worry about what problems might confront you on any given day, and you prepare to overcome them.

> *Though the whole world be full of the fruits of sin,*
> *And unwanted sufferings fall down like rain,*
> *May I see this as exhausting past negative evolutionary actions;*
> *Bless me to use all bad conditions in the path!*

You get set for the worst, you take responsibility for it all yourself, prepare yourself to make a virtue of adversities, take advantage of mischances, see them as opportunities for evolutionary advancement for self and others rather than as undeserved and overwhelming disasters. In this way you transform your usual sense of powerlessness in the face of difficulties, and you take back your own power to use obstacles to your advantage, for the sake of all others.

> *In short, whatever happens, good and bad,*
> *Through practice of the five forces, essence of all Dharma,*
> *Becomes a path to increase the two enlightenment spirits—*
> *Bless me to contemplate indomitable cheer!*

The five forces are the forces of determination not to let mental addictions arising from egocentric delusion dominate your life, even for an instant, your whole life long; the seed of virtue, which is your engaged spirit of enlightenment; preemption of negative habits, proactive countering of your tendencies arising from self-preoccupation; mindful prayer, dedicating any accomplishment to becoming a buddha for the sake of all beings; and familiarity, the power of tiny incremental transformations of negative habits into positive ones, "baby steps," so that your mind will respond to gentle, gradual cultivation by becoming more and more positive. The two enlightenment spirits are the relative spirit—love and compassion for all beings that will not be satisfied until you are a buddha and can really help them find true happiness—and the ultimate spirit—your wisdom-awareness of all things' intrinsic freedom, their voidness of any intrinsic identity as what they seem to be, which allows their infinite transformability by the power of love. Naturally the good cheer that wells up from such realization is indomitable.

> *Bless me to give my liberty and opportunity great meaning,*
> *By practice of the precepts and vows of mind reform,*
> *Applying contemplation at once to whatever happens*
> *With the artistry of employing the four practices!*

The four practices are those of gathering merit, overcoming negativities, making offerings to demonic obstructors, and seeking help from protective angels.

We have resolved to become bodhisattvas, children, sons or daughters, of the Buddha. We resolve to achieve the spirit of enlightenment and develop the heroic concept of saving all beings from suffering. In this wonderful mind reform method, we focus very closely on our self-preoccupation habit, to see how all of our troubles come from being self-preoccupied. We also see that all virtues, happinesses, and benefits come from being other-preoccupied, from exchanging the self-preoccupation for the other-preoccupation. Recognizing that we have harmed others immeasurable times over previous lives, we see that by those negative karmic acts, words, and thoughts we have harmed ourselves. By seeking our own self-interest, we never really will fulfill our own self-interest.

In the mind reform transformation, you reverse the normal behavior, self-aggrandizing and self-promoting, and you substitute other-promotion for self-promotion. You substitute other-preoccupation for self-preoccupation. You live in a way that is the opposite from the people of the world.

Geshe Chekawa, one of the greatest mind reform practitioners, was the twelfth-century author of the famous *Seven Point Mind Reform* text, a favorite of the Dalai Lamas', including the present one, and of the Panchen Lama who wrote the *Mentor Devotion.* A famous story about this geshe tells of his disappointment on his deathbed. He said to his chief disciple, Seychungwa, "Alas! Things have not turned out as I had hoped. Please make special offerings to the Three Jewels." Seychungwa asked him, "What had you hoped for?" He replied, "I have always prayed that I could draw in the sufferings of all beings at my heart like a cloud of black smoke, but now I am having only the vision of the Land of Bliss, where I do not want to go!" * The geshe's mind reform practice was so powerful, his inner bliss so tightly connected to his other-preoccupation, he wanted only to share such bliss with others to relieve them of their suffering, not wishing any external relief of apparent stress for himself. According to Geshe Chekawa, these are some of the commitments in the practice of mind reform:

- Be consistent, carefully mindful, and impartial.
- Use force to abandon addictions and develop virtues.
- Overcome excuses for self-preoccupation.
- Consciously prepare for difficulties.
- Don't rely on extraneous coincidences.
- Change your attitudes but remain natural in behavior.
- Don't criticize the faults of others.

---

* This story and a different English version of much of the information on mind reform in this section are available from H. H. Dalai Lama, 1995, pp. 170 ff.

- Don't meddle in others' business.
- Don't expect rewards.
- Avoid toxic food; don't spoil practices with selfish motivations.
- Be critical of yourself, and don't stubbornly hold grudges.
- Don't tease people maliciously.
- Don't wait in ambush.
- Don't go for the jugular.
- Don't overload or jeopardize others.
- Don't always try to get ahead, and don't exploit the Dharma teachings.
- Don't turn a god into a demon by being spiritually self-preoccupied.
- Don't seek happiness through others' suffering.

Each one of these commitments has extensive instructions on how to observe and practice it in daily life. Each is a training for someone who has taken a vacation from the pursuit of his or her normal, mundane goals. In mind reform, we're not seeking normal success, normal status, normal ego space, normal victory, but we're looking for something completely different out of all of our relationships. In every exchange, we're looking for the happiness of the other.

In mind reform, you let the enemy have the victory. Let him win, let him have it. You take the defeat yourself. If someone abuses you, you take the benefit of the abuse by building your tolerance and patience, and do not think of retaliating. In the commitment to be critical of your own delusions, you go after your own faults and biases. If someone harms you, you do not hold this in mind and wait for an opportunity to take revenge. Instead, strengthen your patience and find ways to forgive the harm done to you. Don't go for the jugular with others: In other words, be careful not to offend others, whether humans or spirits. Never humiliate them by pointing out their weak spots in front of others.

Do not exploit the Dharma to promote yourself. The purpose of the Dharma teachings, and the mind reform in particular, is to gain enlightenment to benefit all beings. You should, therefore, avoid using the teachings just to promote yourself, to gain wealth, reputation, or other worldly success. If I were giving these teachings and this retreat with a view to trying to gain worldly success, that would really be the wrong thing to do. Far from getting success, I would get all kinds of negative results.

I do love the mind reform tradition, as little as I'm able personally to practice or perform it, because it really is so radical, so marvelous. It engages enlightened self-interest, but not as some sort of sentimental altruism. It recognizes that, if you are preoccupied with your own condition all the time, it will always be unsatisfactory to you, and you will only narrow your being and make yourself smaller, and close up more and more, and become less and less enlightened.

We tend to listen to this voice within that we identify as ourselves telling us constantly, "Well, now, is that going to make you happy? Is this going to be nice? And what should you do for yourself today?" We constantly engage in this inner attention to our own situation. Yet those times when we really feel happy—we have a moment of relief from this constant inner griping, restlessness, and discontent—are precisely the times we forget ourselves when something special happens to us while we are engaged with others. When we are doing something really wonderful and others manifestly benefit from it, we forget our usual dissatisfaction and just enjoy their enjoyment.

Mind reform recognizes that the essence of the happiness of those moments in life is that we're no longer thinking about our own condition. The minute we have an experience and stop to evaluate it, asking, "How fun was that for me? How much did I enjoy them enjoying their new toy? How great was that van Gogh I saw?"—when we have that thought, then we completely lose the enjoyment. We begin to think it was fun enough, but we could have enjoyed it more ourselves, it was never good enough.

Since those times of other-preoccupation are the times when we are happy ourselves, let's stop waiting for them to happen somehow and just go straight to it, taking the other-preoccupation straight up. Let's not be self-preoccupied and then be surprised by something so that we become other-preoccupied and momentarily distracted from our cycle of inner despair and misery. Let us go for the other-preoccupation, let us focus on others, let us always think of being there for sentient beings. What we're doing is for sentient beings. Forget about the results for our self. Act without focusing on the results of your actions, act purely out of the joy of the action, out of the virtue of the action, and do not think about any result.

This is the yoga of positive evolutionary action. This is what is called acting transcendently. When you give a gift, you don't perceive yourself as the giver, you don't perceive the gift as a gift. You don't perceive the receiver as the receiver. Something flows from this part of you to that part of you, and you don't perceive yourself doing it. You don't take note of it or say, "Oh, I'm so great, I gave a gift." Or "Gee, was it too big a gift I gave?" Or "Gee, am I going to miss that myself later?" All this kind of reflection ruins the transcendence of any gift or act.

Mind transformation was taught by all of the great saints of Tibet, who also acted in this amazing, unconventional way. As Milarepa used to say, people of the world seem crazy to a spiritual person, because the people of the world are seeking wealth and security and shelter and comfort and possessions and status, everything that the spiritually insightful sees as completely insubstantial results melting away like dew with the rising of the sun. And truly spiritual people see the inner world of the opening of the soul to generosity and tolerance and wisdom and openness and freedom as the only thing worthwhile. This opening can be enhanced sometimes by poverty, by accepting injury, by accepting defeat. It can be enhanced by not retaliating, by not seeking to compete with others but only with yourself, competing against your self-preoccupation, bringing other-preoccupation to bear against self-preoccupation.

The way that the spiritual person such as Milarepa lives looks insane to the people of the world. For example, Milarepa observed that most mothers and fathers have a big thing about giving wealth to their children. They want to leave a legacy, some money or a house, possessions, social status. But all of those things simply trap the offspring into feeling that those things are worthwhile, and they may be deceived into spending their whole life seeking more wealth, status, fame, and possessions instead of freedom and happiness.

I'm reminded of the story of Milarepa meeting the young dandy on a horse crossing a river. In Tibet, fording the icy rivers at some times of year can be truly harrowing. Mila sensed an openness and intelligence in the dandy, but he also saw he was hopelessly absorbed in his worldly trappings and pursuits, so could not hear the Dharma teachings he needed. Mila used his supernormal powers to make the stream rise uncontrollably so the dandy's horse could not get across. Mila then walked across the surface of the water and eventually led horse and rider to safety. Impressed, the dandy wanted to repay Mila's kindness, so he offered him a nice jacket, a pair of pants, some fine boots, and so forth. Mila kept refusing, saying he preferred his nearly naked free condition, and object for object, Mila sang a poetic song, beginning with the jacket Mila had, made of insight, compassion, transcendence, and bliss. The dandy kept trying to compete, even offering his silver saddle and beautiful stallion, and each time Mila sang about how his "horse of well-trained inner neural winds" was preferable, bearing him effortlessly across the swollen rivers of the life cycle and onward to ever greater levels of bliss and wisdom. Finally, the dandy realized there was something more to life than having the latest gadget of utility and pleasure or the finest object of art, and he became Mila's disciple—though the tale ends with the implication that it will take some time for the dandy to develop the deep transcendent attitude required to motivate the more intensive practice of Milarepa's closer circle.

If you really want the full happiness, the total enlightenment, of your offspring, give them teachings of the realistic Dharma rather than material things. Or at least give the Dharma in addition to some sort of material assistance, which they may need to leave them free of the preoccupation with getting by. But to leave them your wealth as if that were the only important thing, and not to have a higher aspiration for your children is, in an evolutionary sense, actually harmful to the children, for it traps them more and more deeply in the endless cycle of worldly concerns.

That's a little taste of the mind reform tradition. I have a new English proverb for it: I say, "Buddha is as buddha does," meaning that we shouldn't hold buddhahood or enlightenment so far away from ourselves. Sometimes when you're too religious, you think, I've got to concentrate, I've got to be on retreat, I've got to become enlightened so I can help all beings, but meanwhile, I don't want to help this one being over here. I refuse to give a dollar to this being. I'm going to squabble and quarrel with that being about who gets to sit where in the retreat. If we were buddhas, we would naturally become focused on the day-to-day mindfulness of our day-to-day being.

We think, "Once I am buddha, then I'll be nice, then I won't struggle to the top, I'll perceive you as more important than myself." Or "When I am buddha, that's the way buddha-consciousness is, but until I get that, I better be more focused on myself to get to be buddha." The great eighth-century Indian saint, poet, and adept Shantideva says, "Buddha thinks only of the welfare of others. Buddha has no thought for himself or herself, because Buddha, himself or herself, is utterly self-satisfied in total blissful freedom." Buddhas don't need anything. However, they don't shut out of their awareness the neediness of other beings, and therefore, the only thing remaining for them to do in the world is to satisfy the needs of the other beings. Of course, satisfying them ultimately doesn't just mean giving material things or palliating their suffering. It means giving them the realistic Dharma teachings, which they can use to develop their clear understanding and to liberate themselves from suffering and its cause.

One of the great practitioners of mind reform, the exchange of self and other in daily life, was Geshe Bangungyel, Geshe Ban for short. He was a member of the Kadampa school, which flourished for several centuries after the time of Atisha in the eleventh century. Once he was in a ceremony with his fellow monks and lamas, and a lay patron came to give some yogurt to each of the monks. Geshe Ban was some distance down the line, and he took note of the thought in his mind that the patron should give the monks smaller portions or he might run out before getting to Geshe Ban. He took note of this thought, and when the patron reached him and held out the ladle full of yogurt to place in his bowl, Geshe Ban suddenly withdrew his bowl. The patron asked him, "Don't you want your yogurt?" And the geshe replied, "No thank you, I've had quite enough already!"

Another exploit of this geshe always stays in my mind. He was visiting a merchant patron in his shop in town, and the merchant was out front talking to a customer. Geshe Ban was enticed by the aroma of excellent Chinese tea in several bins in the shop. He thought, "He'll never miss a little piece of this brick of tea," and so he reached into the bin and took out a chunk of the tea brick. Suddenly he shouted, "Stop, thief! I've caught a thief!" and he rushed out and turned himself in to the merchant, still shouting, "Thief!

Thief!" His left hand had firmly gripped his right wrist and forced the right hand to open and show the merchant the chunk of tea brick it was holding. In these ways, Geshe Ban guarded himself against the demon of self-preoccupation and continued his mind reform practice even in the midst of ordinary comings and goings. There are many other good tales of the famous Geshe Ban and his determination to keep to the path and bring others into enlightenment also.

THE BODHISATTVA VOW

Now we come to the bodhisattva vow. In order to take the bodhisattva vow, however, we first have to know what it is. There are said to be the eighteen root vows and forty-six branch vows of the bodhisattva, although the central gist is saying, "I vow to save all beings from suffering." But taking and following the vows are not as simple as that. They also comprise specific ways in which you determine to guide your interaction with others when you become spiritually reborn, born again in a mode in which you are living for others more than living for self. The vows guide you to live for self primarily through living for others, having exchanged self-preoccupation for other-preoccupation.

The specific eighteen root vows and the forty-six minor vows all together constitute a kind of ethic and etiquette of altruism, a very strong, detailed, well-thought-out ethic of replacing the habit of self-preoccupation with other-preoccupation. This ethic and etiquette give us the opportunity to carry our meditation into daily life, to bring focused mindfulness with us into everyday interactions with others and even into our thoughts that concern others.

For example, Shantideva mentions in his great work on the bodhisattva career how he commits never to sit idly and nervously rip out blades of grass as he waits on the ground for someone. He commits to move gently like a cat or a thief, so as not to disturb others when he enters or leaves a room. And my favorite one—he commits never to point the way with his index finger when someone asks him directions but always to use the gesture of welcome with his full hand outstretched, as if inviting the person to go in the indicated direction, thinking to himself, "Now I invite you to go where you have asked to go; in the future life I will invite you on the path to buddhahood." These are ways of meditating with the body and with your speech as well as with your mind.

The reason it is so important to learn the specifics of interactive meditation is that they immeasurably deepen solitary meditation. We can always retreat now and then, but we do spend a great deal of time interacting with others. We should try to interweave these two phases of development as much as we can, so we can maintain a constant progress. I like to invoke Bill Murray's famous precept, given in his role in the movie *What About Bob?* to make progress in "baby steps." We develop our minds, we improve our lives, we deepen our insight and increase our love little bit by little bit, by baby steps of progress. It is unrealistic to try to get there all at once; we inevitably fail, become discouraged, and too often decide it's no use trying.

The bodhisattva vow is so like the good aspects of other world religions. It evokes Jesus' Sermon on the Mount, the great compassion he taught, and the great compassion for others taught by Allah al-Rahman in Islam and exemplified in the deeds of the great adepts of Sufism. It is reminiscent of Confucius' notion of being loyal to others and gracious with them, and feeling true love—*ren*—for them. *Ren* means "love." The master wanted his disciples to be loving with others, not merely humane or genteel, though those virtues move in the right direction. When you are loving with others, then everything you do with them will be automatically gracious, exemplifying *li*, the complementary Confucian virtue of "graciousness," not mere "propriety."

Hindus call the love of God *bhakti*, but they also have *maitri*—

love—and all of the other loving virtues—gentleness and nonviolence, *ahimsa*, a common human religion of kindness, of friendliness, of love and compassion. Every human being needs love from others. We couldn't live without loving relationships with others, and we would never be happy ourselves unless we loved others. You don't need religion to know that; it's a common biological fact. We humans are a kind of group being, and the bodhisattva vow acknowledges that.

The eighteen root downfalls, or transgressions, of the bodhisattva vow, for example, are:

- To praise yourself and deprecate others.
- Not to give the Dharma teaching to those who need it, or not to give material things to those who need them.
- Not to forgive someone when he or she sincerely apologizes.
- To abandon the idea that all beings deserve full happiness and full enlightenment.
- To make personal use of offerings given to the Three Jewels.
- To abandon the Dharma, saying that some teachings of the Dharma that we don't personally like or that do not fit with our ideas are no good or stupid: "Oh, Buddha couldn't have said that."
- To push monks or nuns to disrobe and go off and be normal worldly people because of ignorance of the great virtue of the true vacation realm, the resort of the monastic Sangha.
- To commit the five heinous crimes: killing one's father, killing one's mother, killing a saint, wounding a buddha, or creating a division in the community.
- To hold unrealistic views.
- To completely destroy a town or city, civilian bombing in general. The bombings of Germany, Japan, Yugoslavia, and Iraq were unfortunately too much like this. People who have

made such attacks, even though they're on the righteous side, say, against a horrible genocidal dictator—Hitler, Saddam Hussein, or Slobodan Milosevic—by going too far and destroying entire towns, are certainly losing their bodhisattva vows in case they took them in a previous life.

- To teach voidness or radical freedom to the uneducated.

This danger is well guarded against in the Tibetan Buddhist tradition; the lamas tend to feel that voidness or selflessness is a little bit like a secret teaching, or an advanced teaching, because it can be confusing for someone to realize that he has no fixed identity without being prepared in some other way for how to deal with that freedom. Freedom is dangerous for someone unprepared for it; it may freak him or her out, causing downfall into nihilism. Although the Tibetans are a little reserved about teaching freedom in its full form of wisdom, I believe that people in the modern world already have a kind of involuntary experience of identitylessness. Many modern people already start out thinking that they are nothing. So it's not so dangerous to them. People in more traditional societies were quite comfortable with the cultural matrices in which they lived, and they didn't have this nearly commonplace encounter with nihilism, or with nothingness, that modern people have.

It's dangerous for someone with a naïve sense of identity to lose that and then mistake the loss of it for their being nothing and therefore become nihilistic. But all of us in the modern realm are "educated" in nihilism already. I think we need the medicine of emptiness and selflessness as a critique of nothingness.

The other root downfalls are:

- To persuade a bodhisattva who wants to save all beings by becoming a perfect buddha that it would be too difficult. To say, "Why don't you just go do some other things?"

- To cause someone who is a monastic to abandon his or her individual liberation vow, whatever his or her particular ethical vow or level of discipline is, by saying, "That's useless, forget it and have a good time."
- To disparage the monastic vehicle. The bodhisattva vehicle presupposes the monastic vehicle. It's essential that people have the mind of transcendence, and the ethic of transcendence, before they can begin to have the mind of universal compassion and the ethic of universal salvation. If they don't have the mind of transcendence, if they have not experienced the first sort of relief of transcendence themselves, they don't really know what is the salvation they want to make for everybody.
- To claim to have realized emptiness when one hasn't.
- To receive and resell icons or other property of monastics.
- To give away gifts or treat them disrespectfully. If you're a yogi, for instance, and you're doing retreat and intense practice and you are given gifts by donors to support your practice and performance, but because you're irritated with the donor you give those gifts away to someone who's not seriously practicing, that's a root downfall.
- Most serious, to give up the spirit of enlightenment. If you get discouraged when someone really angers you, and you feel bitter hatred for that person, and you decide, "I cannot be a bodhisattva, I cannot save all beings, because I won't save this one. This person is just too horrible, and I refuse to embark on the quest of buddhahood for the sake of saving this Hitler, this Saddam Hussein, this terrible, creepy person who does all these nasty things. That one I'm leaving out," if you leave out even one sentient being once you have taken the vow of determination to save all beings, this is considered really not good.

So you shouldn't rush to take the bodhisattva vow.

The Tibetans have a ceremony for vowing *to try to learn* to take the bodhisattva vow. You don't rush into it. However, if you do have the vision of the infinite continuity of life, then it actually becomes easy and natural to take the bodhisattva vow and really mean it, and you can't possibly lose it. Once you know that your personality will change in other lives, as will that of all the other beings that you know, and you recognize that all are in this together, forever, that we are in each other's faces for the infinite future, if you really feel that vision, you cannot give it up. If you have the commonsense feeling that such is the nature of reality, that you're never going to get away from these other people here, these other beings, even the animals, the bugs—they're all going to be with you forever, not always in the same form, the bugs will become humans—that this is the cosmos you live in, and you're bound to live in, even as a buddha, you cannot give up the quest of making all beings perfectly happy. If you feel infinitely connected to all those beings, you cannot give up your vow.

You can break it, in a moment of anger or something, but you can repair it. In order to break your vow irreparably, you have to think that what you did to break it was right, that you were not at fault. You have to have no intention of trying not to break it again in the future, you have to think what you did was right. You even have to be happy that you broke the vow, and have no regret about it.

Preparing to take the bodhisattva vow is like embarking on a discipline of altruism. The vow is so other-sensitive, it's also a spiritual etiquette. Just as being a monk or a nun is like a boot camp for learning gentleness, becoming a bodhisattva is a training in sensitive altruism.

When you reach the point at which you want to take the bodhisattva vow, when you want to have the venturing vow of the bodhisattva, the activated mind, then you enter a space like the space of the wish-granting generation tree refuge field, and you call to witness all the buddhas and bodhisattvas from all the universes, and all the three times—past, present, and future—and all the ten directions. You call all the enlightened beings from everywhere to witness as a great host in the sky, like a close encounter of the third kind, like the refuge field jewel tree assembly. Then you also must arrange very elaborate offerings for this invited assembly; voluminous flowers, marvelous cakes and cookies, fruits and bags of rice, incense and lights in a very big, very lush display. They obviously don't eat it or use it, but you do it for the generosity, the feeling of offering, of connection.

When you take the vow, you solemnly swear, "I will become a buddha, for the sake of all beings, as all the buddhas did when they awoke from being individualistically oriented beings, self-preoccupied beings just concerned with themselves, when they awoke from that delusion to become other-preoccupied beings, other-cherishing bodhisattvas, just as they did and then eventually became buddhas, so I, too, will become a bodhisattva. I, too, will conceive the spirit of enlightenment. I, too, will practice the bodhisattva deeds, and become a perfect buddha for the sake of all my mother beings."

You repeat it three times, and you call all the beings to witness.

When you take the vow, it is said you truly are born in the family of the buddhas. As a child, son or daughter, of all the buddhas, you have a new clan. You have gained a new gene, your spiritual gene, your bodhisattva gene, which you take with you from life after life. And you now insist that your evolution and all of your experiences in life have the meaning that you give to them. They are your way to buddhahood for the sake of all beings.

And then you use everything, even the most adverse conditions, even accidents and disasters and sicknesses, to assist you on your path. Everything becomes fuel for your vehicle of enlightenment. Even when sleeping, you are generating vast masses of merit. Even when you do the smallest thing with the view that you do it to help someone else become free and happy, you are acting as Buddha would. "I give this coin to this beggar with a view to becoming a perfect buddha, so that someday I can help this beggar become perfectly happy and give him the teaching, so he can become a perfect buddha."

Having achieved the bodhisattva mind, you are happy and delighted, like someone who is born again. In fact, you *are* born again when you really take that bodhisattva vow. You have done something truly magnificent. You have changed your life, your whole orientation. You use the words of Shantideva, "Just as the previous lords of bliss conceived the enlightenment spirit, and just as they successfully lived by the bodhisattva practices, for the sake of all that lives do I conceive the spirit of enlightenment, and likewise shall I, too, successfully follow the practices, in order to further and increase that spirit from now on." The intelligent who have vividly taken the spirit of enlightenment in this way should extol it and congratulate themselves.

This is how we will greet ourselves upon taking that bodhisattva vow, or even imagining or deciding or determining that we want to develop ourselves to be able to take the bodhisattva vow, following the words of the great Shantideva:

Today my life has borne fruit, having well obtained this human existence, I've been born in the family of Buddha, and now I am one of Buddha's children. Thus whatever actions I do from now on must be in accord with the family tradition. Never shall I do anything to disgrace this holy, faultless family. Just like a blind man discovering a jewel in a heap of trash, likewise by some coincidence, I have found the enlightenment spirit within me. It is the supreme elixir that overcomes the lord of death.

It is the inexhaustible treasure that eliminates all poverty in the world. It is the supreme medicine that cures the world's disease. It is the evergreen tree that shelters all beings wandering wearily on the roads of life. It is the universal bridge that frees beings from wretched lives. It is the rising moon of the mind that dispels the torment of addictions. It is the great sun that burns away the misty ignorance of the world. It is the quintessential butter from the churning of the milk of Dharma, for all guests traveling the path of life who wish to experience true happiness, this spirit will satisfy them with joy, and exalt them in the highest bliss.

    Today, in the presence of all the saviors, I invite the world to be my guests at the feast of temporal and ultimate bliss. May gods, humans, and all be joyful.

This concludes the meditation on the spirit of enlightenment. If you've ever imagined cultivating this spirit, opening your heart and turning it inside out in this wonderful way, and coming up with this marvelous, magnificent resolution to make all of evolution meaningful—you can make your life meaningful by becoming a perfectly enlightened being, the engine of the happiness of all other beings.

Shantideva's own story is instructive here. He lived in the eighth century in northern India. As a young monk, he was thought to be the worst student in Nalanda University. He never spoke in class, even fell asleep, and nobody had any idea if he knew anything or even studied at all. His nickname was Bhusuku, meaning "he who eats, sleeps, and defecates." Finally, the senior monks decided it was time to send him home, so they challenged him to offer his dissertation to the entire community. To graduate from the university, students had to give a full address to all the scholars and then defend their thesis against challenges in debate. Shantideva said, "Okay, when and where?" The monks set a date but actually thought it was a big joke, as they were sure he was incapable of giving such an address.

When the day came, he ascended the dais. There was a large crowd, since everyone thought they would enjoy teasing the ignorant

Shantideva. First he asked the senior faculty present, "Do you want to hear something heard before? Or something previously unheard of?" They laughed and said, "From you, Bhusuku, the unheard seems appropriate." "Okay," he said, and then he launched into the eight hundred or so verses of the *Introduction to the Bodhisattva Way of Life*, one of the greatest works of Dharma teaching, poetry, just good literature, in the Sanskrit language. They were all astounded, and soon rapt with the beauty and profundity of his magnificent teaching. When he neared the end, he began to levitate on the dais, and he slowly floated off out of the university headed southeast from Nalanda in Bihar toward Orissa province, on the Bay of Bengal. Monks had to run after him to extract the final hundred or so verses before he left for good. Shantideva later resurfaced as a Tantric adept, but that is another story.

MEDITATING GIVE-AND-TAKE

In the *Mentor Devotion*, the Panchen Lama next puts forth the meditation of "give-and-take":

> *Bless me to cultivate the spirit of enlightenment,*
> *To save beings from the great ocean of existence,*
> *Through the universal responsibility of love and compassion,*
> *And the magic of mounting give-and-take upon the breath!*

"Universal responsibility" is an alternative translation of the Tibetan *lhag bsam,* literally "overflowing aspiration," or my favorite, "messianic resolution." The give-and-take meditation—meditating on giving your happiness to others and taking their sufferings upon yourself—is an extremely effective method of reinforcing your exchange of self-preoccupation for other-preoccupation. You will live more harmoniously by seeing things from others' perspectives equally with your habitual way of coming only from your own perspective.

Focus now for a moment upon the host of beings around you under the jewel tree refuge field. Reflect how they are receiving the luminous light of blessing from you, as you receive it from the jewel tree assembly. It overflows out around you equally to all the loved, neutral, and unloved beings you can imagine. Intensify the radiation toward them, thinking that the bliss is welling up within you, stimulated by blessings flowing down upon you from above, but by now also welling up out of your spirit of enlightenment, loving resolve for others. Now think about them, their real condition, how much they suffer from loss of pleasure, from pain, from the deep anxiety about future loss and pain. Think about how they cycle through the different life-forms, including the hot, cold, crushing, and cutting hells; the hungry ghost realms of endless hunger and thirst; the animal kingdoms, wherein one is always eating another and being eaten by another; the titan realms of endless warfare; and the god realms of extreme pleasures doomed to eventual exhaustion.

Visualize them in all the dreadful conditions in the human realm, suffering loss of loved ones, torture by enemies, sickness, old age, death, birth, humiliation, poverty, famine, war, terror, and so forth. Feel great compassion for all of them, willing them to be free from their sufferings, and also great love for them, willing them to be happy.

Visualize that your body, possessions, and even virtues all become like wish-granting gems. Visualize yourself on your own as being like a wish-granting jewel tree. Imagine these beings one by one, beginning with those you know, your friends and enemies, and including those you merely know about, perhaps those whom you have seen on television news—a starving Sudanese, a wounded Iraqi child, a bereaved black or white or Asian American or Native Amer-

THE JEWEL TREE OF TIBET 167

ican parent, a Polish wife, a Kurdish father. Think of what they need, specifically, individually, something material—food, clean water, medicine, wealth, a friend, a pet, a house, a boat, a vehicle; something by way of protection—a policeman, a guardian, a fierce angel; some sort of knowledge—especially knowledge of Dharma, understanding of reality, education. And emanate to them teachers, books, media programs, whatever they need of material things, protection from danger and fear, and provision of knowledge and insight into realities of life and death in order for them to find their own freedom and awakening. Think of giving your own body, your own happiness, your own possessions, your own virtues.

As you exhale your relaxed, contemplative breath, send light rays out from your heart of bliss upon it, and let those light rays transform into whatever each of all the many beings needs. Let them find relief, freedom from fear, and openness of awareness. As you inhale, think of their physical and mental suffering and draw it away from them in the form of dark smoke, sucking that back to yourself and swallowing it down the center of your mind and body into the center of your heart. Let it fall upon your habit of self-preoccupation there, giving it energy to see through the delusion of the fixed "self," which pretends to be so important an object of preoccupation, and let it dissolve into the infinite voidness of intrinsic identity, which releases the self in its very core and turns it into an inexhaustible well of bliss. The self-preoccupation focus is like a black hole consuming inescapably all the dark energy of others' sufferings, which then bursts forth in a blazing pulsar of infinite energy of light and joy coming from infinite other interconnected dimensions, making it effortlessly possible to expand your awareness of other-preoccupation, which is the engine of your buddhahood and the accomplishment of all others' deepest wishes.

Contemplate like this: Exhale brilliant light rays that provide all that others wish for and truly need; then inhale the dark, smoky cloud of all their sufferings and burn it up like rich coal in your heart furnace of compassion and love. Don't worry if you can't at first encompass many beings. Pick any single one of them you know well and focus on her or him. Don't think about how this practice will benefit you, although it will of course—think only of benefiting others. Ironically, it benefits you only when you do it with no thought of that benefit. To really benefit yourself, forget about yourself, think only of benefiting others. As the Dalai Lama likes to say, "If you have to be selfish, at least be a wise selfish! If you want to be a success at being selfish, don't be selfish!"

This is the meditation of give-and-take.

THE BODHISATTVA DEEDS

Now the bodhisattva way of life strives to make no difference between meditating and not meditating. Therefore, once you have conceived the will to enlightenment, once you have taken up the bodhisattva vow and so activated the spirit of enlightenment, given birth to the awakening soul, you must venture forth into the transcendent deeds of the bodhisattva. The Panchen Lama gives us the following verses in the *Mentor Devotion* text:

> *Bless me to intensify my efforts*
> *On the sole path of the all-time champion buddhas,*
> *Binding my process with pure messianic vows,*
> *And practicing the three ethics of the supreme vehicle!*

The three ethics are the ethic of self-restraint from harmful actions of body, speech, and mind; the ethic of positive actions to help other beings; and the ethic of accomplishing beings' aims by the attainment of perfect buddhahood.

Bless me to perfect the generosity transcendence,
The precept increasing giving without attachment,
Transforming my body, possessions, and all-time virtues
Into just the things each being wants!

The first of the six transcendent virtues of the bodhisattva is generosity, the willingness to let go of all attachments and give away everything to all beings. It does not necessarily require that you give everything away all at once, but it requires that you be able to, should it indeed be helpful to all beings. In evolutionary progress toward buddhahood, the bodhisattva who eventually became Prince Siddhartha and then Shakyamuni Buddha recounted the stories of his own heroic deeds of generosity in previous lives; how as a young prince he gave away his body and life to a famine-starved mother tigress and her four cubs, which five beings were reborn as his first five disciples when he became a buddha; how as the Shibi king he gave away both his eyes in a transplant operation; and how as Prince Vessantara he gave away all his possessions, his kingdom, even his children and his wife, these last being more difficult than giving away himself.

These stories are unsettling to us in our ordinary frame of mind, since these heroic bodhisattvas make these great gifts with such joy and total transcendence. It is as if they are living in a way no longer identified with body and possessions as "I" and "mine," and rather identify with the awakening soul, which blissfully grows and thrives with each self-transcending accomplishment. The morals in these stories always warn us not to try to imitate these deeds literally until such time as to do so would seem natural and easy for us, not when it seems a tragic sacrifice. The point for us is to cultivate generosity bit by bit, baby step by baby step, using meditative visualization at first.

Bless me to perfect the justice transcendence,
Not surrendering, even to save my life, my vows
Of individual liberation, bodhisattva, and secret mantra,
Collecting virtue, and realizing beings' aims!

The three vows are those of the monastic vehicle, either as renunciate nun or monk, or as ordained layperson, refraining from killing and so forth; the bodhisattva vows as we have described them; and the Tantric vows, which aim to restrain even the subtlest negative habits of the subconscious mind. Justice is the virtue of treating others as if they were yourself, just appropriately in an optimal way for their actual situation. It is a transcendence when it is performed with the insight of wisdom, which does not differentiate between self, other, and the just right action.

Bless me to perfect the patience transcendence,
So that, even if every being in the world were furious,
Cut me, accused, threatened, even killed me—
Feeling no stress, I could repay their harm with benefit!

As you slowly gird yourself with the shining armor of patience, you develop the ability to tolerate any harm anyone could possibly inflict, even unto death. Experiencing yourself transcendentally as your awakening soul, you joyfully embrace all harm as expiation of your own previous negative evolutionary actions. This does not mean you necessarily allow others to harm you all the time, making a martyr of yourself, since harming you may actually be rather bad for them. But it means that no matter what might happen to you, you will never succumb to hatred. You become invulnerable to internal eruptions of anger and aggressiveness. You might act forcefully to prevent another from committing harm, but only out of compassion and love, never out of anger. Therefore, even your forcefulness will be beneficial and never harmful—and thus far more effective.

Bless me to perfect the creativity transcendence,
So that even if I had to spend oceans of aeons
In the fires of hell for the sake of each and every being,
My compassion would never tire of striving for enlightenment!

Creativity here means the joyous energy with which you address positive activities of body, speech, and mind. It means inexhaustible resourcefulness, artfulness, and effectiveness in pursuing the welfare of all beings, yourself included.

Bless me to perfect the meditation transcendence,
Through the one-pointed samadhi *that transcends all flaws*
Of distraction, depression, and excitement,
Focused on the insubstantial reality of all things!

Finally the bodhisattva engages in transcendent meditation. It is transcendent because meditator, meditation, and the act of meditating are not perceived as separate entities. This is where the bodhisattva develops real fluency of mind control, going through nine stages: focus, compensating focus, intermittent focus, solid focus, mindfully disciplined focus, serene focus, serenity, one-pointedness, and stable absorption. You ascend these nine stages by avoiding five obstacles: laziness, forgetfulness, manic oscillation between excitement and depression, noncompensation, and overcompensation.

Once you have achieved solid concentration in the ninth stage, you need to continue to practice it steadily until you gain what is called "fluency" of mind and body, which brings to you an especially intense, serene bliss of body and mind. This bliss gives you endless creativity and energy for meditation on all virtuous evolutionary development.

There is a delightful Tibetan chart of these nine stages, which shows the mind as an elephant being led by a monkey up a winding path. At first the elephant is of a storm-cloud dark hue and behaves wildly and intractably, making it difficult even to harness him. Gradually he becomes more tamed and is led along the path. He turns lighter and lighter as he rises. Finally, he looks peaceful and luminous as he reaches the top.

Many traditions in Buddhism emphasize the practice of meditation above all others. Without the mastery of one-pointedness of mind, none of the other accomplishments is attainable, since the mind needs to be a highly polished instrument to reach profound understandings. However, there is a danger in pursuing meditative adeptness if it is not accompanied by the transcendent attitude, the compassionate spirit of enlightenment, and at least some sound level of the profound wisdom of selflessness. That danger lies in the special blissfulness of the higher meditative states, as well as in the supernormal powers that naturally accompany their attainment.

Once you break free from being caught in the compulsive flow of uncontrolled conceptual thinking, your mental energy is released within and you begin to attain states of loving ease, intense joy, visionary expansiveness, and extreme serenity. If you come to these states with your self-preoccupation unquestioned and intact, you will definitely think you have attained some sort of ultimate essential state, some sort of ultimate reality, and you will shut off your further evolution toward compassion and wisdom, bodhisattvahood or buddhahood. The world of other beings will seem all jangly and troublesome to you, and you will become addicted to a kind of spiritual escapism. According to Buddhist cosmology, you are likely to leave the human world eventually and then be reborn as a long-lived deity of the realms of pure form or formlessness. Such rebirth is not considered fortunate at all but rather is seen as a long delay in your evolutionary progress toward the far greater bliss of buddhahood, wherein your buddha-being can remain in touch with suffering beings and truly be of help to them.

The long-lived deities, by contrast, remain utterly aloof and serene in their isolated quietude, with no sense of the passage of time, too jaded to experience a need for space until, after millions of years—but suddenly in their experience—they fall out of their anesthesia, land smack-dab in the middle of a war zone, and once again suffer the inexpressible anguish of being squeezed between internal addictions and external stresses.

Their experience is like getting sodium pentothal at the dentist's. I look forward to getting out of my consciousness with the anesthetic so the dentist can deal with my cavity or root canal; I feel a buzz and start to relax into oblivion; and then, without my having any sense of a moment passing, the nurse is rousing me, unpinning my bib. I am forced up out of the comfortable chair and told that an hour has gone by and another patient is coming. I never have the pleasure of a moment's sensation of being really gone! But at least, unlike the poor long-lived deity, I have my loved ones back at home and friends around town, I can return to my Dharma practice; I can continue to try not to waste my precious human life endowed with liberty and opportunity.

The last, and most important, of the six transcendent virtues of the bodhisattva is wisdom. But that we will save for the next chapter. Here we conclude the second big theme, the spirit of enlightenment—following the first, the transcendent attitude—which we contemplate under the jewel tree. As the mentor beings in the jewel tree refuge realize we have been contemplating and rehearsing the conception and production of the spirit of enlightenment, the mind reform practice, the bodhisattva vow, the give-and-take meditation, and the bodhisattva deeds, they become so delighted that they radiate out so much light they actually dissolve themselves into light, and descend to us in a Niagara flow of blessings and merge indivisibly into us. We ourselves feel securely one with these our wonderful mentors, and we then dedicate the merit of our meditation together to our attaining of buddhahood for the sake of all these suffering mother sensitive beings. And we ourselves dissolve into light and merge indivisibly with all beings.

After resting a moment in this luminous dissolution, someone wonders where we have gotten off to, and we arise again in our ordinary embodiments in our ordinary environments.

❧

FIVE

THE KEY ROLE OF WISDOM ON THE PATH
Liberation Through Understanding

In this chapter, we'll contemplate the role of philosophical thought in the Buddhist meditative path, and the questions, What is the role of intellect and intelligence on the path to enlightenment? and What is real wisdom?

WESTERN CULTURE VERSUS TRANSCENDENT WISDOM

Many of us in the West come to Buddhism from too many years of being in school, having crammed too many facts into our heads, having memorized too many equations and formulas and axioms and dates of battles. We are generally sick and tired of overworking the brain. And so, when we first hear about meditation, or we hear about the teachings from the East, whether yoga, Hinduism, Christian mysticism, Buddhism, Taoism, moving meditation, the martial arts, we think, Aaah, relief. Pleasure. No more thinking. No more of this wearing out the brain.

In past decades, almost all the teachers of these traditions used to teach that the solution to everything was simply not to think. The traditions were introduced simplistically, so that people thought, Well, if I go and I just breathe, and I disidentify from any particular thought train, and I let my thoughts kind of come and go, and then really let them go, then a big silence will well up in my mind like a resonating bell. And somehow, this big silence welling up in the mind will be the blessed silence of enlightenment, the blessed silence of fulfillment.

Generally students would go on retreats, or take classes in meditation, and they would release their thought trains, and they would get different types of silence. A certain type of energy would stop circling in their brains, and it would flood the body with a feeling of bliss, or a sort of buoyancy. The neural energies would go out into the body from tight little cycles of conceptualizing thought, and people would feel a kind of soaring feeling, pleasure, or warm energy circulating.

And people would, naturally, flip out. They would think, Eureka! This is it! They would do this for one year, two years, five years, ten years, depending on how gung ho they were, and how much time they could afford to do it, how much their predilection was. And then they would begin to notice that the silence could actually become a kind of deadening or deadened state. It could become sort of dullness. Everything else would seem too complex for them. They would become almost addicted to the silence, and going out in the world would be too irritating to them. The sound of the bus in the street, other people's irritating behavior, a jackhammer drilling were just too jangling. And some would just abandon the practice. Later they would feel disappointed. What they had thought was complete freedom because they were free from the surface level of compulsive thinking turned out not to be complete freedom. It turned out to be a kind of quiescence.

The lucky ones among the people who made this discovery went back into the yoga, Buddhist, or mystical tradition and began to learn more. They began to learn that you can't separate your meditative states from how you live in the world, and how you interact with others. They began to learn about the nature of reality and the psychology of other traditions and cultures. They began to question the ingrained sense we have of the superiority of the West, that we are the great scientists and intellectuals and that power over physical matter made us supreme. Many people came to my classes over the years who wanted to know about the wisdom of the East, but then, when challenged about the science of the West, would become very aggressive and defensive about how it was superior. I think overall the culture still is at that point. But the Chinese and Japanese, and especially the Indo-Tibetan traditions introduce us to the possibility that the Buddha and the great Buddhist teachers and masters were the leading scientists of the earth—the supreme knowers of the nature of reality. They gained valid knowledge of the nature of reality through internal observation and empiricism, not through microscopes and telescopes, atom smashers and cloud chambers. Through introspective awareness about the nature of their own neural networks—not just the nature of their spirits, some vague, nonmaterial thing—they learned the nature of language and concept function, how thought works and how nonthought works, how altered states function and how ordinary states function.

Therefore, their view of the actual nature of reality may be superior. Their choice not to develop a superpowerful, potentially self-destructive material technology was perhaps a conscious choice. They saw that would be a foolish thing to do, although their ancient culture had plenty of would-be generals, world conquerors, egomaniacs, and exploiters. Without self-control, any control that you try to exert in the outer world is dangerous.

When we seek to enter the path of enlightenment, we have to engage with society. We have to engage with the negative ethical actions and ethical patterns in our society, take responsibility for how our culture is exploiting other cultures, and how it exists in the world. Even if we are involved in a nonprofit meditation center, for instance, we may need to look at a gift or stocks given by a grateful practitioner that include a corporation that is destroying a rain forest. If that funding is at the basis of the center, the meditations in that center will not actually lead the people to liberation, freedom, and happiness. There'll be some nagging element in the atmosphere that this base is being supported by the horrible bulldozers and chain saws destroying the lives of species and beings somewhere.

We must engage with life and people around us. The *shila*, as the Buddhists say, justice, the ethical path, is foundational to the meditational path. Yet there is no consensus about the monastic life being essential to the path. Many of us teachers of Buddhism have been monks and/or nuns at some time, but then, in interacting with our society, or because of our own inability—our imperfection, our temptation, self-indulgence—we couldn't maintain that lifestyle. I myself was a monk for four and a half years, fully ordained for only a year and a half of that, but I still lived as a monk that way. Later, after I resigned, I held the view for a while that we don't need monks and nuns in America. I thought that, since America is such a secular society and such a lay society, it should have lay Buddhism and everybody should be a layperson. I was rationalizing, in a way, my own behavior.

After studying the history of the Buddhist institutions and the history of America, and taking a good look at the militarism of America, and taking a good look at the Protestant Reformation, I realized that the monastic institution that was invented by the Buddha, the Sangha, is not exactly the same as the Christian monastic institution in its ethical disciplines. It is very, very close but not the same. The Buddhist tradition is an amazing social institution. We actually need more of it. In a way, our universities, schools, and colleges are a kind of monastery, and we should acknowledge, honor, and support them with lifelong fellowships or longer fellowships anyway. People who go to them are really on a vision quest within our society. They want to experience themselves and their lives, and they want to endow their lives with true meaningfulness under a religious, secular humanist, or philosophical framework. That's what school is for, for some, who don't want to be pushed into graduate school as a dentist, or doctor, or lawyer before they have really come up with their own set of values.

In medieval Europe, for example, there was a high degree of monasticism. Martin Luther was an ex-monk, a failed monk. He became furious at the Church and at the monks, and came up with a theory that it was impossible to obtain salvation as a monk or a nun, that you couldn't purify your mind, you were such a sinner, and you could only depend on the faith of God and the grace of God given to you freely. According to his theory, it's even wrong for people to be monks and nuns. They're fooling themselves thinking they're developing their minds or evolving their spiritual insights.

Subsequently, princes and authorities in the Protestant countries used Luther's theory as a way of denying individuals the freedom to pursue their self-perfection. They were not faithful people, like Martin Luther was. Luther was a person of great faith. Princes and authorities just saw his theory as a chance to dominate and monopolize people's effort, and prevent them from pursuing their spiritual life in a monastic community that was outside the rulers' secular reach. So they created the Protestant ethic, as Max Weber, the sociologist, called it, and the Protestant atmosphere, which is what we are suffering from still in America. It's the ethic that everyone has to work all the time to justify his or her individual existence, and that no one should be supported to pursue some sort of inner creative prompting, or vision, or happiness.

Chinese culture had this same kind of ethic in ancient times.

When Buddhist monks initially went to China, the Chinese people and the culture begrudged them the offering of the free lunch that was the basis of the monastic institution in India. The monks adapted to that situation and said, "We'll just grow our own food, since the culture isn't generous enough to give us a free lunch. We'll grow our own lunch." And they developed the "no work, no lunch" ethic in Ch'an, or Zen. So it's not only a Protestant ethic, it's also a Zen ethic. So the idea that people who are monastics, monks and nuns, are gold-bricking, not working or justifying themselves, is both an Eastern and a Western prejudice.

It took me fifteen years as an ex-Buddhist monk to realize that the ungenerosity of the American culture, of the industrial, Protestant culture, leads us to believe that we don't need to support people just to meditate, just to develop themselves, and give them a free lunch, so to speak. Because most people in industry are not Protestants, they're secular humanists, I had to trace the idea back from the Industrial Revolution, which was connected with the Protestant ethic in northern Europe.

So, in our ethical turn, I think we have to move our consciousness forward a little bit to embrace the importance of monks and nuns, of renunciates dropping out of the community. We need to be willing as a community to embrace the idea that some people would like to have the mind of transcendence as the full effort of their lives, to be on vacation from their worldly duties, and develop their spiritual knowledge and meditative experience. We should be willing to support them, and we should have that kind of generosity to invest in their liberation. We should not invest out of self-interest—because once liberated they can do great things for us—but just for them to be liberated.

Thomas Merton, a Catholic monk, wrote that he didn't want to be thought of as a "prayer factory" for laypeople. He didn't believe that every monk had to give back good vibrations in exchange for receiving the free lunch. He wanted, really, to be free. We can argue sociologically that the free people in the monastic community *do* give back a huge blessing to the community, but it isn't a quid pro quo. If it is, it's not a free lunch.

A NEW WAY OF THINKING

Besides the meditational orientation to the path to enlightenment, we need a wisdom orientation. We need to learn a new way of being and thinking and of not thinking. Now we can see that the intellect is not the problem; thought, even, is not the problem. The distorted intellect is the problem, erroneous thought is the problem. In other words, all thoughts are not the same. There are creative thoughts, and there are destructive thoughts. There are insightful thoughts, and there are ignorant thoughts. There's prejudice, prejudicial thought, and there's critical, wise thought.

And so, if we're going to meditate effectively, we have to make our thought more accurate. Now nowhere is this necessity more evident than in the issue of realizing emptiness and selflessness, which is, after all, key to enlightenment. It is a synonym for enlightenment, the realization of selflessness or emptiness. We need reliable information about the nature of the self, the body, and the nature of reality—but especially the self, which is the core of our experience of reality.

Poet and essayist Gary Holthaus has described what he calls a word totem or truth totem, which shows the progression of what we sense, from the basic, most fundamental level up to the ultimate level of wisdom. It being a totem, which is read from the bottommost figure to the top, you should start reading the words starting with "Data":

Wisdom
Knowledge
Information
Facts
Data

This actually illustrates what the Buddha teaches us, too. We start with information about the world around us—what we get from our senses. And we proceed up the ladder, refining our insights into a clear sense of reality—wisdom.

Our feeling of the here and now as we sit within the refuge of the wish-granting gem tree is a gut feeling. Everyone feels a solid sense of presence. Even if we're not thinking, we feel we're here. I feel I'm me even without thinking. Then, when I add thought, I think, Oh, I'm really me, or I'm great, or many other things that I will add that build upon the foundation of the gut feeling, what the Buddhist psychologists called the unconscious misknowledge, or the instinctual misknowledge, or the instinctual self-habit. That instinctual self-habit is just the feeling that I'm it. I'm the one.

But everyone feels he or she is the one. We all feel that as a gut feeling, because that's the unconscious misknowledge, the unconscious ignorance, the unconscious self-habit that has driven the ego-centric life cycle, samsara, since beginningless time. Every Gila monster thinks, I'm the one, and jumps on its prey to feed the one. And we all have that instinctual feeling of self-centeredness. It is not imposed on us by some acculturation, some confused thinking. That instinctual feeling of self-centeredness is the primal ignorance, and it cannot be dislodged, in fact, by simply not thinking. If it could be, animals that do not have language and cannot have discursive thought in the same sense would be all unself-centered. They would be enlightened. But they are not. They kill one another. We can see that. They are self-centered.

That's why wisdom includes the wisdom of learning, the wisdom of critical reflection, and the wisdom of meditation, in that order. What is it that you learn? The learning in the learning of wisdom is the correcting of the instinctual distortion of our experience of life. We learn that the feeling we have of self-centeredness is based upon a sense of solidity in the core of ourselves, which is a kind of investment or habitual creation at a subliminal level, a feeling that there's an absolute in there, that I am, and that's me, and I'm it, and I'm that one. We learn how that takes place. We observe how we feel that way. Then, we investigate and analyze how that feeling relates to our concepts of relative and absolute, and self and other, and many things. And then we can come to the clear knowledge that such a solid self-feeling is a distortion.

The simplest way of describing such knowledge, perhaps, is what Buddhists call the "royal reason of relativity." This means that anything you can experience or relate to is relative and not absolute because you can relate to it. The royal reason of relativity is a negation, technically; all things we can encounter are empty of absolute essence, because they are purely relative. When we encounter a chair, table, body, or person, we perceive it, we touch it, we investigate it, we encounter it, we relate to it. It is relative. All things are empty of intrinsic reality, or an absolute in-itself-ness, because they are merely relative. That's the royal reason of relativity.

Absolute and relative are opposite. Once you can encounter something, you are relating to it, and that means it's relative. Absolute means it cannot have limit or boundary, it cannot have parts or pieces, it cannot come into existence or be created, and it cannot be destroyed, therefore. It is infinite, uncompounded. It can be described only negationally, as lacking all the properties that relative things have.

So when we understand that reason of relativity, we can get a clear understanding, which is called an "inference." Here is the classic example of an inference in Buddhist logic: There is fire on the mountain (though I do not see it behind the trees), because I do see smoke rising on the mountain, and I know that wherever there is smoke, there is fire, as in the fireplace.

Now we know something that we don't see or directly experience with sight, because it's obscured by the trees. We come to know that it's there, and we walk over to that campsite, to that fire, because we see a sign of it in the smoke. That's valid inference, we infer the fact from the sign. So I can infer that things are empty of absolute essence, although I can't directly see that, and I feel even that they have absolute essence. I feel it about myself, I feel it about things. But I know that they're empty of that absolute essence because they are merely relational—because I relate to those things, I can see them. Even if they seem to me to be absolute as I see them, I realize that my sense of their absoluteness is an irrational prejudice, a distortion.

Because all relative things are not absolute, by definition, any relative thing that I see here I can take apart. A watch is not an absolute watch; I can smash its atoms to smithereens. My experiences, I can take them apart and realize there's no absolute essence in them. I look at the watch again as a watch, and it seems like a real watch, like an absolute watch to me. In other words, when you use emptiness or selflessness intellectually, what you understand about yourself is contrary to your instinctual feeling about yourself. It's counterintuitive.

You know that you can take yourself apart. You may have had experiences in meditation of dissolving. Even without meditation, you may naturally have had this experience as a child, or in some state of intoxication, when you just sort of melted into the woodwork, then there was no you, you went down the cosmic drain. Naturally or artificially, throughout all cultures, people have had this experience. Sometimes it's frightening, but from it you can intellectually understand that nothing about you can be absolute, because you can completely dissolve, you can take yourself totally apart.

That is inferential understanding. You still intuitively feel that you're absolute, although you know you're not. Now, you may question, "Well, I don't intuitively feel I'm absolute." We might feel that ourselves. But just go and stamp on a person's toe, run over his foot with your car, harm her in some way, and he or she will go berserk. She'll be ready to kill. Someone comes and destroys my beloved, I'll be ready to kill in her defense. I can kill because of a feeling that my one-ness—I'm the one—has been violated to such a degree that is intense enough to be absolute.

That's beyond relationality. That's why killing is the first negative path of evolutionary action, and saving life is the first positive path of karmic evolution. You may question whether you really do feel so absolute about yourself, and you can simply test yourself by putting yourself into some sort of extreme situation, either imaginatively or in memory. Think of when life is threatened, when the dearly beloved is threatened, when the sacred thing is blasphemed, when the archcrime is committed. Then you are ready to kill.

Our sense of self-absoluteness emerges when we kill. We feel that a certain absolute is worth taking the life of another. That's the experiential measure of absoluteness, let's say. We could also say, of course, there is no absolute killing, killer, or killed, but emotionally or instinctually, when you want to kill is when you know that in you there is an investment, an absoluteness about your life essence. When death appears to us as an absolute, it reveals that we feel we are absolute.

But we can have a correct understanding of selflessness, of emptiness. We live by inference; so don't think that inference has no power. We gain knowledge of many things that are directly or intuitively obscured from us by inferring about them and other experiences.

So now we're in a position, as seekers of enlightenment, seekers of knowledge of the nature of reality, seekers of wisdom, where we have the inference that all things are empty of intrinsic reality, absolute

separateness, and that all things, therefore, are relative and interconnected, and yet we still feel intuitively and instinctively that we are
separate, absolute, and that our essence is disconnected from reality.

Now, how do we bring that inference into sync with our instinct?
Or, how do we bring our instinct around to that corrected critical
knowledge? This is the role of *vipassana* meditation. There are two
types of meditation in all the Buddhist traditions, and they're called
shamatha and *vipassana*. *Shamatha* is a one-pointed, concentration type of
meditation. It is the kind of meditation you do to have the valuable
experience of divorcing yourself from your thought flow, disidenti-
fying from your individual thinking pattern. You don't identify with
the "I" that thinks a thought, you let it just fly away. You broaden
your sense of identity, your sense of being, you become the radio
rather than the particular channel on the radio. And then, eventually,
you calm down, you come into the quiet that I mentioned earlier, that
people find so powerful and rewarding when they first discover it.
Shamatha is peaceful, soothing, calming. It enables you to develop the
ability to think something in which you put your whole effort, without all these other chattering thought flows.

Because by doing it you become able to maintain a state of non-
thinking in a concentrated way, *shamatha* meditation is extremely
valuable. But by itself, *shamatha* meditation does not dislodge that instinctive sense of self-centeredness, that instinctive sense of absolute selfness. In fact, unfortunately, it can reinforce it, because in
shamatha you disidentify from all the thoughts and all the thinking,
and come into a state of silence and mental stability, but then your
mind simply stands still, and you feel, I am the one now with my
mind standing still.

You may feel even more solid. Shockingly, we have discovered in
the West what many Buddhist societies already knew, that many
people who had long years of meditating could emerge even more

selfish than when they went in. They would even demand to be worshiped as gurus and behave unreasonably and, in fact, even have special powers because of that higher power of the mind developed from their practice of concentration. They can cause a tremendous amount of trouble rather than act as enlightened, loving, helpful, benevolent people.

Gaining higher mental power by achieving mastery of meditations by itself does not dislodge selfishness and therefore does not produce enlightenment. The type of meditation that produces enlightenment is *vipassana*. *Vipassana* insight meditation is the same as what Zen calls the great doubt, the koan-puzzle type of meditation. It is the critical investigation of something in which you break through your habitual awareness of it and see through your superficial, habitual ways of seeing. You start from mindfulness of the body, mindfulness of sensations, of the mind, and of mental phenomena, to come to a deeper, more open sense of pure presence. *Vipassana* insight dislodges the sense of self-centeredness, so that we get to a situation where we feel less self-solid, and we confirm our valid inference that we are not self-solid, and that our habitual feeling is in error.

Then we bring our one-pointed power of concentration onto this corrected understanding of the self and place it, like a hot steam iron, on top of the distorted I'm-the-one feeling. We hold them together, with strong concentration. When we do that in a sustained way, we can come to seeing through the self. The seeming rock of self-centeredness, the rock that is the focus of self-preoccupation, crumbles. It dissolves. And, ultimately, our intuitive feeling will become the same as our critical feeling. This is the process of achieving transcendent wisdom.

Now most cultures and most parts of most cultures have philosophies, cosmologies, and worldviews. People all have world pictures and models that support the way they live and the way they feel. Almost all of them reinforce a gut feeling of self-centeredness. Of course, they control that feeling because they don't want everyone at each other's throats at all times, so they say, "Well, yeah, you're self-centered, but that's because you're a member of this chosen nation." Or, "Your god, who is the real self-centeredness of all time, supports you in being that way." Or you are taught to be polite to other people because you realize that they feel they are the one, even though you know they are wrong. You share your being-the-one-ness with your own children, because they're part of your clan. That's what most cultures and psychologies and philosophies do.

So, you will not likely find the critical correction of instinctive self-centeredness by being with nature or within a culture. You can only find it through science. The Buddha, in his process of discovering, was functioning as a scientist. He was investigating himself, investigating the atoms, investigating the trees and the earth and the air and the water, the fire. He was looking for that absolute essence in everything. Science originally was a branch of philosophy. Philosophy, the love of truth, the love of reality, is like the Dharma philosophy. Philos and Sophia are compassion and wisdom, love and wisdom, the same. Philosophy is, in fact, the science of reality, pursued from the human subjectivity. It doesn't pretend that there is no human subjectivity, which materialist science has done for three or four hundred years, with rather fascinating results.

This is why wisdom has first a level of learning, and then the level of critical reflection and debate and inquiry and investigation. This is why the Buddhist traditions value words and speech and reasoning—all of them can help us drill through the rock of self-centeredness. Critical wisdom demands that we look at sexism, look at racial prejudice, look at religious prejudice. People get a strong gut feeling that another person is inferior, or evil, because of his religious belief, or because of her racial characteristics, or because of his or her sex. They can reason, they can read every book about biology or philosophy, and realize that we're all really the same human beings, but that gut feeling is still there. Whenever they sit down next to a prejudicial person on the bus or subway, they want to crawl away. In situations of great stress, this will become lethal. Jews in Germany were massacred, blacks in America and in the Sudan get murdered. This deep gut feeling of race prejudice can still seem absolute. And it is not easily overcome. But we also know, having tried, that we *can* overcome this feeling, we can uproot it, we can continually review what's wrong with that gut feeling that we inherited or became acculturated to. We continually review the evidence against it, we meditate on it, and eventually we will experience the other in an open way.

But if you were to take a racist, a white supremacist, and say, "Sit down, don't think for a month," and then expect him to get up and be a Rainbow Coalition member, you'd be naïve. He would have to carefully think about the error of being a white supremacist, then sit on it with deep concentration for quite a while, before he could get up and join the Rainbow Coalition; which we hope he and they all will. Many wonderful texts have been written on the psychology of transforming self-centeredness into freedom, into love and compassion and wisdom. Tremendous knowledge is available. The door is wide open to a feast of delight and a treasury of knowledge. We can all study and learn.

There's a tendency in our current climate to talk about practice as if it is only sitting and meditating. But when you read a sutra or treatise on the path to enlightenment—from the Nyingmapa Order, or the Gelukpa Order, or the Sakyapa Order; or from Chinese Buddhism, or Japanese Buddhism, or Indian Buddhism, or Burmese, Thai, or Vietnamese Buddhism; or Taoism or Hinduism; or Western mysticism (Judaic, Christian, Muslim); or secular humanist developmental psychology, transformative psychology, transpersonal

psychology—all contribute to the practice of the path of enlightenment. That study and that learning, making notes and memoriz-
ing a little pattern, learning a little scheme so that when you
meditate you can bring this scheme to bear on your focused reflection, *that* is practice.

So you are an ethical person, and you walk around the street, and
a beggar asks you for a coin, and you feel revulsion—and you don't
want to support a crack habit, or you don't want to give that coin, or
you feel a paranoia that if you give this one a coin, you have to give
thousands of them a coin and you'll be destitute yourself, or you feel
annoyed that the mayor doesn't take care of them, or that the president doesn't take care of them, or that there's been the wrong kind
of welfare reform—and you're just clutching your hot little quarter
in your pocket, and then you suddenly remember the Dharma, and
you think, "What a wonderful opportunity, I can overcome this
clutching, sweaty palm with a quarter, and I can reach this hand out,
I can open the hand, I can place respectfully this quarter in this little
cup, and say, 'You're welcome.'" The joy of giving that quarter is
practice.

Giving is not only practice, it's performance. That's the Dharma
in performance, that's achievement. And when you read and study
the teachings of whatever enlightening, liberating teacher, and you
make notes and you remember them, and you become critical about
some prejudiced idea you find that you had about something, that is
practice, and that is performance. Then, when you enrich your meditation on the two sides, by the wisdom on the one side and the
ethics on the other side, then you're walking the path of enlightenment, then you are living in the spirit of enlightenment.

Now let's open the visualization of the wish-granting gem tree field.
Let's meditate together for a few moments. Get in a good posture,

calm down. Slow the breath. Feel yourself melt a little. Remember that you exist only insofar as you don't look for yourself to be existing. When you look for yourself, you seem to dissolve into thin air. So, take a good look for yourself introspectively, and you begin to lose track of who and what you are. You feel lighter, and you feel looser, and you float into empty space and dissolve. The world around you dissolves as well, and you're no longer sure where you are—what country, what planet, what continent, what era. Focus on the ultimate nature of reality, where nothing exists as a thing-in-itself, nothing exists as pin-down-able by any concept. Everything exists in the inconceivable matrix of relativity.

Rest and keep this awareness, as if you were in empty space, as if you *were* the empty space. From the empty space, we arise together on the top of the world overlooking Lake Manasarovar, on a grassy bluff surrounded by all beings. Above us shines the gem tree, the wish-granting refuge tree. On the tree are all our mentors—Buddha, Socrates, Mary, the goddesses, the gods, Krishna, Jesus, Muhammad, and the many sages of world spirituality. Our human teachers, mentors, people we admire, even people we've never met are conversing casually with each other, sitting on the different lotuses of the tree, shining. Their lights flow down to us. We feel buoyed up, bathed, anointed, exalted, relieved, soothed by the flowing jewel energy.

The energy drives away all of our self-doubts, all our anxieties, all our frustrations, irritations. They flow out of us like darkness. The light reflects back from us to the beings around us—friends, strangers, enemies. They start to glow with gratitude, inspiration, challenging alertness.

We're in our meditative shrine space. We make boundless offerings radiating from our hearts' wish to see the world perfected and see the world beautiful. We visualize beautiful forms, flowers, sculptures, jewels, gems, beautiful objects streaming forth from our hearts, presenting themselves to the mentor beings.

Exquisite music emerges from the offering array, clouds of incense, delicious foods, fruits. We salute the refuge field host. "Buddha, wonderful to see you there. We take refuge in your presence, in all the deities' presence." We think of whatever negative things our bodies have done and regret having done them, and resolve never to do them again. We resolve to do the opposite, good things. We rejoice in all the accomplishments and virtues of all other people and in our own. We're delighted when people advance, happy when they succeed.

We request, "O you beings. Stay with us in the world. Thank goodness you haven't gone away. We implore you not to abandon us for the quiescence of ultimate transcendence in any sort of aloof Nirvana. We request from you the rain of teachings, the rain of Dharma. We dedicate whatever virtue we accomplish here to the freedom and happiness of all beings, and we aim to become buddhas ourselves to secure their freedom and happiness."

We reflect on the planet. We imagine that it's a little shining ball in front of us in space. We pick it up in our hands gently, holding it up as an offering, and offer it to enlightened beings. We unenlightened ones can't take care of it anyway. We decide to give them the whole world.

Now that we're established in the jewel tree's field, we run through the familiar steps of thought we use to develop the transcendent attitude. As you read and review this meditation, you can do it as slowly or as fast as you like. We reflect on the first thought—on the preciousness of our human life endowed with liberty and opportunity. We appreciate the amazing embodiment we have. We're happy we're using it at this very moment, focusing it on our higher purpose of achieving freedom and enlightenment. We reflect on the immediacy of death and the soul force that is all we have through the death transition. We take the third step, the inexorability of evolutionary cause and effect and the infinite importance of every tiniest improvement; we see that each moment is infinitely pregnant with potential. And with the fourth step we accept the inadequacy and inherent painfulness of all egocentric states of existence. We think through these steps and feel the release of mind of the transcendent attitude.

We run through the eleven steps to the spirit of enlightenment, of love and compassion for all sensitive beings. We reflect, step by step, on the impartial equanimity we feel for all living beings. We recognize that they served as our mothers many times in previous lives. We remember their kindness and are grateful to them, and we vow that we will repay that kindness by loving them unconditionally. We exchange self-concern for other-concern, giving up self-preoccupation by seeing its terrible costs and taking up other-preoccupation by seeing its tremendous benefits. We develop universal love for all beings, willing and giving them happiness. We develop universal compassion for all beings, willing and taking from them all their suffering. We resolve to be messianic in taking responsibility for all beings' liberation from suffering. We conceive of the will to enlightenment and produce the spirit of enlightenment. Once we have taken, or have rehearsed taking, the bodhisattva vow and so have activated the spirit of enlightenment, we visualize and practice the transcendent virtues: generosity, justice, patience, creativity, meditation, and wisdom.

And now, remaining within the jewel tree refuge field, we turn to focus especially on the cultivation of transcendent wisdom.

TRANSCENDENT WISDOM,
REALIZING THE EMPTINESS OF REALITY

The *Mentor Devotion* says,

Bless me to perfect the wisdom transcendence,
Through the yoga of ultimate-reality-spacelike equipoise,
Connected with the fierce bliss of the special fluency
Derived from the wisdom that discerns reality!

Bless me to complete the magical aftermath samadhi,
Understanding the process of truthless appearance
Of outer and inner things, such as illusions, dreams,
Or the reflections of the moon in water!

Bless me to understand Nagarjuna's intended meaning,
In which life and liberation have no jot of intrinsic reality,
Yet cause and effect and relativity are still inexorable,
And these two laws don't contradict, but mutually complement one another!

We come to the actual root of freedom itself by achieving the mind of transcendence, and then developing the mind of universal compassion and realizing that our ultimate freedom depends upon creating freedom for all beings. As I mentioned before, the Buddha realized that the key to complete liberation cannot be compassion alone, although compassion is a powerful cause of the quest for wisdom. But we can't actually free beings from suffering simply by willing their freedom. We must fully understand the cause of suffering in order to know how to prevent it. And then we have to help beings understand that cause for themselves. Compassion itself, to become universal, powerful, and effective, must also be based on an understanding of the nature of reality. Wishing for one's own and all beings' liberation is very crucial and powerful, but it will not by itself accomplish that liberation. Giving up all mundane preoccupations is essential, to give ourselves the space and time to focus on the nature of reality, but finally, we have to come to an understanding of profound reality.

This liberating understanding is called "transcendent wisdom" because it is a profound awareness, a thorough and total knowledge, not merely a resignation or existential acceptance of some "way things are." It's a real knowing of the true nature and structure of everything. It is a knowing of everything by *becoming* everything. It's symbolized by the sword of wisdom with flames at the tip, the flames being like a lamp, a laserlike light that pierces the darkness of delusion. So wisdom is the actual tool that accomplishes our liberation. It is the actual vehicle of our liberation.

The wonderful thing about Buddha's teaching is that it is not just a religious teaching about something in which we have to believe. It is a scientific teaching that says the nature of the world is such that, if we understand it, we will be free from suffering. But we can be free only by understanding it. We won't be free by just believing that somebody else understands it. We have to come to the understanding of it ourselves.

There are three types of wisdom by which we come to know reality. The first is the wisdom born of learning. The second is the wisdom born of critical reflection. The third is the wisdom born of meditative insight.

Sometimes people think that they need to begin meditating right away to get going on the path of enlightenment. And it is good to meditate right away, because if we don't meditate on something positive, and instead keep going about in the world and involuntarily thinking along in our minds, we're unconsciously meditating on our negative habits of self-preoccupation. So, you don't have a choice to meditate or not meditate. A human being is always meditating. As you read this, you are meditating. When you walk down the street thinking something such as, "Where am I? What should I do?" that, too, is a meditation. The problem is that the mind has its own habit energy of self-preoccupation. And our culture has a very powerful habit energy that it imposes on us—repeating and repeating its theory of reality, its cosmology and story of what we are and where we are—in a constant stream of reinforcement of our habitual world picture.

So, to meditate specifically on the nature of reality, to make our meditation effective and yield insight, we first have to learn something. We have to use our heads. First, we have to do the learning meditation to learn what our false beliefs are. Second, we have to do the meditation that involves critical reflection, which often involves discussion and debate with others. In the Tibetan tradition and the ancient Indian tradition, debate was a crucial link between learning and meditation. Once you learned something new, you had to debate with others, you had to argue and reason and see the fallacy of your prejudices. Then you could develop a strong critical awareness, and your meditation would be effective.

When you're meditating on your own, if you don't bring up and analyze what you think, then you'll never get through false beliefs and come to true knowledge.

We've already encountered the proposal that the nature of the universe is selfless, empty, free from any intrinsic reality. To investigate this possibility, we need to examine the two levels of the selfless universe: its subjective selflessness and its objective selflessness.

Subjective selflessness means that you are not a fixed, independent, absolute thing in yourself. But I will start with the concept of objective selflessness because it connects nicely with modern science's view of the universe, though traditionally, when you meditate, you don't begin with the selflessness of objects. Objective self-lessness sounds funny at first; talking about the self of an object is odd, since we think self is a personal thing. But actually we use the expression *self* with objects, if you think about it. We say "the table itself," "the sun, the moon itself." *Self* is like a reflexive pronoun that goes back to the thing we've mentioned and seems to hit as if it were the essence of the thing.

For example, when we say "the table itself," we're thinking of a table as having some sort of essential "thingness" about it that gives us its tableness. We don't think, "Oh, we're creating the table by thinking of it as a table." Our perception, even without thinking anything, includes having the table loom up at us as if it were a thing-in-itself. Now, let's do a thought experiment with the table—it's easier to start with the table than with our own self—and look to see, what is the table? I put my finger on it. I could take a little saw and cut off that piece of wood I just put my finger on, but the table would still be there, although without the part I just hacked off. It would be a table with a little hole in it. If I took one leg off, and it had only three legs, and I propped it up on a stack of cinder blocks, it would still be the table. So that leg wasn't the table. None of the legs is in fact the table. In fact, none of the parts of the table is the table. We could disassemble all the parts and put them in a box and mail it to our friend, and say, "Here's the table," but it would be in pieces and not really the table as we think of a table. If you did a subatomic analysis of the atoms in the wood of the table, you would see other aspects of the table, which aren't the table either, in and of themselves. Basically, the table dissolves under analysis. In fact, any-thing in the universe dissolves under analysis.

Modern investigative science has come up with a conclusion sim-ilar to the Buddha's insight of thousands of years ago that every-thing dissolves under analysis. There is no indivisible particle. We are living in a universe that is gossamer. It is essentially illusory.

Seemingly solid objects are made of atoms, cells are completely diaphanous, mostly empty space. Even the nuclei and smaller energy particles themselves dissolve at quantum level into inscrutable "charms," "quarks," "mesons," and "bosons."

As we experience things dissolving under analysis, we mustn't take their disappearance itself as the absolute. Any seeming absolute itself dissolves under analysis. The absolute is also the absolute's emptiness of itself. And that emptiness does not impede—in fact, it enables—the infinite relativity of all things, the surface reality where we all live.

Take, for instance, a mirror's surface. It contains no images itself, but it reflects all of the objects in front of it. Similarly, all of the universe is reflected on the surface of emptiness. The reflections are nothing but the surface; they're not something extra on the surface. It won't reflect anything if it's held toward empty sky. It will seem empty. If it's held toward differentiated objects, it will reflect differentiated objects. Objective selflessness, or objective emptiness, is like a mirror—empty in itself yet still reflecting the images that surround us.

We live in a world that is illusory. It isn't just an illusion, that is to say, utterly unreal. It's *like* an illusion; it's somewhat unreal. It is not absolutely unreal, only somewhat unreal. It is also somewhat real, with relative processes and relative things. Each thing in the world habitually seems absolute to us as a thing-in-itself, but when we investigate, we discover that it is not absolute.

We might assume that there would be some sort of nonapparent absolute, or an absolute that would appear to us if we had the wisdom of emptiness. Some people will even say, "Oh yeah, I achieved the direct experience of emptiness," as if emptiness were a big giant space that they saw. But whoever saw space? No one can see space. When you say, "I see space," it means "I didn't see anything. I didn't see anything seeming to fill a space." You never see the space. Space is a negation, defined as the "absence of impenetrability."

Similarly, *emptiness* or *absolute*—*absolute* meaning "away from solution," away from relationship—is a negation. Negations are different from objects. Negations are inferred when you don't see what they are negating. You look for the elephant and you don't see an elephant, and you negate that the elephant is there. You don't ever see a nonelephant. Emptiness is known by a different type of awareness. The absolute is known only through that negative awareness of failing to see any other thing that is absolute in itself.

Therefore, when you look for the nature of things, and you analyze them and they dissolve under analysis, your nonfinding of those things is your discovery of emptiness. Your nonfinding is your discovery of ultimate reality, your direct experience of ultimate reality. Yet if you then were to turn around mentally, in some deep state of concentration, and to look for the emptiness itself, you wouldn't find it. You conceive of it as if it were something different in kind from what you had presumed it to be, but you still can't find it. That realization is called the "emptiness of emptiness," or the "emptiness of the absolute."

Yet emptiness is not nothingness. The emptiness of the table does not mean that the table is nothing. The emptiness of the table means that the table is empty of a fixed essence that makes it a table. It becomes a table only when we use it like a table, interactively, relationally, in various ways—in relation to its causes, in relation to its parts, in relation to our use of it and our designations for it. In other words, it is a table in relation to our minds. It does have a relative existence; it is not nothing. But it is empty of being absolutely a table as it seems to be when we originally encounter it. When we originally encounter the table, it seems like a thing-in-itself to us.

Throughout history, so many philosophers, Western and East-

ern, have come up with ideas about the table. But the thought experiment we just went through should give you some sense of how the
table is empty and how that emptiness confirms its relativity rather
than annihilating it. This is very important to understand from the
beginning. Understanding emptiness in this way gives us an initial
feeling about the nature of the world as the Buddha understood it
and as the great Buddhist philosophers and scientists explained it.

SELFLESSNESS AND THE FOUR KEYS

Now we come to the theme on which traditionally we would first
meditate to develop wisdom—the theme of personal selflessness
and personal self. Here I take my hat off to the Tibetans in particular for making this process more accessible. When Buddha pro-
claimed ultimate selflessness, he always taught a relative self. That is,
when someone asks, "Who is it who understands my selflessness?"
Buddha says, "It is you yourself." What does he mean by that? He
means your relative self. If there is no self, who is it who is reborn?
The answer is, "Your relative self is reborn, since it is not ultimate."

   If there is no self, who is it who becomes a buddha? Your relative
self becomes the buddha. Anything that exists in the world exists relationally. Even the absolute we can conceive of is simply our notion
of the opposite of the relational. If you say *absolute* means "uncreated, unrelated, unconnected, undestroyed, the opposite of all relative things," it cannot possibly be in any kind of contact with relative
things and retain its absoluteness. And therefore if it ever existed as
a thing-in-itself, it would be irrelevant to anything relative. A self-
subsistent, absolute God, for example, could not relate to relative
beings, and so would be irrelevant to them.

   However, your understanding of this fact is not irrelevant. Understanding this fact is liberation. Our mental habit is to absolutize
every relative thing. We live in a world of "book," "table," and espe-

cially "self," which we think is really real. To me, my inner self is absolutely, indubitably there. And so is this book and the floor. And so is the world. When I am free from thinking this way, then I am free to be a relative self, content with impermanence and change. A relative self realizes that it is not isolated from other things, and that its sense of difference and sense of individuation are only arbitrary and temporary.

The Tibetans were great about unpacking the relative self, which they call the "conventional self." Even Buddha has a relative self. Even an ignorant person has a relative self. The teaching of selflessness frees that relative self from false suppositions of absoluteness and so changes suffering to happiness.

In the ancient Indian texts, the Buddha often stressed selflessness, meaning absolute selflessness. He also often referred to the self in many other contexts, and he mentioned the need for self-control and self-reliance. But he rarely explained that such words referred to a conventional, verbally constructed, relative self. This was probably because the absolutist tendency was so strong in his time that he felt that elaborating on the self would seem to be condoning a concentration on the self. More than two thousand years later, Tsong Khapa, who attained enlightenment in 1398 and taught extensively for the next twenty-one years, faced a different cultural problem. His contemporaries had taken voidness and selflessness too far, and they tended to verge on nihilism. So Tsong Khapa drew together a reinvigorated interpretation of his predecessors' teachings and beautifully articulated the nature and function of the relative and conventional self. This is the wise view of reality and the self that we study to this day.

Now, how do we mediate on personal or subjective selflessness? How do we mediate on wisdom as it relates to our own personal self? This is the next step on the path. But before we begin, I want to warn you that, when you start to meditate on selflessness, you must be prepared to avoid the common trap of believing that you are nothing, and that everything is nothing. That's not liberation, and that is absolutely wrong. The fear of nothingness is wrong, and the delight in it, the escapist mentality, is also wrong. Both the simple grasp of language and the Buddha's greatest insights prove that there is no nothing. Therefore, you cannot become nothing, and you never have been nothing. "Nothing" clearly means there is no nothing.

Thus, when you meditate you need not fear becoming nothing. Because you have been living so long with your relative self, when you see through the absoluteness of that self, it seems as if you saw through the relative self, and you can have moments of feeling as if you have disappeared. You could have such a moment, so prepare for it. Because the real relative self and the unreal absolute self have been so fused in your habitual psychological perception and your self-experience for so long, when you see through the harmful illusion of the unreal self, it kind of takes away the helpful real one, just for a second.

You control that tendency by recognizing that you could not be experiencing nothing, because it isn't anything that can be experienced. What you are experiencing is your own notion of nothing; but since it is nothing, you will come right through its experience and you will then be free from the false edge of absoluteness of your existence, and you will be closer to wisdom.

Now we come to the actual meditation on selflessness, which has four steps of thought, known as the four keys for the attainment of personal selflessness. The first is called the key of the identification of what is to be negated. That which you need to negate is, of course, the self you presume is there, to which your ego adheres. The suffix -*lessness* means "lacking, the absence of." So selflessness is a negative expression meaning that such a self is lacking. But what kind of self is there *not?* You have to know what the self would be if it were there. How can we identify our absolutized self—the self that we habitually consider to be the real self?

Try this: Remember a time when you were falsely accused. It doesn't have to be about something big. It could be a parking infraction, or the accusation that you drank up the last of the milk in the icebox. Whatever it is, you can easily think of a time when you felt righteously indignant about having been falsely accused. At that moment, when you feel that righteous indignation, especially when you *are* in the right and your accuser has made a mistake, though he still accuses you with vehemence, you feel a strong feeling of "I am innocent. I am right."

When the "I" comes out, it has a slightly strangled or choked feeling to it, because what it refers to seems to be so solid. "I know it's I, I know I'm I, and I didn't do it." I can safely be righteous about my "I" because I'm right, and I didn't do it. So I say "I" and I feel really solid inside. Also, when you feel furious anger, when you've been harmed, your "self" feels absolutely outraged. But you see, that's not a good time to remember, because you can't witness yourself at that time, you're too blown away.

If you are merely feeling righteous indignation, however, you can still have some presence of mind. To meditate on personal selflessness properly, you have to be subtle, observing yourself being righteous as if from a corner of your mind. Only by developing a subtle splitting of awareness and by watching yourself demurely, secretly from a hiding place in the corner of your awareness, so to speak, will your own self-habit emerge in full glory, in all its splendor. And it is absolutely crucial that it do so.

I believe it was the Eleventh Dalai Lama who wrote that we should spend six months doing just this meditation on the self, sneakily observing the self. Without it, we should not proceed any further in the meditation on selflessness of transcendent wisdom;

because without being clear about what the "real self" feels like, we'll get no realization. The Buddha doesn't say, dogmatically, "All things are selfless, and I expect you to believe that." It would do us no good to believe in selflessness. If we did, we would inevitably misunderstand it as some sort of real nothingness, and we would think we are nothing.

I know people who think of themselves as Buddhists who misapprehend selflessness as meaning they are nonexistent. And therefore they are meditating as hard as they can, hard as rocks, expecting themselves to disappear, at least experientially. The most unfortunate ones have actually had an experience of disappearing, and they become attached to that, and they feel that was their enlightenment peak experience. Those beings are cut off from their compassion; they're cut off from the life of liberation, and they're stuck in the anteroom of liberation—the momentary experience of nothingness. They are stuck thinking of nothingness as an absolute, solid, concrete, ultimate reality in itself.

So, for that reason, the Buddha doesn't say, "You must believe in selflessness." The Buddha says, "I recognize that you don't believe in selflessness. And *you* must recognize that. You must recognize it when you really observe your solid self-habit, arising out of your solar plexus, in your throat, in your chest and heart. You must recognize your 'you,' the real 'I' for you, your real 'me,' your life-and-death, ready-to-struggle you. Only then you can see that you do not feel selfless." Buddha is not asking for belief. Buddha is challenging you. He is saying, "Granted, you feel you're really you. And I'm glad you now can feel how strongly you feel that feeling, and how much that feeling powerfully dominates your experience of everything. So you can begin to identify the thing to be negated, the sense of absolute self, the independent, self-sufficient referent of 'I,' the referent of the Greek pronoun *ego*, the Indian *aham*."

So then Buddha says, "Okay, I know you feel that way. I felt that way, too, I can remember. I was unquestioning about it. I was going to find my enlightenment with my real self. But now I challenge you, because you now have noted that this is in the core of your habitual existence, this solid sense of self. Therefore, if it is really there, as you habitually feel it to be there, then if you look for it with all your effort, as if it were the most important thing in your life to find it, then you should be able to find it. So I challenge you to verify it. When you act, when you are filled with a powerful emotion, the self seems even more absolute than your body. So now you must find that self."

So this first key to selflessness is identifying the seeming "I."

One of Nagarjuna's greatest disciples was a thief called Matangipa. He was caught by Nagarjuna lurking outside of Nagarjuna's house, waiting to steal the master's famous alchemical golden bowl. Nagarjuna suddenly threw it out the window toward Matangipa, who pounced on it in delight and began to run away with it. But the thought arose that the master would not have thrown out the bowl if he had not been clairvoyant and if he had not had things even more valuable inside. Besides, what sort of self-respecting thief takes what the victim freely gives him—no challenge in that. So Matangipa sheepishly went back to the house and threw himself at the feet of Nagarjuna. The master adept then sat him down in a small hut, ordering him to contemplate a pile of jewels placed in front of him. After some weeks, horns began to grow on Matangipa's head, and soon they grew up into the rafters and the thatch roofing. The reformed thief couldn't move at all and was uncomfortable and crying in pain. Nagarjuna came to visit him and noted his predicament. He explained to him that the horns were his sense of intrinsically real subject and object and that they would disappear and he would experience freedom to do what he wanted if he contemplated them critically and realized their illusoriness. Matangipa complied with this instruction and quickly attained freedom. The horns were a symbolic experience of the substantial sense of presence of the intrinsically real *ego* underlying the habitual sense of self. Matangipa certainly identified it very graphically.

AN ANATOMY OF MEDITATION

The second key to meditating is to admit that if you can't find the self, then you will cope with the fact that it is not there. You will not allow any third option. You will not say, "Well, it's sort of there and not there. It's sort of here and not here." You will not keep yourself in limbo on the question by thinking you couldn't find it but maybe it's still there. In this deepest vital quest, you will commit to a practical outcome.

The third key to this meditation is investigating our body-mind processes to discover whether the self is the same as they are or different from them. We look to see whether the self is the same as the aggregate of body and mind. The Buddhists found, over centuries of meditating, that it was most helpful to use a diagnostic scheme of five levels of body-mind systems: the physical systems, the sensational systems, the ideational systems, the emotional systems, and the consciousness systems.

Next we begin an introspective inventory of our five systems to see whether we can uncover a unitary, solid, substantial, absolute self there. We look through the physical systems, which are all of the sense organs—eye, ear, nose, tongue, and skin—and their sense-object forms—sounds, smells, tastes, and textures. And we go through all the bodily systems—organs, spine, nervous system, brain. Pretty easily, because of modern medicine and our understanding of the physical body, we dissect every single thing and find no self. This has a powerful liberating effect when we realize how much we do identify our habitual identity with our body. I think of myself as a man because I have a male anatomy. But my self is not my anatomy at all, however much I pound my chest to refer to my-self.

Second we go to the sensational systems, which are the beginning level of mind, the neural impulses of pleasure, pain, and numbness, and we zoom around through the nervous system, and we don't find any stable, unitive thing, like a sensational self.

Then we go to the ideational systems, and they're more compli-cated. Even the conception we have of ourselves as having a body, even the map we have of our nervous system, these are all ideas. So we're sort of looking into an idea of our ideas. We find a cloud of imagery and verbal discourse. We see pretty quickly how unstable it is, and how multifaceted. No single image or concept can be un-changing, absolute, or fixed in itself.

Next we examine the emotions, those times when we feel so ab-solutely concrete and solid in ourselves. In times of fury, in times of righteous indignation, in times of fear and terror, in times of great lust or great greed or great depression or alienation, we feel solid. When powerful emotions seem to be emanating from that self, or seem to have that self in their grip, the self feels most solid. So it's logical to think that maybe the self resides in the emotions. But when we look at them, we find them completely transient, mercurial, powerful but ever-changing, a buzzing, blooming confusion.

So then we look into the fifth system, the greatest candidate for the fixed self, consciousness. And then we break consciousness down into five sense consciousnesses and a mental consciousness. None of the sense consciousnesses is unitive, all are changeable. When I'm lis-tening intently, for instance, I don't see something. When I'm look-ing intently, I don't hear something. When I'm tasting intently, I don't see or hear. The mental consciousness jumps around, aligns with this sense and that sense, fluctuating.

The sixth, or mental consciousness, coordinates all of the im-pressions, functions, motor realities, emotions, ideas, and sensations. It seems to be trying to bring all of these things into a unitive experience, but it's always changing, too. It's constantly dealing with new inputs from here and there, with new inner surges of emotion. There's nothing stable, fixed, or absolute about consciousness that we can discern.

As we meditate on the self further, we move from the senses and consciousnesses to examine the formless, abstract mental states. There (as we can imagine) we seem to be pure being, pure infinite space, infinite consciousness, absolute nothingness, beyond conscious and unconsciousness. But even there, we recognize that we go in and out of those states. Even though these states seem vast and absolute when we are in them, there's a time before we were in them. When we were in the sensory world, we withdrew from them. So even they do not appear to be absolute, things in themselves, when we really investigate them. They're all changing, affected in altered meditative states or in constantly changing sensory states.

In the last-ditch effort of trying to get to the deepest core in consciousness, we come into a situation in which we seem to be like whirling dervishes. We feel that the reason we're not finding this unaffected observer, my unchanging self, is that it's our self that's looking. I keep turning back on my looking, looking for myself, like a dog chasing its tail. We feel as if we are whirling on ourselves, trying to catch ourselves. We whirl and turn on the subjectivity, and as we do this we become what is called the diamond cutting drill. We don't allow ourselves any veering off into some inchoate zone of nothingness or boundlessness. With that deep inner turning of the diamond drill of wisdom, it is said that the whole knot of the self begins to erode.

Sometimes this process is described as being like using a fire stick, which is wound in the string of a bow that you pull back and forth to make the stick spin on another piece of wood with a little bunch of kindling around, to kindle fire without flint. The spinning of a

fire stick—critical insight—ignites the wood—that feeling of absoluteness—and burns it away. We feel it as if we were dissolving in
empty space, into pure, clear voidness. This is called the direct experience of emptiness or selflessness. It is like water being poured in
water, and we feel beyond vast. We don't feel like a subject looking
out into an empty space. I, the subject, become a vast empty space at
the same time as the realm is a vast empty space, yet I am still looking for the self here. I don't start looking and enjoying that, because
I'm still looking for the self. But then looker and looked-for both
dissolve and there is an ecstatic experience of release.

Recall the *Mentor Devotion* verse here:

Bless me to perfect the wisdom transcendence,
Through the yoga of ultimate-reality-spacelike equipoise,
Connected with the fierce bliss of the special fluency
Derived from the wisdom that discerns reality!

Even though I don't find the self, neither am I finding my failure
to find it. And this sustained nonfinding erodes me further, launches
me into vast spaciousness, the threshold of which feels a little like
death. Going into this melting can be frightening. It has nothingness
states and boundlessness states very close to it, and if I'm not careful, I might veer off into and hide in them. But if I keep focusing on
the quest of the self, I will not veer off into them. When I stay focused, the quest, the quester, everything dissolves, and there is a feeling of vast space, although it's not like I have a feeling of vast space.
And therefore it is a huge relief, a freedom that is timeless, bound-
aryless, dualityless. At some point, the momentum of my intellect,
my wisdom, empowered by concentration, evaluates being in vast
space. It doesn't all of a sudden think about it clumsily, because in
the experience there are no words, no mouth, no language, no hu-
manity, no life, no death, yet there is still a subtle probing. I stop and

have a sense of this space, which immediately disappears. The moment is like looking through a pane of glass in winter when your breath has frosted the glass: Your attention is on the frost, on the surface, but then perhaps you turn your nose down and the frost slowly dissolves. And you find that your vision sees through the glass and you see everything on the other side, out the window, the world with the trees and the forest and the snow. And so the differentiated world, the world of relativity reemerges in this realm. But it reemerges in a way that is not divisible from the vastness of the space, because the space is not a thing that could impede the relative world.

You enter into what is called the mirrorlike, or dreamlike, or illusionlike aftermath. You are immediately attracted to the living beings among all the differentiated things in the world. Inside and outside are perceived as equal; self and other are perceived as equal in this illusionlike aftermath; you are free at the same time as you are engaging with the world. You're not stressed out or trying to collapse everything into the absolute, but instead you are aware of both the surface of the mirror, the transparency of the void, and the infinite colorfulness and the shape and the beauty of differentiated relativity—you're aware of everything simultaneously. In this way, nonduality embraces relativity.

Again, we return to the *Mentor Devotion* verse:

> *Bless me to complete the magical aftermath samadhi,*
> *Understanding the processes of truthless appearance*
> *Of outer and inner things, such as illusions, dreams,*
> *Or the reflections of the moon in water!*

Going through the anatomy of these meditations is a rehearsal for the realization of freedom: Know what kind of self you're looking for. Be aware that either you find it or you don't, and never give up looking and never finding. You will be catapulted into a vast, spacelike experience of the dissolution of subject and object in the void, and then you will see the void itself dissolve. This is an initial taste of the wisdom of selflessness.

After you have developed the freedom from true sameness of self and body-mind processes, you deploy the fourth key—the freedom from true difference between self and body-mind processes. Here you think that since you did not find a self within the body-mind processes, the self might be different from them, either their foundation, their content, their owner. You remember that something absolute cannot be distinguished from something relative. Therefore, the supposed absolute consciousness that is the supposed self cannot exist meaningfully as your self in any sort of relevant connection with the relative processes of your body-mind. When you combine the critical gaze with one-pointed concentrated contemplation, you enter again into the spacelike balanced *samadhi* and then to the dreamlike aftermath *samadhi*. You oscillate between them again; you unify the two states gradually again.

You have to do it again and again and again. Now that you've begun the meditation and cultivation of transcendent wisdom, you are drilling down to the level of beginningless instincts that are ingrained in your being, gut feelings that you are real, that you really exist. These are such powerful gut feelings. Meditation again and again pounds and pulverizes this upwelling. It transforms even the most basic instincts. The deeper you go, the less absolute you feel, and the more broadly and vastly connected you feel. And even when you're meditating formally, your compassion is developing. Relativity and absolutity mutually reinforce; they become not contradictory but complementary. And you become happier and happier, lighter and lighter, and more and more open.

This is actually the ultimate transcendent insight *(vipassana)* practice, built up out of the foundational mindfulness of the body, the sensations, the mind, and ideas. Wisdom, from basic mindfulness to transcendent wisdom, sees through the apparent intrinsic reality of every little sensation, of every little thought, of every little identity manifestation. This is the real meditative path to the discovery of liberation, awakening from being just a mechanistic, machinelike being. And the consummation of transcendent insight is when it goes beyond the awareness of impermanence and beyond the awareness of suffering and comes to the awareness of selflessness, and penetrates through the deepest core sense of identity, and realizes identitylessness.

This realization—far from crippling you into feeling that you are nothing, or that you are stuck in the experience of being nothing— frees you finally to become responsible for imaginatively creating yourself. You realize that what you imagine is what you are, and that what the world imagines you to be also is what you are. It's not solipsistic; it's the combined interface of the imaginations of you and all beings. It's what you and what all things are.

Emptiness means all things are open to being transformed into any form, depending on how the beings perceive them, what the beings agree to, how they work together. Therefore, emptiness means you have the potential of being a buddha. And others do, too. So you begin to take responsibility for the art of developing the buddha-self, of developing that self that interacts with other selves in a totally altruistic way, where its manifestations are only for the benefit of producing happiness in the other selves and removing suffering from the other selves.

The *Mentor Devotion* verse, again:

Bless me to understand Nagarjuna's intended meaning,
In which life and liberation have no jot of intrinsic reality,

Yet cause and effect and relativity are still inexorable,
And these two laws don't contradict, but mutually complement one another!

We need to work out our own liberation. We can refer to the verse's wisdom, but we are not to believe it just because a great sage or teacher said it. We are to question everything. The Buddha told us, "Don't believe something just because I said it. Don't believe something because it appears in ancient books. And don't believe something because it is said to be of divine origin. Believe only what you yourself have tested and questioned and have found to be true."

Now, we'll close the refuge field by looking around in it, seeing the mentor beings up there, high above us, and in front of us, and all around, seeing all the beings around us looking all happy and delighted. And the mentors in the refuge field are ecstatic and enchanted because we have been meditating and reflecting on these useful things. We have a sense now of the structure of the path. We know the different points at which we really want to exert effort and come to critical awareness of ideas different from our own.

Because of their joy, the beings just melt into light, and they become light that flows into us. They dissolve, and the whole sky and the clouds and the crystal Lake Manasarovar and everything just flows into us in the form of diamond, ruby, emerald, topaz, and sapphire light. They become one with us, and we become one with the mentor, one with the Buddha; we feel the Buddha and the mentors living in our heart. And then the light flows out from us to all the beings around us—friend, stranger, enemy—who now have come to seem, all of them, more familiar; all of them are our mother beings, although they are temporarily behaving in these different roles with us in this life.

We are delighted with them. We're happy to be one with the

refuge field, and like the refuge field, we melt into light, our meditative persona melts into light, flows out into them, as we dedicate the merit of whatever we have done here to attaining perfect buddhahood as soon as possible for the sake of all beings. And then, someone wonders, "Where is everybody? What happened?" And now we're back in our ordinary reality, and ready to practice wisdom in the world.

SIX

REVVING THE ENGINE TO ENLIGHTENMENT

Empowerment from the Subtle Realms

Then bless me to embark in the boat to cross the ocean of the Tantras,
Through the kindness of the captain Vajra-master,
Holding vows and pledges, root of all powers,
More dearly than life itself!

Bless me to perceive all things as the deity body,
Cleansing the taints of ordinary perception and conception
Through the yoga of the first stage of Unexcelled Yoga Tantra,
Transforming birth, death, and between into the three buddha-bodies!

Bless me to realize here in this life
The path of clear light-magic body union,
Coming from you, Savior, when you put your toe
In my eight-petaled, heart center's central channel.

If the path is not complete and death arrives,
Bless me to go to a pure buddhaverse
By the instruction for implementing the five forces
Of mentor soul ejection, the forceful art of buddhahood!

In short, life after life forever,
You, Savior, care for me and never part,

Bless me to become your foremost heir,
Upholding all the secrets of body, speech, and mind!

Thou, Savior, when you're a perfect buddha,
May I be foremost in your retinue.
Grant me good luck for easy, natural achievement
Of all my goals, temporary and ultimate!

Thus having prayed, may you, best mentor,
Joyously come to my crown to bless me,
Sit securely, your toenails glistening,
In the corolla of my heart-center lotus!

The pure virtue of performing this practice,
I dedicate to the success of all the deeds and vows
Of all the three times' bliss-lords and their heirs,
And to uphold the word and practice of the holy Dharma.

By the power of that dedication, through all my lives,
May I never lose the four wheels of the supreme vehicle—
May I consummate transcendence, spirit of enlightenment,
Realistic view, and progress on the stages of creation and perfection.

We have completed our retreat on the exoteric path, the three principal themes of the transcendent attitude, the loving spirit of enlightenment, and the wisdom of selflessness. These themes consist, respectively, of four steps, eleven steps, and two insights, each of which can use four keys—though we can always subdivide these processes in more elaborate ways.

When you master these three principal themes, at least to some degree you are prepared to enter upon the esoteric vehicle of the Tantras—spiritual technologies and arts that accelerate enlightenment. However, you also must have the personal authorization, empowerment, and instruction from a qualified mentor and possess the compassion, intelligence, determination, and opportunity for the practices. So, we will enter the jewel tree field together one more time, recapitulate more fully what we have understood, and open the door to take a peek at the possibilities and the magnificence of the Tantric sciences and arts.

Some teachers think that Tantra should remain esoteric, only for the initiated. Even the full-scale practice of the jewel tree of the *Mentor Devotion* normally requires authorization, empowerment, and instruction of a real mentor, since the visualization of the jewel tree itself is drawn from the spiritual technology of the Tantras. Nevertheless, systematic visualization is widely used in most Tibetan systems that propel us along the path to enlightenment. Tantra is the fastest, most powerful technology for accelerating your evolutionary progress toward buddhahood. As long as you have developed the transcendent attitude, have conceived the spirit of enlightenment, and have clearly understood, at least inferentially, the selflessness of subjects and objects, Tantric practice is not excessively dangerous. So let's take a look at it, as revealed by the *Mentor Devotion*.

Turning to the Tibetan wish-granting jewel tree, we'll begin again by opening our special refuge environment. We let ourselves dissolve, let our whole world picture dissolve. We merge into an experiential taste of selflessness. We arise on the top of the world, at the crystal Lake Manasarovar, sitting on a grassy bluff, with all beings around us looking at us. We behold the jewel tree growing out of the island in the lake before us, filling the sky and the heavens, and glowing and glistening like a giant Christmas tree. We see the wish-fulfilling jewels of all our mentors from all the cultures—Buddha, Zoroaster, Isaiah, Moses, the Goddess, whoever our mentors are.

And the whole heavenly host is radiating jewel light rays down to us—diamond, ruby, emerald, topaz, and sapphire. We fill up with light ourselves and radiate the light out around us to all the beings, filling each one with light and energy and hope and pleasure. Their gratitude comes back to us; our gratitude goes back to them and to the refuge tree.

Once you're in this environment of the gem tree, you review the thought steps of the contemplative path to enlightenment: First, you offer the world to the mentors, take refuge, praise and salute the beings, confess and repent of your wrongdoings, rejoice in the virtues of others, request the rain of Dharma to fall from the mentors, and ask them not to go away. You dedicate everything you do to buddhahood, for the sake of all living beings' freedom from suffering.

Now, you are firmly settled in the refuge tree field and are beginning the actual path of development. You recognize the preciousness of human embodiment, endowed with liberty and opportunity; the immediacy of death; the infinite continuity of life, beginningless and endless; the cause and effect of evolutionary actions; and the inevitable suffering found in all egocentric life states, or samsara. These four realizations lead you into the first mind of the transcendent attitude; self-release and self-appreciation; and a new, evolutionary ethic of interrelationships with all beings. You feel a definite release from your habitual preoccupations, a new freedom to look more carefully and meaningfully at your life.

Next, you turn your mind toward the second great theme, the spirit of enlightenment. You survey the condition of all beings, and your relation to them. As you develop equanimity, you recognize that each and every one is your mother. Remembering your mothers' kindness, you wish to repay them all, so you exchange self and other, trade away self-preoccupation for other-preoccupation. You reflect more deeply on the disadvantages of self-preoccupation and broadly over the advantages of other-preoccupation. You develop universal love, the giving of all your happiness and pleasure to all beings, and you see them as lovely in their happiness. You exercise universal compassion, taking from others all their suffering, bringing it over to yourself to convert it into bliss through understanding. You adopt the messianic resolution that you will be the one to help all of them, and to save them from their suffering. First you free yourself, and then you teach others how to do it themselves. Finally, you conceive the spirit of enlightenment of love and compassion to all beings. You vow to become a buddha for the sake of all living beings, and you move to activate that enlightened mind by taking the vow of the bodhisattva and determining, "Yes, I will become a buddha for the sake of all living beings." Now you have added the second mind, the spirit of enlightenment, of love and compassion, to the first mind of transcendent renunciation.

You go then into the third main theme of the path, the wisdom of reality and selflessness. Realizing there is "subjective self" and "objective self," you implement the four keys on the personal self: First, you recognize the instinctive, solid gut feeling of absolute self-identity and independence; next, you commit to find that self or to give it up if you cannot find it; next, you seek the self in the life systems but affirm that it is not there; finally, you turn to look for the self as something truly separate from, but connected to, the life systems, but you fail to find it there, either.

Each time you fail to find the self, you experience a meditative dissolution: Your subjectivity dissolves along with all objectivities, and you experience a spacelike, balanced state. Each time you emerge from that spacelike state, you seek the self or essence of the spacelike state itself. That state itself then dissolves under analysis, and you discern the inconceivable entirety of the universe on the surface of the space, so to speak, as if in a dream or a reflection in a mirror. You oscillate from spacelike to dreamlike and from dreamlike to spacelike states. As you do so, they become more and more fused together, until they are ultimately experienced as nondual, the nonduality of voidness and relativity. At that time, your wisdom of selflessness manifests simultaneously as unconditional compassion—you feel one with all beings and so feel their sufferings as your own sufferings and so naturally are moved to end them. You realize the nonduality of your wisdom that is aware of everything's emptiness and your compassion that is committed to everything's relational presence. This nondual insight enables you to effectively help beings terminate their suffering and to begin to live relationally in a harmonious, happy, nonsuffering way.

Now, we come out of the meditation, having run through the contemplative summary of the path. You should now have this under your belt, so that you can play with these themes and reflect on them again and again. Even when you focus on just one particular step of thought, say, the precious human life endowed with liberty and opportunity, it's good to do so within the context of the whole path. Before settling on one step, try running through all the steps briefly, and then come back and really practice your focus on that one theme. All the different principles reinforce each other and lead to a harmonious, unified mental state.

Once you've practiced one principle and move on to the others, however, you mustn't think you know it forever. For example, if you meditate on the cause and effect of karmic evolution, it's not as if you don't have to think about that ever again. In fact, the first time you learn something, your knowledge is not that deep. Usually, you have gained mere intellectual knowledge. It won't necessarily come out in your experience of life and the world right away. Often, we think we understand something, think we've got it all settled, and the next day we're sort of confused, and we go through it again, gaining a much deeper experience of it. Then we really feel, "Now, today,

I really understand it." Yet we come back again, and we know it again, and we seem to find an infinite depth of experience and reexperience. Reality is infinite openness, infinite potential, infinite possibility, and, therefore, it's no wonder that you can go on and on, become more and more amazing, more and more miraculous, more and more wondrous, the deeper and deeper you go.

Now that you have the path as a whole, you can even memorize the different points and count through them regularly. Doing this is very helpful. The Asian traditions in general use memorization, which is why they like to number things—the four noble truths, the three principal themes, the four steps of this, the eleven steps of that, and so forth. This is not because they are all would-be accountants, but because structuring things makes them more useful in meditation. To really understand something, whatever it is, any subject, you have to meditate, to engrain that understanding more deeply in your mind. Memorization is very useful, because it focuses your mind without distraction. If you just read something and feel you understand it as you read it but leave it in the book, then when you do meditate, your mind will wander here and there, and you won't really be able to go more deeply. But if you memorize the main points of what you've learned, when you meditate you will have a clear framework for your thought, a set of points to serve as parameters for your critical inner gaze, and you can drill more deeply at each of the main points and deepen your understanding.

To drill deeply, you can't just accept a surface realization. You have to develop a more critical penetration. You can do this by questioning, by debating, by arguing and discussing. You don't passively accept any one idea but see where you stand in relation to it. You work the ideas, argue with someone else about them, see where your own thinking and perceptions are ill founded or well founded. Even if they are well founded, you may not really know how to explain that well foundedness. And you want truth. You don't simply want to adopt an idea for your life and enlightenment without making sure it is bedrock solid. You deepen your reasoning, you deepen your insight, and as you do so you also deepen your inner meditation. You drill to deeper levels of understanding.

Even at over sixty years of age, I'm still kind of suspicious of what I think I understand, because I have had so many experiences of having thought I understood something really sharply, even having a eureka-type insight, only to have a further insight a couple of years later that turned my previous understanding upside down. Sometimes I have even been embarrassed about the way I previously understood something! And yet, every new understanding has a quality of, "Wow! Eureka! Now I've got it!" Later that dissolves, and I go more deeply still, and I am embarrassed that I had thought the other thing. Again and again, it goes like that.

So, you shouldn't be defensive and think you have one thing you know for certain, and hold on to that because you think it will never change. It will change, the deeper you live your knowledge. And the deeper you live and examine your knowledge, the more wonderful it is. We have the assurance of the enlightened beings that reality is goodness, that reality is freedom from suffering, that reality is bliss. So we should never fear to open ourselves to reality, to cast aside our preconceptions and biases, and to open more and more to whatever turns out to be real. You can have faith in enlightenment, faith in evolutionary potential, faith in infinity, faith in your infinite self.

ACCELERATING YOUR BUDDHAHOOD

Now, think back to your conception of the spirit of enlightenment, your determination and vow to achieve perfect buddhahood. Even though at that point you established the bodhisattva mind and the soul of enlightenment, you're not yet at the full awareness of enlightenment. You have planted and sprouted the seed, however, the determination for enlightenment that changes all of our subsequent evolutionary experience.

Also, think about the tenth step toward enlightenment, the step of messianic resolution, "I must do it all for everyone, I can't wait." We vow to proceed as bodhisattvas, but we don't have to be high holy people or reincarnate lamas to be bodhisattvas. Sure, an advanced, even angelic bodhisattva such as Avalokiteshvara, the bodhisattva of perfect compassion, or Tara, the female bodhisattva who symbolizes the dynamic redemptive activity of all buddhas, is like a celestial archangel. But even we can be bodhisattvas just with our deep vow and deep determination to become buddhas for the sake of all beings, to focus all our life experience on that.

The bodhisattva is ready to be patient and enduring; ready to practice generosity for three incalculable aeons of lifetimes; ready to practice justice and sensitive, ethical interaction with others for three incalculable aeons of lifetimes; ready to practice tolerance and bear with the injuries of others, sacrifice the self, and leave the victory to others for three incalculable aeons. The bodhisattva is ready to do all of that from her or his own perspective; the bodhisattva is in no rush. For once we have tasted a single drop of the bliss of bringing others into that freedom, with the spirit of enlightenment of love and compassion, once we have loosened the grip of the solid, separated, alienated self that is the core of self-centeredness, then we are already happy in a certain way. The bodhisattva is always joyful, even when suffering. Bodhisattvas are always happy and cheerful under pressure, because they have felt the essence of reality as freedom, even though they haven't fully experienced it. So bodhisattvas can pretty much undergo whatever comes their way.

However, bodhisattvas will never be patient or tolerant about the suffering of other beings. They basically can't stand to wait around the three incalculable aeons of lifetimes that it takes to create a buddhaland, to create a world for all beings that is a buddhaverse, in which everything is openly the mirror wisdom. They're unwilling to wait these three incalculable aeons because of the plight of other beings, of their mothers. How can we stand by when our mothers roast in hell, fight and kill each other unnecessarily and endlessly?

To help the bodhisattvas, the buddhas teach Tantras, which are almost miraculous methodologies. *Tantra* means "continuity." Even enlightenment has infinite continuity, which we studied and accepted during our first steps on the path. Tantra is the definitive system that arises when you finally abandon the notion of a separated state as your inner nature and final destiny. You've set aside all those misinterpreted visions of liberation as being an ultimate separated place, and a state apart that you can enter—some sort of great formless quiet. In Indian culture about a thousand years after Buddha's time, people had become committed to seeing their interwovenness and interrelativity. It had become more normal, and more commonsensical, to see continuity. At that time, the Tantras that buddhas had always taught in secret became more explicated, and they emerged among the educated public as a separate discipline, as scriptural and commentarial texts, although they had always been there in secret.

One of my great teachers, the late Tara Tulku, once said something that surpassed any wisdom I have read in any book, although it was in total harmony with all teaching. In response to the question "What is Tantra?" he said, "Once critical wisdom demolishes the world built on the foundation of ignorance, the world of the samsaric life cycle, the world of self-other conflict, then you are free to build a new world on the foundation of wisdom. *Tantra is the art of building such a world of wisdom.*"

A wisdom world is a mandala, a perfected environment that provides all beings with the optimal opportunity to evolve toward enlightenment. It is a world in which every lotus teaches selflessness. Every passing dragonfly—when its wings buzz, the teaching of universal compassion can be heard. The gurgling water says, "Impermanence, suffering, selflessness, freedom." Everything in the whole world itself is a teaching of liberation and freedom and enlightenment to beings. And that world is built of wisdom by enlightened beings, and the technology of building such a world is called Tantra.

Some people talk of enlightenment as if it were the end of life rather than the aim of every life. They say, "No more rebirth for me, this is my last life." Sometimes Buddha encourages them. But they mean that this is their last egocentrically imprisoned life, their last self-preoccupied life, last life of suffering, of self struggling with the overwhelming other. To them, life is so unbearable, they're actually looking to escape. But if you told them, "Well, sorry, even Buddha is going to have boundless, endless lives, infinite emanations benefiting all others and interwoven with all other beings," this type of person looking for escape would be just terrified and might figure, "Why become a buddha, since I'd be having the same horrible time I'm having now?" So Buddha lets them say "No more rebirth" rather than impose on such timid people the magnificent vision of infinite continuity and infinite life, wherein Tantra serves as the supreme art of building wisdom worlds.

Therefore, to protect such timid people from the unnecessary fear of being overwhelmed with too much life, Buddha decreed that for at least eleven centuries Tantra should be kept a secret, and even after that time it should be treated reverently as esoteric. It was not hidden because Buddha was some sort of elitist and didn't want to share this teaching with people. Tantra is esoteric because if people were not prepared, if the society was not prepared, people would become confused, and they would do the wrong thing, even as they tried to base their actions on the teaching of the right thing.

Say you have a bicycle, and you also want to glide off a cliff. If you use the bike, you'll crash and die. It's not the right equipment for gliding. This is not a mystery. You also need the right equipment to build the world of wisdom and fly into it. The right equipment in-

cludes the mind of transcendent renunciation, first of all. To develop that mind, you recognize the infinite continuity of life, appreciate your own human sense of that life, and envision the possibility
of freedom. Then you understand that there is no escape, that you
are infinitely involved. That's the first wing. Then you recognize that
the only thing to do is also the most essential thing to do—you conceive the messianic spirit of enlightenment. Infinite compassion is
another wing, the second prerequisite for Tantra.

Why have compassion, if other beings are just illusions? You have
to maintain a view of the unity of life and to have compassion for
others, or you would not have cared to evolve a body. A buddhahood,
a body, is only for the purpose of reaching out to others, to hold
them, to caress them, to communicate with them. That's the only
purpose of a body when you are enlightened. Only love and compassion would make you willing to undergo the heroic efforts of re-
building a whole universe. If you didn't have the messianic resolution
of the bodhisattva, why would you want to rebuild the universe? You
wouldn't even think it were possible to rebuild the universe.

The final essential prerequisite of Tantra is some degree of wisdom. You do not necessarily have to be at the brink of buddhahood,
but you need enough wisdom to be secure in the emptiness and relativity of the self. You have to have unseated and dethroned your gut
feeling of solid self, which is our only enemy in the world, and to
understand that no absolute thing can ever be experienced by any
relative thing. You allow that any sense of person you have is relative,
made up of experiences, and infinitely transformable and malleable.
Therefore, you are open to change and won't get stuck rigidly in any
particular sense of self. The motivation is the spirit of enlightenment; the knowledge of infinite continuity provides the horizon of
possibility; and the drive for freedom is the engine. And wisdom
safeguards the openness for self-transformation. So, the path that

we have taught following the *Mentor Devotion* also comprises the pillars, the tripod, on which the palace of Tantra is built.

The need for Tantra arises from the messianic impatience of the bodhisattva—"I want to become a perfect buddha sooner, even in this life, if possible, in the between-state after death, or at least in a couple of lives. I want to become a buddha because I can't leave my mothers in this predicament longer than that." Buddhahood is not just a change of your mind, leaving your body as it was. Thus, the bodhisattva usually has to develop transcendent generosity, justice, patience, creativity, concentration, and wisdom in many, many lives, in body after body. In one life, perhaps, the bodhisattva may perform transcendent giving and give her life for another. Such bodhisattvas live lightly within their bodies, realizing that the body is something that is easy come, easy go. They are transcendently detached. They feel it is just bliss to make a gift of their life, because of the pleasure the one who receives the gift gets.

Without the methodology of Tantra, the bodhisattva has to be born again, grow up, study, make sure he gets to be human, then learn again until, maybe, finally, he accomplishes another great deed of love and compassion. You make one evolutionary leap per lifetime, and it takes millions and billions of lives to evolve into this extraordinary magical being that is a buddha. With the power of Tantra, however, this evolutionary process accelerates. Tantra can speed up the evolutionary process.

The doorway into Tantra itself is the guru, the mentor, the person already adept at the method. The mentor creates a mandala, a sacred place, a magical circle, a divine palace and environment that is totally secure and ultimately beautiful. He or she then introduces the practitioner, reveals the potential of enlightenment, and anoints her or him with the empowerment to practice. Then the practice can begin within a transformed space. This is why the *Mentor Devotion*, as well as most Tibetan versions of the path of enlightenment, introduce the practitioner to the secure and sacred space of the jewel tree. And the practitioner develops the relationship with the mentor and the sense of presence and empowerment within such a space *ahead of time*, while still practicing the foundational practices, developing the foundational insights into life, without going through formalities of formal consecration.*

How does the Tantric vehicle provide its acceleration of positive evolutionary development? Say you have a dream at night in which you do a heroic act—you give your life for the sake of your beloved or your community. In that dream, this supreme sacrifice is difficult for you to perform, because you feel greatly attached to yourself— and yet you do succeed and give yourself away. But then you wake up and realize that actually you didn't die or lose your recognizable self, but you went through the whole spiritual achievement of giving yourself in the virtual reality of the dream, without having to go through the clumsy, heavy process of dying and being reborn. Tantra opens the doorway to such a virtual reality. It helps you open your imagination, your nervous system, your neural net, to the possibility of being a much vaster type of sensibility and being. It teaches you how to dream lucidly, how to use the virtual, subtle body in a dream,

---

* The *Mentor Devotion* can also be done, of course, as a formal empowerment, but only when the practitioner is ready and demands it. This happens only when the practitioner has boosted her or his self-esteem immeasurably through the transcendent attitude, has expanded his or her evolutionary motivation through the spirit of enlightenment, and has opened herself or himself to the immediate possibility of radical transformation through some degree of the transcendent wisdom of selflessness. He or she can no longer abide to postpone radical transformation until the consummation of countless lives and deaths have enabled him or her at last to really be able to help all the mother beings effectively. At this point, it would be wrong for the mentor to deny such a practitioner empowerment.

and how to cultivate more merit, develop more experience, and develop deeper knowledge in a dream. And that is also why you have to have understood some degree of emptiness to do that. You couldn't do it if you didn't understand the insubstantiality and malleability of the seemingly solid self. You have to have come to the understanding that you are actually imagining yourself in the embodiment you now have, so therefore you can reimagine yourself in another, completely different world. You won't have the creative power of visualization or imagination if you have not dissolved your imagination's habitual perceptual patterns, which are stuck on you by your inheritance and acculturation and which constitute your normal sense of self.

TANTRIC PRACTICES

Tantra is the great treasure of Tibet, but it is not ultimately different from the rest of the Buddhadharma path. There are four main kinds of Tantra. In the Buddhist tradition, there are the outer ritual Tantras, the inner ritual Tantras, the Yoga Tantras, and what are called "Unexcelled Yoga Tantras." The Tantric mandalas, taught most elaborately in the Unexcelled Yoga Tantras, are sacred spaces in which you train and develop your deepest sensibilities. They can have the form of magnificent palaces, beautiful magical environments, and alternative universes. In the Unexcelled Yoga Tantras, you begin to train in two stages, the first of which is called the "creation stage." You train as an architect of worlds of enlightenment, as an engineer of the embodiments of enlightenment. You experiment with different virtual embodiments for yourself. A man may visualize himself as woman; a woman may visualize herself as a man; either sex may visualize himself or herself as male and female, two beings in union. You may visualize yourself as an entire community of seven hundred beings, or as each one of the different beings.

There are many degrees of complexity and sophistication in

Tantra, but basically, the practices all aim to expand your mind and imagination. I think it's the most amazing, most subtle, spiritual psychoneurology that the world has ever seen. But I believe that most mystical systems—including Hindu Tantra, Taoist Tantra, Kabbalah, Sufi Tantra, Christian mysticism (like the many mansions of Saint Teresa of Ávila and the union with the Christ that she experienced, or the visions of Hildegard of Bingen)—are all in the same ballpark.

In the process of creation-stage practice, you visualize exquisite virtual realities, in which you rehearse the experience of death. In fact, you learn to see death not as a fearsome thing, not as an annihilation, but as a gateway into ever greater transformation, as a gateway into new birth, the space wherein you can find freedom to shape yourself in such a way that you can interact with any being, to mirror to that being its own potential, its own future development. You learn the exact process of unentwinement of soul and body. You see how the subtle mind, the spiritual gene, is embedded deeply in the central cells, the heart cells of the body. You see how the spiritual gene was originally embedded there at the time of conception, and how at normal death the cells unravel, and the physical connection unravels, and then the soul gene flies free from the body without actually dying. This is the training ground of becoming a buddha, so that you know exactly how to teach another being.

After the creation stage, you enter into what is called the "perfection stage." By realizing deeply the meaning of emptiness, you realize that the shapes of life, the forms of life in which we live are basically created by mutual imagination, not only some sort of god's imagination, but by our mutual imaginations. We imagine ourselves and each other. These intersections of the imaginations of sentient beings are the shape of reality. You discover this insight through knowledge of emptiness, voidness; once everything is void, nothing does not exist. But things exist as they are being shaped by mind.

The intersecting, subjective minds of many beings shape the world through language, through the word. You can't reshape the world alone by force, because other beings also have to understand. But you can lead them to the teaching, you can reason through it for them, you can exemplify it for them, you can illustrate it for them. But you can't understand it for them—they have to do that for themselves.

In the ancient Tantric arts and sciences for building the world of beauty and evolutionary fulfillment for all beings, you use all the energies of life. You transform anything that may have seemed negative—even negative passions, even fierce, frightful things—into various wisdoms of selfless, loving, compassionate benefit. Even the way in which we have been meditating on the wish-granting gem tree path is a kind of Tantra. After canceling the context of the ordinary, dark, confused world with our ordinary limitations, when we bring up our vision of the wish-granting jewel tree, with all our mentors and all the great mentor beings of all traditions, cultures, and civilizations throughout history, that is Tantra. That is creating a mandala within which we are capable of new understanding, a sacred space that helps us meditate and transform ourselves. In our habitual world, we're always incapable and imperfect, and so we never can get past our normal awareness. The mandala, an exalting environment, is immensely empowering, and the mental practice of being there actually is Tantra. It is not esoteric. You don't need to have made a vow. You just use those imaginative arts, surround yourself with them and are empowered by them to create positive change for yourself and for other beings.

NAVIGATING DEATH CONSCIOUSLY

The Tibetan Book of the Dead was developed as a set of instructions for everyone to use at the moment of death. We hope that, by being aware of the immediacy of death, we will not be shocked by it, and we actually will be prepared way ahead of time. So death will not be such a big deal for us, it will be just a transition, a doorway, like leaving a cocoon and moving into a butterfly state. It is an opportunity, something joyful, a release—but it's not a release into some fantasized nothingness, or some fantasized passive place where we're just going to be sitting in some heaven. It's a release into a new embodiment in which we can develop even more.

In fact, *The Tibetan Book of the Dead* in Tibetan Buddhism is called *The Book of Natural Liberation Through Learning in the Between State*, or *bardo-toeudroeul*. That is to say, you will become naturally liberated when you learn about this nature of your own reality, when you learn about it in your subtle body-mind complex that you inhabit during the between-state, in the after-death experience, the bardo.

When I first translated *The Tibetan Book of the Dead*, spent time with it, and steeped myself in it, I had many incredible revelations. I like to say that the main thing I learned from it is the opposite of its Western title, *The Book of the Dead*, because I learned that there are no dead. No one is dead. That was a big thing for me. Many cultures believe that people continue after they die in various ways, and many human beings are afraid of the dead and of ghosts. But the great message of *The Tibetan Book of the Dead* is that there are no dead people. Nobody has time to be dead. Death is just a doorway into further existence.

Now it can be frightening, of course, to go through a doorway. If you hurtle through with no control, and you don't know what's on the other side of the door, that can be very frightening. I think that's really what people are afraid of—letting go of the known and falling into an unknown that would be unpleasant, without having any control. Death is a doorway, a line with no width. When you walk through a doorway, when are you in the doorway? A doorway, the exact boundary between one room and another, has no width. A threshold, however, has a width. You can stand on a wooden threshold that's six inches wide. But when are you actually in the doorway? When your toes just touch that threshold? When you're in the middle of the threshold? Where is the line that is the actual doorway that divides one room from another? It's arbitrary. In a way, the doorway doesn't exist, it has no width. Just so, death is a line with no width between one life and the next one. It's when mind detaches from embodiment in this body and moves into a dream body, called the "between-state body," a virtual-reality body made of subtle energy and shaped according to how the mind is used to feeling itself embodied.

A minute after I die, my out-of-body may have approximately the shape of my former body, because that's how my mind is used to being embodied, with eyes and ears and limbs. In dreams, you seem to see, you seem to hear, occasionally you touch something, so you seem to have a body, limbs, eyes, and ears. But your mind in the dream is in a virtual-reality zone, not in the body, operating it mechanically, creating a virtual body like the body to which it's accustomed. Death is nothing but that line. So, therefore, nobody stays dead; there are no dead people.

My mother, my father, my grandfather, my friend who died— they're not sitting around being dead, they immediately went into new experiences. They immediately became embodied in new ways. Some may have remained in a between-state, which can happen if they were strongly attached to the previous life, although the sages say that everyone goes through little deaths and rebirths even in that state. They periodically dissolve and arise again in a new between-state embodiment, a virtual-reality embodiment, as if they were having a series of dreams without ever awakening. And they can have a ghostlike way of being connected with their previous material reality. It can happen. That is actually how a ghost is defined in the Buddhist tradition. Even then they are not dead but living in a ghostly existence. They're staying close to their previous form, but they're not dead.

If you've been really very, very bad, if you have a very negative, fearful, paranoid, hostile mind, you may go into an all-consuming negative state of experience. If you have a very good, open, generous, loving, luminous mind, you will very soon go into an experience that is positive, that seems to you much more delightful than whatever you were having on Earth. Everything is luminous and nice, and you don't feel any regret about having been on the middle-level, rather grimy planet Earth, although it is beautiful. It is said that Earth is kept in this noncelestial way on purpose by enlightened beings and deities, in order to give us more opportunity to practice compassion.

HOW WE REALLY DIE

The Tibetan Book of the Dead grew out of the learning of the great Indian and Tibetan adepts of the Tantra. They carefully, empirically, and experimentally studied the process of dying and being reborn, of being in the dream state and being awake, and of the most subtle transitions between these phases of consciousness and phases of embodiment. They developed the ability to maintain awareness through those transitions, and from those experiences they developed instructions and guides. For example, when you die, they say, at first you experience a kind of melting feeling. All the hardness in your system gets lost, and you melt in a heap, or in a puddle, internally. You experience a kind of hallucinatory mirage because the hard edges of your vision, the distinct edges of the things you are used to seeing, begin to melt. They become swirling, fluid patterns. You lose your ability to see, and you lose your connection to form.

In the next level, you have a kind of internal vision of smoke (but not with your eyes). You're in a realm in which you feel as if you were in smoke; instead of feeling liquid and melted, you feel hot and agitated, except that you've already lost the feeling of your limbs and all your senses. Your hearing is going, and you sense roaring sounds, like the crackling of flames, or the rushing of floods within you, but you don't hear an external sound. If people speak, you don't hear what they say.

Next, the inner zone of experience becomes like a field of shooting sparks or a cloud of fireflies, flickering and humming, or like raindrops gently falling on a smooth pond surface, creating interference patterns of ripples. It's a sparkier vision than the others.

Then you get the feeling of a single candle flame, absolutely unflickering, a whitish, yellowish light with a little tinge of blue perhaps, like the flame of a candle that's standing perfectly still. It is perhaps at the moment before guttering out, this moment of total stillness, this pure, internal candle flame. You don't see it with your eyes, because they are not functioning at all. No motor energy is functioning at all by this time. Your body has all gone to sleep, as when you sit uncomfortably and a leg or foot falls asleep. Here, the body as a whole has tingled, has gone past tingling, and has become completely numb. You have no sensation of being in it.

Then you go into a stage known as "luminance." You completely disconnect from coarse energy but have a very subtle, virtual energy, what they call "wind," or "subtle wind," like neural energy. And you go into an inner state that feels like a vast space filled with moonlight, luminance, peaceful, cool space.

From there, you go into a state called "radiance," which is like a vast sky full of sunlight. There is no sun or moon, no separate objects. Instead, your whole space is pure sunlight, bright and intense, hot, energetic, a reddish orange. You go from that stage into a deeper stage called "imminence," or "dark light," in which everything is pitch-black, so black it's like a shining black. When you first are aware of going into it, it's like becoming nothing or going into nothing, and the untrained person will become totally unconscious in this state. The untrained person doesn't feel like a person in those states. His or her own sense of subjectivity is pretty muted in the previous two states, the vast, moonlike state and then the vast sunlike state. In the dark light state, you just lose consciousness. But a yogin can retain a very subtle awareness, indivisible from unawareness at this point, and she or he won't completely lose consciousness.

The last state is known as the "state of transparency," popularly known in America as the "clear light," which is okay if one understands *clear* as "transparent." Unfortunately, I think many people think *clear* means "vivid" or "bright," and they think of it as a white light. This isn't white but more like gray, between light and dark, like glass, a transparency. It has no brightness, it has no darkness. It's a light that has no shadow. It's a light that doesn't fall on an object; it's within the object as much as not in the object. It's true transparency. That state of transparency is said to be the subtlest state of any mind, of any awareness. It is true freedom, the deepest state of the buddha-mind, transiting through it is actually what death is, and it is where enlightenment conjoins all beings. It's transparent but doesn't obstruct any of the other states, so it isn't separate from anything. Yet it is very creative, healing, and powerful. It is infinite, and yet you experience it yourself.

When the ordinary person dies, because his or her mind is so used to being in the traction of the sense organs, it immediately tries to create another form and a feeling of being a self isolated from other subjects and objects. So he or she just shoots past these vast stages of moonlight, sunlight, dark light, and clear light, and then the person is back struggling for a form. So, the untrained person, the undisciplined, the unaware person, forgets, or doesn't even notice those states.

But those are the best states with which to work. Those are the states that the Tantric yogin in the mandala, in the subtle yogas of the Tantra, has learned to navigate and remain conscious in, and then to build up consciously a form out of those states, and consciously arise in that form, coming back up through those eight signs of light. The yogins move from transparency to dark light, from dark light to sunlight, sunlight to moonlight, moonlight to candle flame, candle flame to fireflies or sparks, fireflies or sparks to smoke, smoke to mirage, and mirage to solid perception of forms.

Now in a dreamlike, between-state body, the yogin can do that, and the yogin can do that consciously. When nonyogins die, as *The Book of the Dead* tells us, we go back and forth through various kinds of vicissitudes over forty-nine days. Yet we want to—and can—guide our subtle body-minds into a positive rebirth. We want to do this, unless we are at the very highest Tantric stage, at which we are using the subtle embodiments in the between-state to attain buddhahood, or unless we're at an advanced enough stage where we can perceive the buddhas who appear during that subtle time and would be willing to install us in their mandalas in their different buddhalands.

In the fourteenth century, Karma Lingpa, one of the great discoverers of Tibetan spiritual treasures, was led by the angels, the mystic dakinis, to the right place, and he found the book inside a hollow pillar in the Samye monastery, which had been built in Guru Rinpoche's time, six hundred years earlier. Karma Lingpa brought out and published the text, and he wrote commentaries on it. The book has been widely used throughout Tibet from that time. I actually had a fight with the Library of Congress, who insisted that the author of the book is Karma Lingpa, the fourteenth-century discoverer, because they would not credit a tradition in which somebody would have written something and not have published it for six hundred years. Because of all the modern people who are desperately trying to publish something all the time, the library couldn't conceive of such a degree of self-restraint, of such clairvoyance. I told the Library of Congress that putting Karma Lingpa as the author in classifying the earlier translations is disrespectful to the original tradition. If the Tibetans thought Karma Lingpa was the author, they would have said he was the author. They put Padmasambhava as the author and Karma Lingpa as the discoverer, so why don't you get it straight? But they wouldn't change. Nonetheless, I put that down on my publication: Padmasambhava the author, Karma Lingpa the discoverer, and I the translator.

But it surprised me to discover that there are no dead people. I came to understand that Tibetans, the more modern ones particularly, have almost no interest in ancestors. They're not into ancestor worship at all, which is a big thing in China and a big thing in other cultures in Asia, still quite big in India. Nomadic people are not too hot on it, but some, Turkic and Mongolian, still do it. But Tibetans are almost unique in that they don't care for their ancestors much. They care for spiritual ancestors, such as Buddha, Marpa, Milarepa, but they don't care about blood ancestors, because the sense of there being no dead people is embedded in the culture. As told in *The Book of the Dead,* they know that the minute someone dies, he is no longer your uncle, aunt, or grandpa, but he immediately becomes a new being, who goes on into a bunch of new experiences. The people they meet in the street could well be their grandpas and grandmas, so they diffuse out over all beings that sense of relationship, kinship, and familiarity. So if I wanted to be nice to my ancestor, I'd be nice to you, you see. This attitude is a wonderful cultural achievement of the Tibetans, a key to transcending racism.

When Padmasambhava was living in Tibet, the country was run by a militaristic emperor. Although the emperor was intelligent and interested in Buddhism, he was running a military empire with a very authoritarian, hierarchical, sexist social structure. His soldiers were marching out, conquering China, conquering the Silk Route, conquering northern India, Nepal, Kashmir, parts of Bengal. It was a fierce, ferocious, uncivilized country, sort of like America today, highly militarized. In such a militaristic country, people are not supposed to think about death that much. You know, when you think about death, as you noted from meditating on the immediacy of death, death is not depressing. Death is liberating. If you're living each day as if it were your last, you're not going to follow the orders of a boss—you're going to smell the roses. You're going to get into your best meditation. You're going to go on retreats. You're not going to slave at the office, work in the factory, fight in the battle, plow the fields if it's your last day on Earth, even if you're well enough to do so. You're not. So, if you live in the immediacy of death awareness, you're going to be insubordinate, individualistic, seeking some sort of freedom, liberation, bliss, being compassionate. You're not going to be easily coercible by authority.

So, after six hundred years of struggling with their own rigidities, confusions, racisms, fanaticisms, and violence, Tibet opened up. It became normative for individuals to seek their own highest transcendence, to be universally compassionate, to become profoundly and comprehensively wise. Then it was possible for death to be published, so to speak, for people to become widely aware of death. In the new death and dying communities here in America, people are recently becoming aware of it. No one has addressed the problem that by hiding death in this way our culture coerces us to be more avid consumers, more avid producers, more obedient followers of the party line, of the military line, more avid taxpayers. Our delusion becomes exploitable into those social channels. We think, "I'll produce, and I'll get some benefit later. I'll consume, and I'll get a benefit later." We don't think, "Oh, this is my last day on Earth. Why should I produce, consume, fight for somebody else with some minor purpose? I have my highest evolutionary purpose of traveling now on to the new life in the best possible way." People pretend Tibet was a feudal theocracy, but the fact that Tibet was one of the most psychically free countries that history has perhaps ever seen, even though they didn't have the formal documents of democracy, is proven by their feeling that they could afford to let their people live in the full light of death all the time.

THE GREAT MANTRA: BE HERE NOW

In order to live in the light of death, you have to be living with a sense of meaningfulness. You have no life to waste when you live in the light of death. You live intensely, demanding fulfillment, security, compassion from the universe.

In Tibet the national mantra, which I will close by making our mantra, is the mantra of the perfection of each instant. It's the original expression of "be here now." It hails and salutes the lord of compassion, the Jesus Christ messiah of the Buddhist popular tradition, Avalokiteshvara—Chenrezig, as the Tibetans call him—the one who looks down from heaven upon human beings with compassion and does not ignore their state of suffering and difficulty. He is represented in many different forms, of course, but in one of the most beautiful he has eleven heads, a thousand arms, and a thousand eyes, with one eye in the palm of each hand. His arms symbolize his power of compassion to reach into every atom, every moment, and every life of every being, like a great king of Dharma. He is the king of reality, a king of compassion, helping everyone along the way to enlightenment, giving each a thousand helping hands, which are symbolic of an infinite number of helping hands. These helping hands are not just helping you according to what he thinks you need, but they are sensitive to what you really need, because he has infinite powers of sight. The palm of each hand has an eye, the most sensitive area of the body, and therefore, he sees exactly what you need and how you need to be helped. Avalokiteshvara also holds a jewel, which is the symbol of compassion, in his two front hands at his heart.

Our wish-granting gem tree, the refuge tree on which such gems grow, is a special Indian and Tibetan vision. But the actual wish-fulfilling gem is everyone's own heart of compassion and love. Wisdom helps you pry open that clamshell of the solid, self-centered gut feeling "I am the one!"—and then you're happy. Then you can fulfill all your wishes. Then not only do you fulfill the wishes of others, but your own wishes are fulfilled when you fulfill those wishes of others. And that is the real wish-fulfilling gem.

Avalokiteshvara holds the wish-fulfilling gem of universal love and compassion. And in another hand he holds a white lotus, which is the symbol of wisdom—delicate and beautiful, growing in the mud and on the surface of the water, but untainted by mud or water. This lotus of perfection symbolizes knowing the perfect freedom of all reality and beautifully embodies that symbolism in its delicate, opening petals. In a sense the jewel and the lotus are indivisible; the jewel is in the lotus, a symbolic integration of body and soul, wisdom and compassion, life and death.

"The jewel is in the lotus" is the often repeated mantra by Tibetans, who feel they are living in this imminent, wish-granting gem tree refuge field: the whole land of a thousand million snowy peaks, the vast land as large as Western Europe, surrounded by snowy peaks like a snow-peaked lotus. The land resonates with the mantra "The jewel is in the lotus": *Om Mani Padme Hum, Om Mani Padme Hum, Om Mani Padme Hum.* The Tibetans actually tend to drop the *d,* and they go *"paymey hoong."* *"Om Mani Paymey Hoong, Om Mani Paymey Hoong, Om Mani Paymey Hoong, Om Mani Paymey Hoong, Om Mani Paymey Hoong, Om Mani Paymey Hoong, Om Mani Paymey Hoong."* Tibetans recite that when they walk down the road. *"Om Mani Paymey Hoong, Om Mani Paymey Hoong, Om Mani Paymey Hoong."* The Sherpa Tibetans recite that when they haul backpacks up Mount Everest for mountain climbers. Tibetans recite that when they drive down the street. They have hand-held prayer wheels with *mani* mantras on and within them, which they spin round and round as they repeat the syllables. When they sew, as they put in each stitch, they go *"Om Mani Padme Hum, Om Mani Padme Hum, Om Mani Padme Hum, Om Mani Padme Hum."*

And they visualize that a great shining wheel is turning in the core of every atom, or perhaps like a wheel above them in the sky, any way they can do it. Or it could be in the heart. They visualize a beautiful wheel, a kind of carousel wheel, on the surface of which is written, *"Om Mani Padme Hum."* As the wheel turns, these six syllables enunciate, and light rays flow from the wheel. And the light rays flow out from the wheel and down into the hells. When they go to the cold hells, they become sun and sand and warmth and rain. And when they go to the hot hells, they become rain and ice and coolness. And when they go to the realms of hunger and thirst, they become food and drink and all delicious things to satisfy the thirst and hunger of the *preta* beings there. When these rays go to the animal realm, they become the light of intelligence, and the animals become sensitive to each other, and they begin to talk to each other. And when the rays go to the human realm, they become the light of the Dharma, of the teaching of liberation and love and compassion. And when they go to the titan realm, they become the light of rejoicing and the light of joy, and they teach the titans not to feel jealous of the gods anymore, not to attack the heavens all the time, not to fight and compete with each other all the time, but to feel content and to rejoice in the fortune of others. And when the rays go to the divine realm, they become the light of realistic awareness, of impermanence, and they let the gods see the short-term nature of their existence in the heavens—even a billion years is a moment at the end of it—and they recite "impermanence, impermanence, impermanence" to the gods.

And so, as you say *"Om Mani Padme Hum,"* these light rays stream from the multicolored jeweled letters of *"Om Mani Padme Hum,"* and they fill the whole universe with the compassion of Avalokiteshvara, the compassion of all the buddhas, with everything that every being needs everywhere in the universe. As you're saying this, your own moment and every cell and atom of your body are filled with that, and should you die at that moment, you would be simply as one of the light rays within the wheel of *"Om Mani Padme Hum."* You would be embraced by the gentle, loving, tender hands of Avalokiteshvara, and he would care for you and see to it that you didn't go to any of those terrible negative places, and see to it that you didn't go to some terribly overly positive place, where you might indulge yourself and goof off all the time, and see to it that you're reborn in the human realm and that you come back again into a place where you can learn the path of transcendence and the path of compassion and the path of selfless wisdom, and then enter into the subtle realm of the Tantras and evolve and accelerate your evolution to become a perfect buddha in order to bring all beings into the bliss-void indivisible wish-granting jewel tree refuge.

So, with that in mind, just join that Tibetan prayer: *"Om Mani Padme Hum, Om Mani Padme Hum, Om Mani Padme Hum, Om Mani Padme Hum, Om Mani Padme Hum, Om Mani Padme Hum, Om Mani Padme Hum."* And it would not be out of place at the very end, as we say the *"Om Mani Padme Hum,"* to think that this *"Om Mani Padme Hum"* sends out the jewel rays of compassion and intelligence and calmness and contentment and satisfaction to the leaders of communist China, and to all of the soldiers who are sitting on top of the Tibetans in Tibet, and to the poor Chinese who are suffering in labor reform camps, who want democracy in that place, and those who are working in terrible conditions on export platforms at slave wages. Think about *"Om Mani Padme Hum"* and the light of freedom, the brave Chinese people who once fully embraced Avalokiteshvara—

Guanyin, they called it, Kannon—with a full vision of that forced love embedded deep in the heart of their culture. But temporarily, as a result of the influence of the industrial compulsion and the productivity compulsion and materialism, they temporarily want to crush every vestige of spirituality, and they're denying and depriving themselves of it out of fear and pain and paranoia and insensitivity. Therefore, they are harming the poor Tibetans, who could be developing so many institutes of learning and retreat, and they themselves could go back to their own retreat and send out their own rays of blessing to the world, and all the world could visit them and have meditation centers there and climb their mountains and talk to them and enjoy them.

And we should send out *"Om Mani Padme Hum"*s to all beings, so that their situation will be healed in our prayer of *"Om Mani Padme Hum,"* and so they will not be neglected. *"Om Mani Padme Hum, Om Mani Padme Hum, Om Mani Padme Hum, Om Mani Padme Hum, Om Mani Padme Hum, Om Mani Padme Hum, Om Mani Padme Hum, Om Mani Padme Hum, Om Mani Padme Hum, Om Mani Padme Hum, Om Mani Padme Hum, Om Mani Padme Hum, Om Mani Padme Hum."*

MENTOR DEVOTION

VISION

Through the great bliss state,
I myself become the mentor deity.
From my luminous body,
Light rays shine all around,
Massively blessing beings and things,
Making the universe pure and fabulous,
Perfection in its every quality.

REFUGES

I and all space full of mother beings, from now until enlightenment,
Take refuge in the Mentor and the Three Jewels! [*3 times*]

Namo gurubhyoh. Namo buddhaya. Namo dharmaya. Namo sanghaya.
  [*3 times*]

DETERMINATION TO PRACTICE

For the sake of all mother beings, I myself will become a mentor deity to
install all beings in the supreme exaltation as being mentor deities themselves.
[*3 times*]

For the sake of all mother beings, in this very life I will very swiftly realize the
exaltation of the primal Buddha Mentor Deity; I will free all mother beings

*from suffering and install them in the great bliss Buddha state. For that purpose
I will undertake the profound path of Mentor Deity Yoga!* [3 times]

OFFERINGS

*Primal wisdom in reality appear as inner offering and individual offerings and
works to create the distinctive bliss-void wisdom in the fields of the six senses,
extending outer, inner, and secret clouds of offering, totally filling earth, sky,
and all of space with inconceivable visions and sacred substances.*

VISUALIZATION OF JEWEL TREE OF REFUGE

*In the middle of the all-good offering clouds arranged in the vast heavens of
bliss-void indivisible; in the crown of the miraculous, wish-granting gem tree,
radiantly beautiful with leaves, flowers, and fruits; on a sparkling jewel lion
throne on cushions of spreading lotus sun and moon sits my thrice-kind, root
mentor—the actuality of all enlightened beings.*

*His form is of a fulfilled mendicant with one face, two arms smiling
radiantly, right hand in the Dharma-teaching gesture, left hand flat in
meditation, holding a bowl of elixir. He wears the three robes of glowing
saffron color, head beautiful with the yellow scholar's hat. At his heart sits the
omnipresent lord Vajradhara, with one face, two arms, sapphire blue in color,
holding vajra and bell, embracing Lady Vajradhatu Ishvaree, goddess of the
diamond realm; both partners ecstatic in the play of bliss and void, resplendent
with multifaceted jewel ornaments, draped with divinely wrought silken clothes,
adorned with the signs and marks of perfection, surrounded by halos of five-
colored rainbows, shining like the sun.*

*He, my lama mentor, sits in the cross-legged vajra posture. His five body-
mind systems are really the five bliss-lords; his four elements, the four buddha-
ladies; his sense media, nerves, muscles, and joints, the eight bodhisattvas. His
body hairs are the 21,000 immortal saints. His limbs are the fierce lords. His*

light rays are protectors and fierce spirits, and the worldly gods lie beneath him.
Around him sit in rows an ocean of live and ancestral mentors, archetypal
deities and divine mandala hosts, buddhas, bodhisattvas, angels, and defenders of
the Dharma.

The three doors of all these deities' body, speech, and mind are marked by the
three vajras: OM on the crown, AH at the throat, and HUM at the heart. The
iron-hook tractor beams of light rays from their heart HUMs draw wisdom-
hero spiritual duplicates of all deities from their natural abodes. Wisdom heroes
and visualized heroes become indivisible and substantially present.

INVITATION

O source of success, happiness, and goodness,
All-time live and ancestral mentors, archetypes, Three Jewels,
Along with heroes, angels, protectors, and defenders,
Out of compassion, come hither and stay here!
Though all things are really free of coming and going,
You accord with the natures of various disciples
And perform appropriate miracles of love and wisdom;
Holy Savior with your retinue, please come here now!

Om Guru Buddha Bodhisattva
Dharmapala saparivara ehyehi
Jah hum bam hoh
Wisdom heroes and icon heroes become inseparable!

SALUTATIONS

Mentor like a gem embodied, diamond bolt,
Live compassion from the great bliss element,
You bestow in the fraction of a second
The supreme exaltation of the three buddha-bodies—
I bow to the lotus of your feet!

Primal wisdom of all victors of the buddhaverses,
Supreme artist, creating whatever tames each being,
Performer in the dance of upholding the monastic form—
I bow to your feet, O holy savior!

Eradicating all evil along with instincts,
Treasure of a measureless jewel mass of good,
Sole door to the source of all joy and benefit—
I bow to your feet, O holy mentor!

Teacher of humans and gods, reality of all buddhas,
Origin of the eighty-four-thousand holy teachings,
Shining axis of the entire host of noble beings—
I bow to all you kindly mentors!

To the mentors in all times and places,
And all worthy forms of the Three Jewels,
With faith and devotion and oceans of praise,
I bow with bodies as many as atoms in the universe!

OFFERINGS

To the noble mentor savior with your retinue,
I offer an ocean of various offering clouds;
From these well-arranged bright, broad jewel vessels
Four streams of purifying nectars flow.

Earth and sky are filled with graceful goddesses,
With beautiful flowers, garlands, and showering petals,
Delicious incense smoke adorns the heavens
With summer rain clouds of sapphire blue,

Masses of lamps lit by suns, moons, and radiant gems,
Shine ecstatic light rays to illumine the billion worlds;
Boundless oceans of fragrant waters swirl around,
Scented with camphor, sandalwood, and saffron.

Himalayas of human and divine food heap up,
Wholesome food and drink with a hundred savors;
The three realms resound with sweet melodies
From infinite specific varieties of music.

The outer and inner sensory goddesses
Pervade all quarters and present the glorious beauty
Of form and color, sounds, scents, tastes, and textures.

MANDALA WORLD OFFERING

These hundred trillion four-continent, planet-mountain
    worlds,
With the seven major and seven minor jewel ornaments,
Perfect realms of beings and things that create great joy,
Great treasures of delight enjoyed by gods and humans—
O Savior, mercy-treasure, supreme field of offering,
My heart full of faith, I offer it all to you!

Here on the shore of the wish-granting ocean
Of actually arranged and carefully visualized offerings,
This is a garden in which the mind is captivated by the blooming
    lotuses
Of offering substances that are all perfections of life and liberation,
In which one is delighted by the scents of all-good offerings
Which are beautiful flowers of the mundane and transcendent,

Physical, verbal, and mental virtues of myself and others,
And in which one is satiated with the rich fruits
Of the three educations, the two processes, and the five paths—
I offer it all to please you, O Holy Mentor!

This delicate tea, rich with a hundred tastes,
Saffron-colored, finely scented,
And the five hooks and the five lamps,
Purified, transmuted, and magnified
Into an ocean of elixirs—
I offer it to you!

A host of attractive, slender, youthful beauties,
Highly skilled in the sixty-four arts of love,
The heavenly, contemplative, and orgasmic herald angels,
Exquisite, magic consorts—
I offer them to you!

Great primal wisdom of unobstructed orgasmic bliss,
Inseparable from the unfabricated natural realm,
Spontaneous, beyond theory, thought, and expression,
This supreme ultimate spirit of enlightenment—
I offer it to you!

I offer the various medicines of goodness
Which conquer four hundred four addiction-sicknesses,
And to please you I offer myself as servant—
Please keep me in your service while space lasts!

CONFESSION

From beginningless time, whatever sinful acts
I did, had done, or rejoiced at others' doing,

I repent before you, O Compassionate Ones,
Confess and solemnly swear never to do again!

REJOICING

Though things are naturally free from signs,
I heartily rejoice in all the dreamlike
Perfect virtues of ordinary and noble beings
That bring them all their happiness and joy!

PRAYING FOR TEACHINGS

Clouds of perfect wisdom and love amass,
In order to grow, sustain, and prosper
The garden of help and happiness for infinite beings,
Let the rain of profound and magnificent Dharma fall!

PRAYING FOR THE MENTOR TO REMAIN

Though your diamond body knows no birth or death,
You treasure chest of buddhas self-controlled in union,
Fulfill my prayers until the end of time—
Please stay forever without entering Nirvana!

DEDICATION

The mass of perfect virtue thus created,
I dedicate to stay with you, my Mentor, life after life,
To be cultivated by your threefold kindness,
To attain the supreme union of Vajradhara!

•   •   •

PRAYERS

Source of excellence, vast ocean of justice,
Endowed with many jewels of spiritual learning,
Saffron-robed, living Shakyamuni lord,
Patriarch, discipline-holder, I pray to you!

Possessor of the ten excellent qualities,
Worthy to teach the path of the blissful lords,
Dharma-master, regent of all Victors,
Universal vehicle spiritual guide, I pray to you!

Your body, speech, and mind are well-controlled,
You are a genius, tolerant and honest.
Without pretense or deception,
You know all mantras and Tantras.
You have the ten outer and ten inner abilities,
Skilled in the arts and the instructions,
Chief of Vajra-masters, I pray to you!

You precisely teach the good path of the bliss-lords
To the savage, hard-to-tame beings of these dark times,
Not tamed before by visits of countless buddhas,
Compassionate savior, I pray to you!

The sun of Shakyamuni has sunken over time,
You perform the deeds of a victorious Buddha
For beings who have no spiritual savior—
Compassionate savior, I pray to you!

But a single of your body's pores
Is better recommended as our field of merit

Than the victors of all times and places—
Compassionate savior, I pray to you!

The beauty wheels of your bliss-lord threefold body
Ecstatically unfold the net of miracles of your liberative art,
Leading beings by participating in ordinariness—
Compassionate savior, I pray to you!

Your aggregates, elements, media, and limbs
Are the five bliss-lord clans, fathers and mothers,
Bodhisattvas male and female, and the ferocious lords—
Supreme Three Jewel mentor, I pray to you!

Your nature is the million wheels of mandalas
Arising from the play of omniscient primal wisdom—
Chief Vajra-master, lord of the hundred clans,
Communion primal savior, I pray to you!

Inseparable from the play of unblocked orgasmic joy,
Universal lord, you pervade all moving and unmoving,
You are actual, ultimate, all-good spirit of enlightenment,
Beginningless and endless, I pray to you!

HEART PRAYER

You are mentor! You are archetypal deity! You are angel and protector!
From now until enlightenment, I seek no other savior!
With compassion's iron goad, please take care of me,
In this life, the between, and future lives!
Save me from the dangers of both life and liberation!
Grant me all accomplishments!
Be my eternal friend! Protect me from all harm!

BLESSING

By the power of thus praying three times, the vital points of the mentor's body, speech, and mind emit white, red, and blue elixir light rays, first one by one and then all together, which dissolve into my own three vital points, purify the four blocks, and grant the four initiations. I attain the four buddha-bodies, a duplicate of the mentor melts in delight and blesses me completely.

TRAINING THE MIND
IN THE UNIVERSAL VEHICLE PATH

*By the power of offering, revering, and praying
To you, holy mentor, supreme field of benefit,
Bless me, savior, root of help and happiness,
And be pleased so kindly to look after me!*

*My liberty and opportunity found just this once,
Understanding how hard they are to get and how quickly lost,
Bless me not to waste it in the pointless business of this life,
But take its essence and make it count!*

*Fearing the fires of suffering in hellish states,
I heartily take refuge in the Three Jewels;
Bless me to intensify my joyous efforts
To give up sins and achieve a mass of virtue!*

*Tossed by fierce waves of evolution and addiction,
Crushed by the sea monsters of the three sufferings,
Bless me to intensify my will to liberation
From this terrifying, boundless ocean of existence!*

*As for this egoistic life cycle, intolerable prison,
I give up my delusion that it's a garden of delight,*

Bless me to educate myself in ethics, meditation, and wisdom,
The treasuries of the jewels of noble beings,
And raise aloft the victory banner of true liberation!

As I think how these sorry beings were all my mothers,
How over and over they kindly cared for me—
Bless me to conceive the genuine compassion
That a loving mother feels for her precious babe!

Not accepting even their slightest suffering,
Never being satisfied with whatever happiness,
I make no distinction between self and other—
Bless me to find joy in others' happiness!

As I see my chronic disease of cherishing myself,
As the cause that brings me unwanted suffering,
I resent it and hold it fully responsible—
Bless me to conquer this great devil of self-addiction!

As I see that cherishing my mothers makes the blissful
*   mind,*
And opens the door for developing infinite abilities,
Though all beings should rise up as bitter enemies—
Bless me to hold them dearer than my life!

In short, the fool works only in self-interest,
The Buddha works only to realize others' aims;
As I keep in mind these costs and benefits—
Bless me to equally exchange self and other!

Self-cherishing is the door of all frustration,
Other-cherishing, the ground of all excellence—

Bless me to put into essential practice
The yoga of exchange of self and other!

Therefore, O Compassionate Holy Mentor,
Bless all beings to obtain happiness,
Letting my mothers' sins, blocks, and sufferings
Entirely take effect upon me now,
And giving them all my joy and virtue!

Though the whole world be full of the fruits of sin,
And unwanted sufferings fall down like rain,
May I see this as exhausting past negative evolutionary actions;
Bless me to use bad conditions in the path!

In short, whatever happens, good and bad,
Through practice of the five forces, essence of all Dharma,
Becomes a path to increase the two enlightenment spirits—
Bless me to contemplate indomitable cheer!

Bless me to give my liberty and opportunity great meaning,
By practice of the precepts and vows of mind reform,
Applying contemplation at once to whatever happens
With the artistry of employing the four practices!

Bless me to cultivate the spirit of enlightenment,
To save beings from the great ocean of existence,
Through the universal responsibility of love and compassion,
And the magic of mounting give-and-take upon the breath!

Bless me to intensify my efforts
On the sole path of the all-time champion buddhas,

Binding my process with pure messianic vows,
And practicing the three ethics of the supreme vehicle!

Bless me to perfect the generosity transcendence,
The precept increasing giving without attachment,
Transforming my body, possessions, and all-time virtues
Into just the things each being wants!

Bless me to perfect the justice transcendence,
Not surrendering, even to save my life, my vows
Of individual liberation, bodhisattva, and secret mantra,
Collecting virtue, and realizing beings' aims!

Bless me to perfect the patience transcendence,
So that, even if every being in the world were furious,
Cut me, accused, threatened, even killed me—
Feeling no stress, I could repay their harm with benefit!

Bless me to perfect the creativity transcendence,
So that even if I had to spend oceans of aeons
In the fires of hell for the sake of each and every being,
My compassion would never tire of striving for
*   enlightenment!*

Bless me to perfect the meditation transcendence,
Through the one-pointed samadhi *that transcends all flaws*
Of distraction, depression, and excitement,
Focused on the insubstantial reality of all things!

Bless me to perfect the wisdom transcendence,
Through the yoga of ultimate-reality-spacelike equipoise,

Connected with the fierce bliss of the special fluency
Derived from the wisdom that discerns reality!

Bless me to complete the magical aftermath samadhi,
Understanding the processes of truthless appearance
Of outer and inner things, such as illusions, dreams,
Or the reflections of the moon in water!

Bless me to understand Nagarjuna's intended meaning,
In which life and liberation have no jot of intrinsic reality,
Yet cause and effect and relativity are still inexorable,
And these two laws don't contradict, but mutually complement one another!

Then bless me to embark in the boat to cross the ocean of the Tantras,
Through the kindness of the captain Vajra-master,
Holding vows and pledges, root of all powers,
More dearly than life itself!

Bless me to perceive all things as the deity body,
Cleansing the taints of ordinary perception and conception
Through the yoga of the first stage of Unexcelled Yoga Tantra,
Transforming birth, death, and between into the three buddha-bodies!

Bless me to realize here in this life
The path of clear light-magic body union,
Coming from you, Savior, when you put your toe
In my eight-petaled, heart center's central channel.

If the path is not complete and death arrives,
Bless me to go to a pure buddhaverse
By the instruction for implementing the five forces
Of mentor soul ejection, the forceful art of buddhahood!

In short, life after life forever,
You, Savior, care for me and never part,
Bless me to become your foremost heir,
Upholding all the secrets of body, speech, and mind!

You, Savior, when you're a perfect buddha,
May I be foremost in your retinue.
Grant me good luck for easy, natural achievement
Of all my goals, temporary and ultimate!

Thus having prayed, may you, best mentor
Joyously come to my crown to bless me,
Sit securely, your toenails glistening,
In the corolla of my heart-center lotus!

The pure virtue of performing this practice,
I dedicate to the success of all the deeds and vows
Of all the three times' bliss-lords and their heirs,
And to uphold the word and practice of the holy Dharma.

By the power of that dedication through all my lives,
May I never lose the four wheels of the supreme vehicle—
May I consummate transcendence, spirit of enlightenment,
Realistic view, and progress on the stages of creation and perfection.

ROBERT THURMAN ON TIBET'S GREATEST TREASURE

The book *The Jewel Tree of Tibet* began as a series of audio learning sessions published by Sounds True. Designed and taught in the oral tradition by Robert Thurman, this full-length course was intended to be a "home retreat" comprised of spontaneous "dharma talks" plus guided meditations.

The Dalai Lama once confided to Robert Thurman: "If Buddhism is taught in a bland or watered-down way, people will not be inspired to use it." Here is a course that honors the full subtlety and hidden depths of the Tibetan Buddhist path—Robert Thurman's *The Jewel Tree of Tibet*.

To listen to a sample or order this recording, visit www.soundstrue.com or call 800-333-9185.

For more information on Tibet's spiritual philosophy, mind sciences, and cultural heritage, please contact Tibet House, 22 West 15th Street, New York, New York 10011, or visit their Web site, www.tibethouse.org.

INDEX

ABOUT THE AUTHOR

ROBERT THURMAN, PH.D., is Jey Tsong Khapa Professor of Indo-Tibetan Studies at Columbia University, the first endowed chair in Indo-Tibetan Buddhist Studies in America. He was the first Westerner to receive ordination as a Tibetan Buddhist monk in 1964 at age twenty-four and a further ordination in 1971, both from His Holiness the Dalai Lama. Cofounder and president of Tibet House US, a nonprofit organization dedicated to preserving the endangered civilization and living culture of Tibet, he is also a popular lecturer on Tibetan Buddhism around the world. His charisma and enthusiasm draw packed audiences. Thurman is the author of original books, including *Infinite Life* and *Inner Revolution,* and he has also translated many sacred Tibetan texts, including both philosophical treatises and sutras. His numerous books include *Essential Tibetan Buddhism, Worlds of Transformation: The Sacred Art of Tibet,* and a classic translation of *The Tibetan Book of the Dead.*

Thurman writes, "What I have learned from these people [Tibetans] has forever changed my life, and I believe their culture contains an inner science particularly relevant to the difficult time in which we live. My desire is to share some of the profound hope for our future that they have shared with me."